# Building and
# Safety Codes for
# Industrial Facilities

## Other Books of Interest from McGraw-Hill

BAUMEISTER AND MARKS • *Marks' Standard Handbook for Mechanical Engineers*

BHUSHAN AND GUPTA • *Handbook of Tribology*

BRADY AND CLAUSER • *Materials Handbook*

BRALLA • *Handbook of Product Design for Manufacturing*

BRUNNER • *Handbook of Incineration Systems*

CORBITT • *Standard Handbook of Environmental Engineering*

EHRICH • *Handbook of Rotordynamics*

ELLIOT • *Standard Handbook of Powerplant Engineering*

FREEMAN • *Standard Handbook of Hazardous Waste Treatment and Disposal*

GANIC AND HICKS • *The McGraw-Hill Handbook of Essential Engineering Information and Data*

GIECK • *Engineering Formulas*

GRIMM AND ROSALER • *Handbook of HVAC Design*

HARRIS • *Handbook of Noise Control*

HARRIS AND CREDE • *Shock and Vibration Handbook*

HICKS • *Standard Handbook of Engineering Calculations*

HODSON • *Maynard's Industrial Engineering Handbook*

JONES • *Diesel Plant Operations Handbook*

JURAN AND GRYNA • *Juran's Quality Control Handbook*

KARASSIK ET AL. • *Pump Handbook*

KURTZ • *Handbook of Applied Mathematics for Engineers and Scientists*

PARMLEY • *Standard Handbook of Fastening and Joining*

ROHSENOW ET AL. • *Handbook of Heat Transfer Applications*

ROHSENOW ET AL. • *Handbook of Heat Transfer Fundamentals*

ROSALER AND RICE • *Standard Handbook of Plant Engineering*

ROTHBART • *Mechanical Design and Systems Handbook*

SCHWARTZ • *Composite Materials Handbook*

SCHWARTZ • *Handbook of Structural Ceramics*

SHIGLEY AND MISCHKE • *Standard Handbook of Machine Design*

TOWNSEND • *Dudley's Gear Handbook*

TUMA • *Engineering Mathematics Handbook*

TUMA • *Handbook of Numerical Calculations in Engineering*

WADSWORTH • *Handbook of Statistical Methods for Engineers and Scientists*

YOUNG • *Roark's Formulas for Stress and Strain*

# Building and Safety Codes for Industrial Facilities

Joseph N. Sabatini

*With environmental chapters by*
**Stephen R. Sabatini**
*and*
**Robert D. Smith**

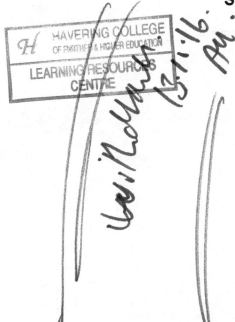

**McGraw-Hill, Inc.**
New York  St. Louis  San Francisco  Auckland  Bogotá
Caracas  Lisbon  London  Madrid  Mexico  Milan
Montreal  New Delhi  Paris  San Juan  São Paulo
Singapore  Sydney  Tokyo  Toronto

Library of Congress Cataloging-in-Publication Data

Sabatini, Joseph N.
  Building and safety codes for industrial facilities / Joseph N.
Sabatini : with chapters by Stephen R. Sabatini and Robert D. Smith.
      p.    cm.
  Includes bibliographical references and index.
  ISBN 0-07-054406-9
  1. Industrial buildings—Law and legislation—United States—
Outlines, syllabi, etc.  2. Industrial buildings—Safety
regulations—United States—Outlines, syllabi, etc.  I. Sabatini,
Stephen R.  II. Smith, Robert D. (Robert Douglas), date.
III. Title.
KF5702.I5352 1993
343.73'0769054—dc20
[347.3037869054]                                          91-12434
                                                              CIP

1 2 3 4 5 6 7 8 9 0  DOC/DOC  9 8 7 6 5 4 3 2

ISBN 0-07-054406-9

*The sponsoring editor for this book was Robert Hauserman, the editing
supervisor was Ruth W. Mannino, and the production supervisor was
Suzanne W. Babeuf. This book was set in Century Schoolbook by
McGraw-Hill's Professional Book Group composition unit.*

*Printed and bound by R. R. Donnelley & Sons Company.*

# Contents

# Preface

If you are in the planning and conceptual stages of a project and are not familiar with all the codes, regulations, and enforced standards in the design and construction of any part or all of your industrial facility, this book can save you tens of thousands of construction dollars and possibly more. If you lack a working knowledge of *all* the significant construction options allowed in codes, regulations, and enforced standards relating to processes that use hazardous materials; to site planning; to building construction itself; and to the environmental regulations for air, water, and hazardous solid wastes, you need to read Chapter 1, which lists all the applicable laws, and Chapter 9, which summarizes all the options in a checklist format. This book also can save the novice code reader considerable calendar time in the preparation of final construction documents.

Extensive growth has occurred over the last two decades in building codes, hazardous process reviews; employee safety regulations; air, water, and hazardous solid waste pollution regulations; and their accompanying enforced industry standards. Those of us who have conducted reviews of some of the more than 35 separate primary volumes of today's codes and regulations, plus the countless enforced standards for industrial facilities that use hazardous materials, realize that it takes weeks of reading and reviewing to select all the applicable words, phrases, paragraphs, sections, and options allowed; to review the economics of the options; and to sort out and resolve the conflicts, contradictions, and unclear statements that exist despite the best intentions and efforts of code-writing committees (see the section Interlocking Maze of Enforced Codes, Regulations, and Standards in Chap. 1 for further discussion). For example, I was involved in a project in which the letter of the state code without question would not allow construction of a certain proposed facility. When I sought the advice of a number of recognized experts, I was informed that the type of facility proposed was commonly built throughout the country. An in-depth review of other codes and standards furnished documentation, from recognized sources concerned with life safety and active in its research, that the proposed facility would be safe. When the local authority was made aware of this conflict between state code and the recognized sources, its code-writing committee confirmed that the state code was unusually severe on the point in question. As a result, the facility was approved for construction and subsequently built.

## Caution

The information presented in this book is simply an outline of the more than 35 volumes that comprise the legal documents governing the construction of an industrial facility using hazardous materials. The reader is reminded that he or she must read and understand the latest enforced edition of the applicable codes, regulations, and enforced standards in detail for the preparation of final construction documents. This book will serve as a guide in the planning process of a project to reveal which of the multitude of documents must be pursued. However, the planner must still contact the local authorities to obtain the latest revisions of the codes, regulations, and enforced standards that are applicable to the project before preparing the final construction documents. Statements made in this book regarding the content of codes, regulations, and enforced standards must be verified by the reader with the actual locally enforced codes before proceeding with the preparation of construction documents, since many of these codes, regulations, and standards are constantly undergoing local, state, or national revisions.

*Joseph N. Sabatini, P.E.*

# Acknowledgments

Chapter 19, Hazardous Waste Regulations, and Chapter 21, Asbestos Regulations, were written by Stephen R. Sabatini, P.E. Mr. Sabatini is a senior environmental engineer and project manager with Environmental Quality Management, Inc., in Cincinnati, Ohio. He has 12 years' experience in environmental consulting. In addition, he assisted the State of Louisiana in writing its hazardous waste regulations and in obtaining authority to regulate hazardous waste management. Mr. Sabatini also managed several asbestos abatement projects at the Dallas–Fort Worth International Airport. He also inspected over 100 buildings for asbestos and assessed the risk where asbestos was found.

Chapter 18, Environmental Water Regulations, was written by Robert D. Smith, P.E. Mr. Smith is a retired senior environmental engineer with MK Ferguson.

In addition to the work of these two authors, indispensable assistance in the areas of their expertise was received from Kenneth A. Wolven, R. A., architect; Don W. Wilhelm, manager, Environmental Group, MK Ferguson; Margaret Acela, librarian and English major with MK Ferguson; and the Cincinnati/Hamilton County Public Library Director and Staff. I would also like to acknowledge the assistance of my wife, Helen, and my daughter, Diane N. Albrinck. This book would not have been possible without the assistance of each of these individuals.

# List of Tables

Many of these tables can be used as design checklists for codes for hazardous facilities.

# List of Figures

# Economical Approach to Code Documents

The first and second focuses of this book, paradoxically, are *economic* in nature, and the third focus is on *compliance* with codes.

## Economical Code Decisions

This book is intended to serve as a guide for economical planning of industrial facilities, especially those which use hazardous materials. It will expedite firm economical decisions in preliminary planning. It will also make the intimidating list of codes and regulations (see Table 1.1) user friendly. A new or existing industrial facility today must comply with the requirements of the codes and regulations listed in Table 1.1 in order to receive all the required occupancy and operating permits.

For a brief outline of the origin and scope of the list in Table 1.1, see Chapter 2. For a detailed discussion of the scope and use of a specific code or regulation, see the chapter or chapters referenced in the right-hand column of the table.

The list in Table 1.1 references over 35 primary volumes. As a result of the shear volume of this material, project managers often overlook code items that add considerable construction costs after their construction budgets have been approved. Chapter 9 of this book provides a quick code and regulation economical options checklist to help reduce this problem. Accommodating the complex and extensive building codes, regulations, and enforced standards that exist today requires a great deal of experience, including familiarity with 12 design disciplines, which will be discussed later in this chapter.

This book will also save the novice reviewer critical time in using any of the documents, such as building codes, OSHA and EPA regu-

**TABLE 1.1    Codes and Regulations for Industrial Facilities**

| No. | Code or regulation | Chapter |
|---|---|---|
| 1 | Local zoning ordinances | 4, 8, and 14 |
| 2 | State and/or local building codes | 8 |
| 3 | State and/or local fire codes | 12 |
| 4 | State and/or local mechanical codes | 13 and 14 |
| 5 | State and/or local energy codes | 13 |
| 6 | State and/or local plumbing codes | 14 |
| 7 | State and/or local electric codes | 15 |
| 8 | State air pollution regulations | 17 |
| 9 | State water pollution regulations | 18 |
| 10 | State labor regulations | 10 |
| 11 | State and/or local road and utility requirements | 8 and 14 |
| 12 | OSHA 29 CFR 1910 Building and Process Regulations | 3, 4, and 10 |
| 13 | OSHA 29 CFR 1926.58 Asbestos Regulations | 21 |
| 14 | Process/System Safety Checklist[1] and/or | 4 |
| 15 | Process What If Analysis (WHAT-IF) and/or | 4 |
| 16 | Process Hazard and Operability Study (HAZOP) and/or | 4 |
| 17 | Process Failure Mode and Effect Method (FMEA) and/or | 4 |
| 18 | Process Fault Tree Analysis (FAULT TREE) and/or | 4 |
| 19 | Process Dow and Mond Hazard Indices | 4 |
| 20 | Environmental Audits | 20 |
| 21 | Emergency Planning and Community-Right-to-Know Act | 3 and 10 |
| 22 | Clean Air Act | 4 and 17 |
| 23 | Toxic Substances Control Act (TSCA) | 3 and 4 |
| 24 | Resource Conservation and Recovery Act (RCRA) | 19 and 20 |
| 25 | Superfund (CERCLA) (SARA) | |
| 26 | Department of Transportation (DOT) Emergency Response Regulations | 3, 4, and 5 |
| 27 | Clean Water Act | 18 |
| 28 | Safe Drinking Water Act | 14 |
| 29 | Solid Waste Disposal Act | 19 |
| 30 | UST Regulations | 20 |
| 31 | Asbestos Hazard Emergency Act | 21 |
| 32 | Special federal agency regulations such as the Food and Drug Administration's or the Department of Agriculture's regulations for food plants | [2] |

[1]The processing of hazardous materials requires Recognized Safety Reviews by OSHA; see Chap. 10.
[2]These regulations are available from the federal agencies.

lations, and the enforced standards, in the preparation of construction documents. All the documents that govern construction of an industrial process and building are listed in Chapter 2, along with references to the specific chapters that cover each item.

### Code options economical checklist

The *maladie du jour* of current building, safety, and environmental codes for industrial facilities using hazardous materials, as those of us who use them recognize, is that they are far from being user friendly. They have been written by thousands of well-intentioned individuals serving on hundreds of different committees. For example, today there are 200 member organizations writing standards. Just one of these organizations has 120 presiding committees, which intermittently revise and reissue the standards. Given this situation, it is impossible that such standards could be written in a sequence that follows the organized method of planning and design of an industrial facility. Compliance with these standards therefore requires a great deal of experience and familiarity or the calendar time to plod through and find each significant paragraph of each of the multitude of documents. In an attempt to resolve this dilemma, a Code Options Economical Checklist has been prepared to assist planners in arriving at competent and economical decisions (see Chap. 9). This checklist details a number of steps in four major areas within the codes, regulations, and standards to reduce construction costs. In addition, the list follows the usual decision-making sequence in the planning of an industrial facility. Also see the section Five Major Economic Decisions in this chapter.

## Unforeseen code cost additions

The increased use of hazardous materials by industry, coupled with the extensive research and advances in fire technology, toxic substances control, and pollution control over the past 20 years, has resulted in the tremendous growth of comprehensive and complex building codes, hazardous process review procedures, employee safety regulations, and environmental regulations. It has become critical, therefore, to use a checklist such as the one presented in Chapter 9 to reduce costs resulting from the proliferation of such code documents, which are cumbersome to read and frequently impede planning. Too often, project leaders discover too late in the design schedule or in a fast-track construction project that an overlooked or unrecalled paragraph or phrase in the codes, regulations, or enforced standards contains an item that adds too much to the construction budget or will interfere with the intended use of the building. This book presents ways to help this problem.

## Needless construction costs

Frequently planners review only portions of the applicable codes and regulations at intervals that may be months apart. For example, each discipline involved in a project may perform its code review on an isolated basis as its contribution is scheduled into the design. Experience has shown that this results in a fragmented approach to compliance and a number of economic pitfalls such as the following:

- Excessive site fire protection costs
- Needlessly severe occupancy classifications
- Needlessly updated existing buildings
- Needless high-rise building classifications for processes that can easily be reduced in height
- Expensive and avoidable structural-steel fireproofing
- Excessive firewater flow designs
- Excessive areas of expensive electrical classification
- Nonrequired automatic fire alarm systems
- Excessive pollution equipment costs resulting from a lack of review of existing process hood designs to reduce air volumes

This book can reduce the number of economic pitfalls and should be used by

1. Project leaders, whenever major conceptual decisions are made and all disciplines are not represented
2. Project team members, whenever all the disciplines do not have an everyday working knowledge of the extensive codes, regulations, and enforced standards
3. Designers, in creating construction documents when they are not familiar with all the codes
4. Constructors and equipment manufacturers who are looking for reduced code cost options
5. Environmental engineers involved in projects that overlap into other codes and regulations

## Five Major Economic Decisions

This book attempts to resolve the problem of needless or excessive costs through use of the five major steps outlined in Table 1.2. See Chapter 9 for an itemized checklist of the second, third, fourth, and fifth major areas of economical code-compliance planning, whether the project is a new facility, an addition to an existing process and/or building, or a retrofit of an existing process and/or building.

### Eliminating hazardous materials

The first step in reducing the cost of an industrial facility is to eliminate, whenever possible, the use of hazardous materials in the manu-

**TABLE 1.2 Five Major Economic Decisions**

| | |
|---|---|
| Decision 1 | Eliminating hazardous materials |
| Decision 2 | Site cost trade-offs<br>Hazardous materials spacing |
| Decision 3 | Building code cost trade-offs |
| Decision 4 | Process versus building cost trade-offs |
| Decision 5 | Environmental regulations |

facturing process. This strategy begins in the process planning stage. Substitute safer chemicals and, if possible, eliminate chemicals that are explosive, highly flammable, or toxic. If this can be accomplished, the increases in worker and environmental safety and the cost savings in process equipment, building construction, and environmental control equipment can be major.

**Site cost trade-offs**

Site selection and layout are the next major economic consideration. Obviously, site selection and layout include many important considerations in addition to code and regulation requirements. Zoning, building, and fire district restrictions, as well as environmental considerations, are of major importance here. For example, high-hazard installations, because they can be a major threat to life safety, are not permitted in densely populated and residential areas. It is necessary, therefore, to consult local zoning ordinances and local building, fire, and environmental officials when selecting a site. See Chapter 4 for site considerations, Chapter 8 for building codes, Chapter 12 for fire extinguishing, Chapter 14 for connections to municipal utilities, Chapter 17 for environmental air control equipment requirements, Chapter 18 for environmental wastewater treatment system requirements, Chapter 19 for solid industrial hazardous waste requirements, and Chapter 20 for environmental audits. The information derived from these sources is essential for establishing project feasibility and for reliably estimating project construction costs.

**Hazardous materials spacing.** The first item generally needed from the building code in site selection and layout is the minimum distances required from property lines and adjacent buildings for hazardous material operation and storage. In addition, the local zoning ordinances must be reviewed for building setbacks. Fire department access is also an economic consideration here, because fire extinguishing system costs can increase where this access is limited and minimum spacing requirements are not maintained (see Chaps. 4 and 9).

### Building code cost trade-offs

The third decision involves economical options in building construction, commonly called *trade-offs*. These options are also itemized in Chapter 9 in the section Building Trade-offs. Unless the owner, architect, engineer, contractor, maintenance planner, manufacturer of industrial equipment, construction cost estimator, or whoever else is involved in the construction, addition, modification, alteration, or replacement of an industrial building, process, or environmental system is familiar with and repeatedly refers to the many documents governing this area, the amount of time demanded to read them is astonishing, frustrating, and potentially a negatively overpowering influence.

### Process versus building cost trade-offs

There are a number of economical comparisons to be made regarding process equipment costs versus building costs. Building costs can be reduced by process design. Since this generally increases the cost of process equipment, careful comparisons should be made.

For example, completely enclosing explosive, flammable, or toxic materials in the process vessels, piping, and materials-handling enclosures—to prevent their being released into the interior building atmosphere and presenting a hazard to employees—will dramatically reduce the building construction costs that would otherwise be necessary to satisfy the life safety requirements of state building and fire codes. Building codes require high-hazard occupancy classifications when hazardous materials are normally present in the building and are not enclosed in the process equipment (see Chaps. 5, 7, and 8 for more information). High-hazard occupancy classifications increase building construction costs by

1. Requiring the addition of firewalls, thereby reducing the allowable area and also the height of the building

2. Requiring the addition of more costly materials and fireproofing to increase the fire rating or fire resistance of the building

3. Requiring more water flow to extinguish a process-fed fire, thereby increasing the costs of fire suppression systems

4. Requiring the addition of explosion vents to the building, in addition to those vents required on the process equipment

5. Increasing the requirements of hazardous (classified) locations, thereby increasing electricity costs

6. Increasing the cost of automatic fire alarm systems

Process equipment can be designed to contain explosions of industrial chemicals (see Chaps. 4 and 5 for more information), and such equipment often will be specified in the planning stage. Most maximum pressure rises of explosion-tested materials listed by the National Fire Protection Association (NFPA) do not reach 150 pounds per square inch ($lb/in^2$). Pressure vessels rated by the American Society of Mechanical Engineers (ASME) can easily contain this pressure because they are often designed for 150 $lb/in^2$. However, process equipment that is too large to fabricate according to ASME ratings can be designed to resist lower explosion pressures, with the excess pressure channeled by explosion-relief vents through the outside of the building. NFPA Standard 68 provides a formula to determine the sizes of such vents and the allowable backpressures on the vessel or building. Also, when the vent area is increased, the backpressure is reduced. See the section Prevention of Vapor/Dust Releases in Chapter 5 for further discussion.

### Environmental regulations

Refer to Chapter 17 for a discussion of the least costly pollution-control equipment allowed under the 1990 amendments of the Clean Air Act and to the nine steps outlined in Chapter 9, section IV-A.

### Compliance

The third focus of this book is on compliance. This book will help planners to avoid design and construction delays caused by changes in the middle of the design and changes after completion of the design that result from local-authority plan reviews. (In the suburbs of major U.S. metropolises, small staffs of only one or two individuals usually review residential and commercial projects. These staffs, which seldom are familiar with the hazardous facility codes and standards, do not have the time and expertise to competently review construction for hazardous materials. Some local building authorities now require letters from the individual in charge of a project stating that all applicable codes, regulations, and standards have been complied with in the preparation of the construction documents.) Some chapters in this book include sample plan-review checklists.

Finally, this book will provide an easy reference, under one cover, to all the building and safety codes, regulations, and enforced standards that apply to the design of industrial facilities. Many chapters contain tables of the more commonly enforced standards for industrial facilities. Plant engineers, consultants, and building owners/managers who are responsible from the start of a project through the final design of the process and/or building will find this book valuable in reducing the time required to review essential documents and in ensuring that none of the safety references are omitted.

## Unprecedented growth of codes, regulations, and standards

The massive proliferation of codes, regulations, and standards includes hazardous process reviews; OSHA employee safety regulations; local municipal ordinances, building codes, fire codes, mechanical codes, energy codes, plumbing codes, and electrical codes; air, water, and hazardous solid-waste pollution regulations; and countless references to other documents. These control the construction, expansion, alteration, retrofitting, modernizing, and operation of today's industrial facilities. This growth has made code review a nearly insurmountable task for an individual or small group. As many of us recognize, code review demands a formidable staff of specialists. Evidence supporting this observation can be seen in the growing number of specialized consulting firms.

## Enforced primary volumes and continual revisions

Codes and regulations that govern the design and construction of industrial facilities are published in over 35 volumes issued by various federal, state, and local agencies. Many additional enforced standards, numbering in the thousands, pertain to the use of a particular code or regulation. In 1991, the American Society for Testing and Materials (ASTM) alone added 637 new standards that apply to building codes.

Most code documents also undergo continual revisions, some every year and others every few years. In many instances this adds to the length and sometimes the number of documents. There is a virtual onslaught of uncoordinated code-writing committees who are not always well informed on the cost consequences of what they write in the codes and who therefore are making industrial facilities more costly every year. Consequently, before any final construction documents are prepared for the local authority to review, planners must study in detail the actual enforced codes of the community in which their facility is to be located and resolve any complexities with the local officials.

## Interlocking maze of enforced codes, regulations, and standards

Most code-writing committees made a good effort to cross-reference codes. However, many code novices are just not aware of the multitude of interlocking sections, paragraphs, and sentences in all the documents. This generally results from a lack of previous experience with the many high-hazard chemicals processed in manufacturing facilities today.

Another reason for difficulties here is that the codes generally are not written in a sequence that follows the requirements of designers for information but rather follow general chapter safety headings. This method of code presentation results in a multitude of cross-references to other paragraphs, sections, chapters, codes, and standards. Cross-references that are not always complete and sometimes are not too clear can lead to omissions and violations unless planners spend sufficient calendar time to thoroughly review the codes and all their enforced cross-references. This problem is particularly magnified in industrial facilities that use hazardous materials.

One typical state code specifies in the administrative section that the rules of the building standards shall supersede and govern any order, standard, or rule of other departments. In other words, in all cases where any orders, standards, or rules are in conflict with the rules of the building standards, except those of the fire marshall, the building standards shall prevail. For example, one typical state code does not list the NFPA 101 Life Safety Code in its Enforced Reference Standards Appendix. However, any industry that brings a quantity of flammable liquid into a building is automatically governed by some of the NFPA 101 Life Safety Code provisions. This is so because the state code enforced NFPA 30, "Flammable and Combustible Liquids Code," as do most state codes.

NFPA 30 Chapter 6 then reads: "The following documents or portions thereof are referenced within this document and shall be considered part of the requirements of this document." The chapter then goes on to list almost 40 NFPA standards, including NFPA 101, about 12 ASTM standards, 10 American Petroleum Institute (API) standards, an American National Standards Institute (ANSI) standard, an ASME standard, and a number of Underwriters Laboratories (UL) standards, all of which are already referenced by other enforced standards listed in the state code.

NFPA 30 also has the usual reference standards list in Appendix G that reads, "The following documents or portions thereof are referenced within this standard for informational purposes only and thus should not be considered part of the requirements of this document."

Furthermore, experience has shown that some local officials read the statement in Chapter 6 of NFPA 30 and choose to interpret it as meaning that the complete NFPA 101 standard is enforced, disregarding the statement "or portions thereof." In addition, there are a number of general phrases in the administrative section that can be used to enforce this position, such as, "for all matters within the intent of this code and not covered by this code compliance is required with the accepted engineering practice standards listed in the appendices under Reference Standards"—a statement that grants carte blanche, according to some authorities, to demanding compliance with all references, including those intended to enforce only a specific paragraph.

Such interlocking cross-references occur repeatedly throughout all codes, regulations, and enforced standards—federal, state, and local. This format creates a formidable interwoven maze that compels either an extensive, time-consuming review by staff or the hiring of a code consultant. For example, one state code instructs its users that after establishing the major code requirements of occupancy, size, fire resistance, etc., the user should review each section to determine the complete requirements applicable to the project.

### Examples of interlocking codes and standards

For a diagrammatic example of this interlocking, see Fig. 11.2. Another serious example occurs with the Clean Air Act amendments passed in 1990. The amendments interlock the Occupational Safety and Health Administration (OSHA), (SARA), and (CERCLA) (see Chaps. 4, 10, and 17).

Often enforced standards contain statements that are stricter than the building code. For example, a 1½-hour fire door was required by a state building code, whereas NFPA 30 required a 3-hour fire door for a flammable liquids storage room. The fire marshall insisted on the more stringent requirement in his final inspection before issuing the occupancy permit. Firewall ratings are repeated throughout this fire code and are not always in agreement with the building code.

For a startling example of the proliferation of interlocking codes and standards, see the lists of over 25 codes, standards, and regulations in Tables 15.2 and 16.1 that must be read to be in compliance in the installation of electrical hazardous (classified) locations and the installation of an automatic fire alarm system in an industrial facility.

### Code and regulation simplification is sorely needed

The time when a designer of an industrial building could glance at one page or one code document and determine the requirements for construction plans and specifications to be in compliance is history. Designers of industrial facilities using hazardous materials, no matter how conscientious, find themselves causing unintended code violations that are prompted by the very codes and regulations whose purpose it is to prevent these violations. Many of today's professional designers approach their tasks with trepidation. This is a growing paradox in the industry that needs to be recognized, understood, and resolved. NFPA may well be one of the first regulating groups to do this. In some of their more recent publications, for example, they have consolidated some of the enforced standards and state that this is done to make the standards more user friendly.

**Early comprehensive reviews**

What is sorely needed is a comprehensive approach to the review of codes, regulations, and standards. Although this is performed informally on some projects by means of a spot-check or shotgun approach, a more organized and systematic approach is needed. As soon as the initial concepts of a facility have been developed, a systematic approach will reduce construction dollars that are too often spent needlessly on equipment and facilities in excess of compliance requirements. With a systematic approach, a design leader can readily list the necessary codes and regulations early in the planning stages. Moreover, a systematic approach will reduce the considerable time and effort required to do the review of the multitude of references needed to prepare detailed construction documents. A more organized approach to code review must be used to avoid repeatedly reading the many detailed paragraphs to interpret the confusion, conflicts, contradictions, gaps, overlaps, and vagueness in the multitude of codes and regulations so conscientiously written by the many committees.

Unless a project is small, the best approach for a designer as soon as the initial concepts have been developed is to conduct a complete review of all the applicable documents. This must include codes, regulations, and enforced standards. The designer should make copies and highlight all the chapters and paragraphs that apply, summarizing them on cover sheets for the repeated references that are required when the design progresses and the construction documents need to be completed. This will avoid repeatedly searching through the endless nonapplicable sections of the documents. Today, when hazardous materials are involved, this is a must. Even with a simple, small building that houses noncombustible materials, the number of enforced standards quickly multiplies. An organized and comprehensive approach to code review more quickly reveals the conflicts among the multiple code documents, and these conflicts can be resolved in the early stages of the design. Code committees recognize that gaps, overlaps, contradictions, and conflicts occur in regulations and standards, and many make an attempt to provide guidance making such statements as "where the code conflicts with other parts of this code, the more stringent shall be used."

## Twelve Design Disciplines Are Required in Planning

Just as important as compliance itself is the economics of compliance, which is the result of the numerous options allowed by the codes. (See Chapter 9.) These options are often interdisciplinary and require project-team planning to resolve the problem of professionals working independently and duplicating costly safety features in the site process or building.

Today, an industrial project can involve as many as 12 different disciplines in the creation of a safe plant design: (1) a chemical engineer (material safety data sheets, MSDS), (2) a process engineer (process safety reviews), (3) an instrumentation engineer (process safety reviews), (4) an architect (state building codes), (5) a structural engineer (state building codes), (6) a civil engineer/surveyor, (7) a pollution engineer (EPA regulations for wastewater, air discharges to the atmosphere, and solid waste), (8) a mechanical engineer (ASME codes for vessel and pipe design), (9) a ventilating engineer (maximum allowable concentrations of vapors or dust substances in the workplace or OSHA regulations), (10) a plumbing engineer (plumbing code), (11) a fire protection engineer (state fire and NFPA codes), and (12) an electrical engineer (electric code).

### Extensive coordination of all disciplines

Fire protection engineering is more than the design of a sprinkler system by the fire protection engineer, as some perceive it. It requires the coordinated attention of all disciplines, because sometimes, for example, if a firewall can be provided, the code will not require a sprinkler system. Or if a sprinkler system is provided, the code may not require an automatic fire alarm system. Without interdisciplinary coordination, all three of these fire protection systems could be installed when not all are required. Code officials and installing contractors will not object to these economic pitfalls.

### Code-experienced "experts" are not always available

Sometimes a code-experienced staff of specialists is not available. For example, the engineering staff might be composed of only a handful of people because its facility and projects are not large. Or, when a large staff is available, it may be overscheduled, meaning that some projects are designed with partial staff or with schedules that are too short.

Should an engineer who functions as a general plant engineer and does, for example, electrical engineering on a part-time basis be expected to know that a fire alarm system for a major industrial facility is covered by 12 different enforced codes, regulations, and standards (see Chap. 16)? Should this engineer be expected to be aware that areas requiring more expensive hazardous (classified) electrical locations are covered by over 20 enforced standards, in addition to the National Electric Code (see Chap. 15)?

**Example of needless construction costs.**   Here is one actual example of a situation in which too many construction dollars were spent as a result of a delay in scheduling the project architect. A flue-gas cleaning process installed in an open structural-steel tower 81 ft high was required by the local building authority to have a stairwell with a 2-hour–rated enclosure for its full height because it exceeded by 6 ft (1.83 m) the maximum height that a municipal fire ladder truck could reach to evacuate victims of a mishap. The process engineer could easily have reduced the required elevation by 6 ft (1.83 m) by rearranging the vessels and connecting piping if he had been advised by the architect of the building code restrictions before specifying and ordering the equipment, thereby saving tens of thousands of dollars in added construction costs, redesign time costs, and construction delay costs. Unfortunately, it was not until the long delivery process vessels had been on order for approximately 6 months that the architect was assigned to the project. Life safety was not a significant consideration in adding the 2-hour–rated enclosed stairwell. The process was automated and did not require any operators at the equipment. However, the process did require the operator, who was located in a ground-floor control room, to climb to the top level of the structure once a day for 5 minutes to manually record an instrument reading. The local authority insisted on enforcing the letter of the code without reviewing the actual threat to life safety, and the money had to be spent for the enclosure.

This manner of scheduling the professional disciplines for a project is a common practice in the construction industry for economic reasons, and the unfortunate consequence is excessive construction costs.

**Professional overkill.**   A second common reason that needless construction dollars are spent is what I call *overkill.* Conscientious professionals, concerned with life safety, the environment, and their professional licenses, when in doubt about a code requirement and rushed by limited design time, will exercise overkill. To prevent a possible omission, a needless costly item is included in the construction documents.

## Variances

The commendable intent of codes, regulations, and enforced standards is indisputably to protect life, property, and the environment. However, codes, regulations, and enforced standards should not always and unquestionably be applied without analysis when they unintentionally result in enormous construction costs with little effect on their intended goal of protecting workers, the public, and the environment.

An example of such a situation is the unnecessary removal of asbestos from some of our public buildings. As reported in *Science* magazine, March 2, 1990, scientists have determined that the asbestos scare is overdone. The scientists contend that the asbestos fiber content in the air of asbestos-containing buildings is harmlessly small, comparable to that in outdoor air. Further, the asbestos fibers potentially released in removing the material pose a greater cancer risk to the workers than that of the asbestos materials in place to an occupant of the building. The EPA now publishes guidelines to encapsulating asbestos building materials in place.

The editorial in *Science* and one in *Science News,* February 3, 1990, also bring attention to the arbitrary lumping together in federal legislation and regulations of disparate minerals under the label "asbestos." Studies in the past two years suggest that chrysotile, the most common substance used in the workplace, poses no hazard at the levels encountered. Crocodolite and amosite admittedly are a definite hazard. Considering the $50 to $150 billion magnitude of the EPA asbestos program, one would have hoped for an accurate analysis of the hazard!

# Industrial Safety and Economic Considerations

In the last two decades, our society has changed its attitudes about industry. The ever-increasing developments in technology that resulted in the creation of new products, materials, and manufacturing methods brought with them a greater concern for the effects our industries have on human safety and the environment.

Particular emphasis has been placed on the use of hazardous materials and their impact on worker safety and the environment. For example, the manufacture of chemicals and allied products is one of the largest industries in the United States. More than 50,000 different chemicals and formulations are produced in more than 12,000 chemical plants, and more than 1.1 million people are directly employed in U.S. chemical production. Many people want closer scrutiny and greater regulation of this huge industry and its products.

Simultaneously, extensive research and advancements in fire technology have occurred over the last two decades, and this has increased the content of building and fire codes as well as environmental regulations. Moreover, this has resulted in an increase in the *number* of federal, state, and local codes, regulations, and enforced standards that apply to industrial facilities. In fact, the number of legally enforced documents that require review for compliance in the design and construction of industrial facilities that use hazardous materials has literally surged to flood proportions, as evidenced by the documents listed in Table 1.1 and outlined in this chapter.

There has been a judicious attempt by society to regulate all possible contingencies so as to protect industrial workers and the environment. The result is an overwhelming number of safety documents, which can be intimidating to today's professionals. To eliminate the atmosphere of confusion and frustration, a comprehensive and ordered procedure for examining these documents is needed.

## Economic Considerations

As one reads through the multitude of codes, regulations, and standards governing any industrial construction project, one quickly comes to realize that there is an added *economic* dimension that can become a *major consideration*. Frequently, opportunities are available for significant savings in construction costs. However, for most projects, an organized approach to these documents is necessary to uncover the cost-saving measures (see the section Five Major Economic Decisions in Chap. 1 and the section Economic Options in Codes in Chap. 9). Such a comprehensive approach involves all the design disciplines in a simultaneous preliminary review of all the applicable codes, regulations, and standards, including the process engineer (before completing the preliminary process concepts), the architect, the fire protection engineer, the electrical engineer, and all the professionals who will be responsible for compliance with all the codes and regulations. (See the sections Early Comprehensive Reviews and Extensive Coordination of All Disciplines in Chap. 1.)

## Complete List of Codes, OSHA Regulations, Standards, Process Safety Reviews, and Environmental Regulations

The origin and scope of all the codes and regulations governing an industrial facility that uses hazardous materials are listed in Table 1.1 and are briefly outlined in this chapter (item numbers refer to numbers in Table 1.1), and their use is explained in subsequent chapters. Both new and existing industrial facilities must comply with the requirements enumerated in the more than 35 primary volumes. When these requirements are coupled with the more than 1000 reference standards that they enforce, compliance becomes a staggering task.

### Local zoning ordinances

Local zoning ordinances (item 1 in Table 1.1) vary with each municipality and are added to the requirements of the state and federal codes and regulations. Local ordinances generally have specific requirements for industry, including specific property zoning classifications; fire district restrictions on using or storing any hazardous materials; and regulations governing noise, smoke, and various other disturbances, such as punch presses. Local ordinances also may include requirements for building setbacks, types of pavements for roads, and the routing of utilities. It is the responsibility of the project manager or engineering staff to contact the municipal officials and obtain copies of their ordinances.

Moreover, zoning ordinances as well as the state's model building code must be consulted to determine if a facility in a particular use group, such as high hazard, can be built on a certain site. However, it also should be pointed out that some states require that any city or county ordinances governing construction must be approved by the state in order to be legally effective (see Chap. 8).

**Municipal services.**   Connections to municipal water and sewer mains are often specified in extensive detail in local ordinances. Types and degree of backflow control to protect the municipal water supply from contamination are specified. State authorities also sometimes address this in their plumbing and fire codes. See Chapter 8 for additional information on local ordinances and Chapter 14 for more specific information on piping and plumbing for hazardous materials.

### Building codes and standards

**State building codes.**   State building codes (items 2 through 7 in Table 1.1) are laws that establish minimum requirements for the design and construction of buildings and structures. They are enforced by state and local municipalities, who are responsible, for example, for responding to building fires that threaten occupants and property. State building codes apply to both new and existing facilities.

**Model codes.**   Some states write and adopt their own building codes, and some local governments pass ordinances to satisfy conditions specific to their region. Most states, however, adopt one of the three model codes in use across the country: the Building Officials and Code Administrators (BOCA) *National Building Codes,* the *Southern Standard Building Codes* (SSBC), and the *Uniform Building Codes* (UBC). The National Conference of States on Building Codes and Standards (NCSBCS) publishes a directory of state building codes and regulations. Local ordinances are available at local government offices.

All three model codes are separated into multiple volumes, and each separate volume covers a different design discipline or construction trade. For example, BOCA volumes include the *National Building Code,* the *National Fire Code,* the *National Mechanical Code,* the *National Plumbing Code,* the *National Energy Code,* and miscellaneous others.

**Reference standards.**   Many requirements found in building codes are excerpts based on standards published by nationally recognized organizations. (See Chapter 11 for 94 organizations that are nationally recognized.) The most extensive use of such standards is their adoption into a state or local building code by *reference*, which makes them legally enforceable by the state or local authorities. The *State of Ohio Building Code*, for example, refers to standards published by approximately 50 national organizations and encompassing about 370 documents. In addition, the *State of Ohio Fire Code* refers to another 100 documents published by about 10 national organizations. See Chapter 11 for examples of some of these references.

Although many reference standards provide only minimal materials specifications and therefore are merely listed in a project's specifications, some need to be examined in detail before the project design drawings are created and submitted for approval. An example of this is the ANSI Elevator Standard, which forbids the routing of sprinkler piping through an elevator shaft. This requirement is not found in most fire codes or NFPA 13 covering the installation of sprinkler systems, but local authorities have required contractors to relocate such piping when it was installed in an elevator shaft. Water pipes in an elevator shaft can be a hazard to electric elevator controls and to individuals in the elevator.

One of the 94 nationally recognized organizations is the National Fire Protection Association which has published NFPA standards, written by over 150 committees. Many of these are referenced directly in state and local building, fire, mechanical, and other codes. About 70 of these are referenced in and enforced by the BOCA *National Fire Code*. Included are NFPA 70, the *National Electrical Code*, and NFPA 101, better known as the *Life Safety Code*. Further cross-references are then found in the standards themselves, and these also can be enforced. Details found in these standards have been developed over almost a century of fire investigations and research by a number of organizations. More than 2400 individuals participate on these committees. The standards are reviewed and developed by consensus as the fairest and best method to achieve standards for safety requirements and codes.

Many of the enforced standards are adopted from the American National Standards Institute (ANSI) and the American Society for Testing and Materials (ASTM), among others. In addition, various insurance organizations, such as the American Insurance Association, Factory Mutual Systems, Industrial Risk Insurers, Insurance Services Offices, and others, also investigate fires, issue detailed reports, and develop standards. Fire research and testing are done by laboratories such as Underwriters Laboratories, Inc., and Factory Mutual Research Corporation. Government agencies such as the United States Fire Administration (USFA) and the National Bureau of Standards Center for Fire Research, among others, also issue reports and standards.

**State and local plumbing codes.**  In 1928, the American Standards Association organized its Sectional Committee on Minimum Requirements for Plumbing Equipment, A40. A preliminary plumbing code was published in 1942 and expanded in 1944. In 1933, the National Association of Master Plumbers published a *Standard Plumbing Code* and revised it in 1942. After 1933, other plumbing codes were published by various agencies, and many of these were followed by state and local authorities in the development of their codes.

**State and local energy codes.**  State and local energy codes (item 5 in Table 1.1) generally first became law after 1974. It was in that year that the National Bureau of Standards (NBS) issued a document entitled Design and Evaluation Criteria for Energy Conservation in New Buildings. In August 1975, the American Society of Heating, Refrigerating and Air-Conditioning Engineers (ASHRAE) published Standard 90-75, Energy Conservation in New Building Design. This standard has since been adopted by the model codes and by other standard-writing agencies as ANSI/ASHRAE/IES Standard 90-75, and it has become code in many states. In the 1980s this standard was revised, and now it is the most recognized national energy standard, called ASHRAE Standard 90.1–1989, Energy Conservation in New Building Design, Except Low-Rise Residential. Each state or municipal code must be consulted to determine which of these documents is legally enforced.

### The Occupational Safety and Health Act (OSHA)

The Occupational Safety and Health Act was passed in 1974 and amended a number of times, including the latest in 1992, and is known as Title 29 of the *Code of Federal Regulations* (*CFR*), Part 1900–1999. It extends to all employers and their employees in the United States. Workplaces covered by other federal agencies under other federal laws are not covered. However, if these other federal laws do not apply in a specific area, then OSHA applies. OSHA states that each employer "shall furnish...a place of employment which is free from recognized hazards that are causing or are likely to cause death or serious physical harm to his [or her] employees." The Occupational Safety and Health Administration, the agency that administers OSHA (also called OSHA), develops safety and health standards (items 12 and 13 in Table 1.1). These standards superseded the Walsh-

Healey Act, the Service Contract Act, the Construction Safety Act, the Arts and Humanities Act, and the Longshoremen's and Harbor Workers' Compensation Act. OSHA standards fall into four major categories:

- General industry
- Maritime
- Construction
- Agriculture

OSHA is authorized to conduct workplace inspections in each of these areas, and these inspections are, with few exceptions, conducted without advance notice. Imminent-danger situations are given top priority; next are accidents resulting in fatalities or injuries resulting in hospitalization of five or more employees; then comes high-hazard industries. In addition, all employers of 11 or more persons must maintain records of occupational injuries and illnesses as they occur, and these records must be available to OSHA. If OSHA violations are found, citations are issued, and there are penalties for each infraction.

An individual state can sign an agreement with OSHA to formally take over all enforcement activities from the federal agency if it submits a plan that is at least as effective as the federal program and is certified. All state standards are available from the Office of Federal and State Operations, Occupational Safety and Health Administration, U.S. Department of Labor, Room 305, Railway Labor Building, 400 First Street NW, Washington, D.C. 20210.

OSHA Part 1926.58 on asbestos regulations must be reviewed for demolition, salvage, removal, encapsulation, construction, alteration, renovation, repair, or maintenance of buildings or products containing asbestos, tremolite, anthophyllite, or actinolite (item 13 in Table 1.1).

### Recognized process safety review procedures

OSHA General Industry Safety and Health Standard 29 *CFR* 1910-106 Section H covers processing plants and Section I covers refineries, chemical plants, and distilleries. These sections also, by reference, require the use of recognized process safety review procedures for industries that process hazardous materials. There are a number of sources for these procedures. A primary source is the American Institute of Chemical Engineers (AIChE). (See Supplementary Sources at the end of the book, and for further discussion, see Chapter 3.)

## Environmental regulations

**Environmental audits.**  Today's extensive cradle to grave environmental regulations make it prudent to conduct environmental audits in order to avoid criminal and civil penalties. Environmental audits (item 20 in Table 1.1) for hazardous material contamination need to be performed, by qualified personnel, for all new sites, as well as for the acquisition of property or existing buildings, to avoid extensive cleanup costs. An *environmental audit,* as defined by the U.S. Environmental Protection Agency (EPA), is a "systematic, documented, periodic and objective review by regulated entities of facility operations and practices related to meeting environmental requirements." Environmental audits involve the "Superfund Act" (CERCLA), the Resource Recovery Act (RCRA), the Superfund Authorization and Reauthorization Act (SARA), and the Toxic Substances Control Act (TSCA) and must include

1. Air—unpermitted emission sources, improper registration, and equipment maintenance.
2. Water—unpermitted discharges exceeding National Pollutant Discharge Elimination System permit limits or sewer ordinances.
3. Hazardous waste—incompatible wastes, uncovered reactive waste tanks, solvent-recovery stills not listed in part A, unplugged floor drains, and incomplete contingency, personnel training, and closure plans.
4. Health and safety—inadequate ventilation, potential work hazards, and right-to-know programs.

One important point to remember is that liability under the Superfund regulations can be inherited in the purchase of a previously contaminated site and/or building. Hazardous waste contamination is seldom apparent and therefore requires review by experienced environmental engineers (see Chap. 20 for more details).

**Right-to-Know and Clean Air Acts.**  The Emergency Planning and Community-Right-to-Know Act (item 21 in Table 1.1) is the third title of Superfund Authorization and Reauthorization Act (SARA) signed into law in 1986. It is known as Title III, and it mandates emergency planning and gives communities the right to know more about hazardous materials used by certain industries. Almost all facilities that produce, handle, store, buy, or transport hazardous materials are covered under this law. As of October 1987, this act mandated specific reporting and provided deadlines. Reporting includes inventories of each chemical produced or handled and the submission of material safety data sheets for each of these chemicals and any annual releases of hazardous materials into the environment.

The Clean Air Act (item 22 in Table 1.1) was passed in 1970, extended and substantially amended in 1977, and extensively amended with sweeping legislation in 1990. The 1990 amendments are 20 times the size of the original Clean Air Act and are over 700 pages in length, requiring a decade to implement. The 1990 amendments impose new standards on industry and include for the first time small industries such as dry cleaners and print shops. The sections that apply to industry cover three titles: Title I, Ambient Air Quality Standards, Title III, Hazardous Air Pollutants, and Title VI, Stratospheric Ozone. The original Clean Air Act authorized the EPA to set source performance standards and national emission standards for hazardous air pollutants. The amendments impose new standards for industry sources for 41 pollutants that must be in place by 1995 and for sources of 148 other pollutants by 2003. In addition, many state and local agencies have implemented toxic air control programs that require planning for the prevention of accidental releases of these materials (see Chap. 17 for details).

**The Toxic Substances Control Act, the Resource Recovery Act, Superfund, and the Department of Transportation (DOT) Regulations.** The Toxic Substance Control Act (TSCA) (item 23 in Table 1.1) was passed in 1976 and amended a number of times, with the most recent amendments in 1989. The *Code of Federal Regulations (CFR)* affects the chemical industry mainly through Section 5. The purpose of TSCA is to regulate chemical substances at their source to reduce human or environmental risks from hazardous chemicals by front-end controls on their manufacture, distribution, use, or disposal. TSCA authorizes the EPA to require testing of chemicals and premanufacture notification for new substances or for significant new uses of existing substances. TSCA applies not only to pure chemical substances, but also to impurities of materials, incidental reaction products, and trace materials.

The EPA collects information on particular substances under Section 8 of TSCA through the Comprehensive Assessment Information Rule (CAIR) and under Section 8(e) requires reporting of substantial risk information. Under TSCA Section 6, the EPA can prohibit, limit, or ban the manufacture, processing, and use of specific chemicals.

The Resource Recovery Act (item 24 in Table 1.1) was passed in 1976 and amended in 1984 and 1988. It is published in 40 *CFR,* Subchapter I, Parts 240–280. It is the prime legislation governing hazardous waste, and it establishes a national program to protect human health and the environment from the improper handling of solid waste and to encourage conservation of natural resources. It authorizes the EPA to generate standards for the storage, transportation, and disposal of hazardous waste and requires:

1. A complete ban on land disposal of hazardous waste unless no migration from the waste facility will occur for as long as the waste remains hazardous or the waste is treated to EPA established levels.

2. Legally mandated deadlines.

3. More stringent standards for the handling of hazardous waste.

4. A schedule for EPA listing of additional categories of chemicals.

5. Regulatory control of and standards for underground storage tanks.

See Chapter 19 for more details on hazardous waste.

Transportation of hazardous materials is governed by Public Law 101-615, Hazardous Materials Transportation Uniform Safety Act of 1990. The law affects those who load, unload, or handle hazardous materials.

The "Superfund Act" (CERCLA, SARA) (item 25 in Table 1.1) was passed in 1980 and amended a number of times, with the latest amendments in 1988. The Superfund Amendment and Reauthorization Act (SARA) establishes controls for emergency responses and the reporting of spills for both industry and public safety agencies. SARA also requires OSHA to adopt regulations designed to protect hazardous materials emergency responders and makes it mandatory for industry to record inventories of extremely hazardous chemicals in reportable quantities.

The U.S. Department of Transportation (DOT) has issued regulations (item 26 in Table 1.1) governing the movement of hazardous materials by air, water, road, rail, and pipeline to protect human safety and the environment in the event of an uncontrolled release. The DOT's *Emergency Response Guidebook* provides recommendations for this protection from releases of specific chemicals and discusses procedures for responding to both large and small spills.

**Other antipollution measures.**    The Clean Water Act (CWA) (item 27 in Table 1.1) was passed in 1972 and amended a number of times, with the most recent amendment in 1989. It is a successor to the federal Water Pollution Control Act legislation that was passed in the 1950s and the 1960s (*CFR*, Title 40). The 1977 amendments severely limit the discharge of pollutants. Industries must control toxic pollutant discharges from plant site runoff, spillage or leaks, sludge or waste disposal, and effluent from industrial manufacturing or processing operations. The CWA controls discharges from point sources into waters of the United States. It regulates five types of discharges:

1. Direct discharges

2. Indirect discharges

3. Sources that spill oil or hazardous substances

4. Discharges of dredged or fill material

5. Sewage from vessels

See Chapter 18 for details.

The Safe Drinking Water Act (item 28 in Table 1.1) was passed in 1974 and was amended a number of times, with the most recent amendment in 1988. This act applies to public water systems. Part C, Protection of Underground Sources of Drinking Water, applies to any person or entity that contaminates an underground source of drinking water. Section 1417 prohibits the use of lead pipe, solder, or flux after 1986 in any plumbing system providing drinking water for human consumption. In May of 1991, the EPA set new nationwide standards to lower the level of lead in drinking water. Up to 1991, the level of lead permitted in drinking water was an average of 50 parts per billion (ppb) measured anywhere in the water distribution system. The new standard requires at least 90 percent of the monitored household drinking water taps to have lead levels of 15 ppb or less or an average level of approximately 5 ppb. The new standards require 79,000 public water suppliers in the United States to monitor for lead. Large water systems (serving more than 50,000 people) must begin monitoring by January 1, 1992, medium-sized systems (serving 3300 to 50,000 people) by July 1, 1992, and small systems (serving fewer than 3300 people) by July 1, 1993.

The Solid Waste Disposal Act (item 29 in Table 1.1) was passed in 1976 and was amended by the Hazardous and Solid Waste Amendments of 1984 (Pub. L. 98-616), the Safe Drinking Water Act Amendments of 1986 (Pub. L. 99-339), and the Superfund Authorization and Reauthorization Act of 1986 (Pub. L. 99-499).

Underground Storage Tank (UST) Regulations (item 30 in Table 1.1) were passed in October of 1988. They are an addition to the Resource Recovery Act as Subtitle I and were developed by the EPA to protect human health and the environment from leaking underground tanks (see Chap. 20 for details).

The Asbestos Hazard Emergency Act (item 31 in Table 1.1) was passed in 1986 and mandates the removal of asbestos from all public buildings (29 *CFR* 1926.58). This act applies to all construction work, as defined in Section 1910.12(b), including (1) demolition, (2) removal, and (3) construction, alteration, repair, maintenance, or renovation of structures where asbestos, tremolite, anthophyllite, or actinolite is present.

## Periodic Amendments

Almost without exception, all municipal ordinances, state building codes, environmental regulations, and federal regulations are periodically amended. You must ask for all amendments when you request copies of these regulations because local authorities generally enforce the latest amendments if they were legally adopted at the time the design is submitted for approval, and sometimes even up to the time the construction is started.

## Conclusion

Reviewing this overwhelming list mandates the only realistic and economical conclusion: *Conduct a comprehensive code, regulation, and applicable standard review early in the project design process,* as described in Chapter 1, not only to achieve compliance, but also (as discussed in the following chapters) *to reduce construction costs.*

The following chapters discuss the application of these codes, regulations, and standards, attempting to make them more user friendly, in roughly the sequence they are needed as the engineers and architects progress through the design process for an industrial facility.

# 3

# Material Safety Data Sheets for Hazardous Chemicals

This chapter provides detailed information on where to find the regulations governing every hazardous chemical that is received, processed, and/or stored in an industrial facility.

## Federal Regulations Governing Hazardous Materials

1. See the section Right-to-Know and Clean Air Acts in Chapter 2.

2. See the section The Toxic Substances Control Act (TSCA), the Resource Recovery Act (RCRA), Superfund, and the Department of Transportation (DOT) Regulations in Chapter 2. Almost all facilities that produce, handle, store, buy, or transport hazardous materials are covered under the Toxic Substances Control Act (TSCA). As of October 1987, this act requires specific reporting and provides deadlines for such. Reporting includes inventories of each chemical produced or handled and the submission of material safety data sheets for each of these chemicals and any annual releases of hazardous materials into the environment.

## OSHA Material Safety Data Sheets

OSHA's Hazard Communication Standard (29 *CFR* 1910.1200) was promulgated in 1975. In 1991, the Laboratory Standard (29 *CFR* 1910.1450) was passed for chemicals in laboratories. Section (g)(1) requires industry to submit a legal document for every hazardous material manufactured. Therefore, in an industrial facility, a material safety data sheet (MSDS) must be submitted for every hazardous material that is received, stored, used, processed, or shipped. An MSDS is a compilation of the health, flammability, and reactivity hazards of a chemical.

Figure 3.1 shows a sample material safety data sheet taken from OSHA Form 174, which may be used to comply with OSHA's Hazard Communication Standard (29 *CFR* 1910, Part 1200). You will note that the required data are grouped under eight sections: Section I gives the source or manufacturer's name and address, as well as an emergency telephone number for use in the event of an accident. Section II lists the hazardous ingredients and provides identity information. Section III delineates the physical and chemical characteristics. Section IV provides fire and explosion hazard data. Section V gives reactivity data. Section VI gives health hazard data. Section VII lists the precautions for safe handling and use. And Section VIII presents control measures.

Although no specific form is mandated, manufacturers of hazardous materials are required by law to publish all the information covered in these eight sections. If a section does not apply, the manufacturer must state this on the form, since all spaces must be filled.

However, four sections have been added to current material safety data sheets to satisfy today's environmental regulations: Section IX lists special precautions. Section X provides shipping information. Section XI lists emergency response guidelines. And Section XII provides product information contacts. The following paragraphs provide a detailed discussion of the 12 sections required in a material safety data sheet.

Section I is self-explanatory, providing the manufacturer's name and address and the emergency telephone number.

Section II, Hazard Ingredients/Identity Information, lists the components, chemical formula, and common names of the substance. This section also gives worker exposure limits, such as OSHA's permissible exposure limit (PEL) and threshold limit value (TLV).

Section III, Physical/Chemical Characteristics, lists the boiling point, vapor pressure and density, solubility in water, appearance and odor, specific gravity, melting point, and evaporation rate of the substance. This information might be required, for example, to determine the need for general room or local ventilation controls.

Section IV, Fire and Explosion Hazard Data, gives the flash point, lower explosive limit (LEL), upper explosive limit (UEL), extinguishing media, special fire fighting procedures, and unusual fire and explosive hazards. The flash point is needed to determine if a liquid is a combustible liquid or a flammable liquid, as defined in NFPA 321, Ba-

| Material Safety Data Sheet<br>May be used to comply with<br>OSHA's Hazard Communication Standard,<br>29 CFR 1910.1200. Standard must be<br>consulted for specific requirements. | **U.S. Department of Labor**<br>Occupational Safety and Health Administration<br>(Non-Mandatory Form)<br>Form Approved<br>OMB No. 1218-0072 |
|---|---|
| **IDENTITY** *(As Used on Label and List)* | Note: *Blank spaces are not permitted. If any item is not applicable, or no information is available, the space must be marked to indicate that.* |

**Section I**

| Manufacturer's Name | Emergency Telephone Number |
|---|---|
| Address *(Number, Street, City, State, and ZIP Code)* | Telephone Number for Information |
| | Date Prepared |
| | Signature of Preparer *(optional)* |

**Section II — Hazardous Ingredients/Identity Information**

| Hazardous Components (Specific Chemical Identity; Common Name(s)) | OSHA PEL | ACGIH TLV | Other Limits Recommended | % *(optional)* |
|---|---|---|---|---|
| | | | | |
| | | | | |
| | | | | |
| | | | | |
| | | | | |
| | | | | |
| | | | | |
| | | | | |
| | | | | |
| | | | | |

**Section III — Physical/Chemical Characteristics**

| Boiling Point | | Specific Gravity ($H_2O$ = 1) | |
|---|---|---|---|
| Vapor Pressure (mm Hg.) | | Melting Point | |
| Vapor Density (AIR = 1) | | Evaporation Rate (Butyl Acetate = 1) | |
| Solubility in Water | | | |
| Appearance and Odor | | | |

**Section IV — Fire and Explosion Hazard Data**

| Flash Point (Method Used) | Flammable Limits | LEL | UEL |
|---|---|---|---|
| Extinguishing Media | | | |
| Special Fire Fighting Procedures | | | |
| Unusual Fire and Explosion Hazards | | | |

| (Reproduce locally) | OSHA 174, Sept. 1985 |
|---|---|

**Figure 3.1**   OSHA sample MSD sheet.

**Section V — Reactivity Data**

| Stability | Unstable | | Conditions to Avoid |
|---|---|---|---|
| | Stable | | |

Incompatibility (*Materials to Avoid*)

Hazardous Decomposition or Byproducts

| Hazardous Polymerization | May Occur | | Conditions to Avoid |
|---|---|---|---|
| | Will Not Occur | | |

**Section VI — Health Hazard Data**

| Route(s) of Entry: | Inhalation? | Skin? | Ingestion? |
|---|---|---|---|

Health Hazards (*Acute and Chronic*)

| Carcinogenicity: | NTP? | IARC Monographs? | OSHA Regulated? |
|---|---|---|---|

Signs and Symptoms of Exposure

Medical Conditions
Generally Aggravated by Exposure

Emergency and First Aid Procedures

**Section VII — Precautions for Safe Handling and Use**

Steps to Be Taken in Case Material Is Released or Spilled

Waste Disposal Method

Precautions to Be Taken in Handling and Storing

Other Precautions

**Section VIII — Control Measures**

Respiratory Protection (*Specify Type*)

| Ventilation | Local Exhaust | | Special | |
|---|---|---|---|---|
| | Mechanical (*General*) | | Other | |

| Protective Gloves | | Eye Protection | |
|---|---|---|---|

Other Protective Clothing or Equipment

Work/Hygienic Practices

**Figure 3.1**　(*Continued*)

sic Classifications of Flammable and Combustible Liquids, and NFPA 30, Flammable and Combustible Liquids Code.

Section V, Reactivity Data, states whether the material is stable, conditions to avoid, incompatibility (other materials to avoid), hazardous decomposition or by-products (if hazardous polymerization can occur), and conditions to avoid. Primary consideration must be given to the following:

1. Is the substance unstable?

2. Will it oxidize with other materials?

3. Will it react with water or air?

4. What is its rate of combustibility?

5. Is it radioactive?

6. Is it corrosive?

Section VI, Health Hazard Data, indicates the danger to skin, the dangers from inhalation or ingestion, whether the effects are temporary or permanent, whether the material is a carcinogen, the signs and symptoms of exposure, medical conditions generally aggravated by exposure, and emergency and first aid procedures. Again, for example, this information may be necessary to determine the need for personal protective equipment for workers and general or local ventilation controls.

Section VII, Precautions for Safe Handling and Use, lists the steps to be taken in case the substance is released or spilled, indicates the appropriate waste disposal method, and suggests precautions to be taken in handling and storing and other possible precautions. Again, this information may be necessary to determine the need for personal protective equipment for workers and to know how to respond to an emergency.

Section VIII, Control Measures, gives the requirements for respiratory protection, ventilation (local, special, or general), protective gloves, eye protection, other protective clothing or equipment, and work/hygienic practices.

Section IX, Special Precautions, provides more information on what situation to avoid, storage requirements, and other precautions.

Section X, Shipping Information, lists primary and secondary hazards, DOT shipping name, hazard class, 49 *CFR* section reference, and what quantities are reportable.

Section XI, Emergency Response, provides requirements for evacuation, containment, and disposal, as well as emergency response contacts and phone numbers.

Section XII, Product Information Contacts, gives the names, addresses, and phone numbers of specialists to contact for further technical information on the product.

With the detailed hazard information provided by a material safety data sheet, the architects and engineers involved in planning an industrial facility can specify the proper requirements to protect life and property and to ensure the continuance of operations. Other codes, regulations, and standards prescribed by the EPA and OSHA from the point of receiving, storing, using, or processing a hazardous material through storing and shipping the finished product and disposing of any hazardous waste are described in subsequent chapters.

### National Fire Protection Association Hazardous Materials Information

The National Fire Protection Association (NFPA) has compiled, from other authoritative sources, a list of the fire hazard properties of 1500 substances (see table in NFPA 325M, Properties of Flammable Liquids, Gases and Volatile Solids). This list provides the flash point, ignition temperature, upper and lower flammable limits, specific gravity, vapor density, boiling point, water solubility, extinguishing methods, and hazard identification for each substance listed.

NFPA 704, Standard System for the Identification of the Fire Hazards of Materials, provides a system of easily recognizable markings that at a glance gives the hazards and their order of severity (rated 1 to 5) of any material in terms of health risks, flammability, and reactivity (instability). In this system, the severity numbers are arranged inside a symbol. Also included is a letter to indicate if water can or cannot be used on the material or if the material is radioactive. See NFPA 704 for further details.

Other useful references are NFPA 49 and NFPA 491M. NFPA 49, Hazardous Chemical Data, provides very detailed hazard information on specific materials. About 20 chemicals are added per year to the list. NFPA 491M, Manual of Hazardous Chemical Reactions, contains information on about 3550 documented reactions. These standards should be used as a supplement to the legally required MSD sheets. Table 3.1 presents the "Topic Finder" from NFPA's *Fire Protection Guide on Hazardous Materials*. See Chapters 4 and 5 and Table 5.2 for more information.

Table 3-2A, "Explosion Characteristics of Various Dusts," found in the NFPA *Fire Protection Handbook* (Table 3.2 includes a sample first page only), lists the following information for over 300 types of dust:

**TABLE 3.1   NFPA Topic Finder**

| Subject | Section no. |
| --- | --- |
| Boiling points | 49, 325M |
| Chemicals causing hazardous reactions when mixed | 491M |
| Clothing contamination hazards | 49 |
| Description of hazardous chemicals | 49 |
| Electrical equipment for hazardous chemical locations | 49 |
| Explosives | 491M |
| Extinguishing methods recommended | 49, 325M |
| Fighting fire in hazardous chemicals | 49 |
| Fire fighting procedures and methods | 49, 325M |
| Flammability hazard identification method | 704 |
| Flammability hazards identified | 49, 325M |
| Flammable limits (explosive limits) | 49, 325M |
| Flash point | 49, 325M |
| Hazard index described | 704 |
| Hazard index applied | 49, 325M |
| Hazardous chemical reactions | 491M |
| Hazardous chemicals data | 49, 325M |
| Hazardous chemicals, description of | 49 |
| Health hazard identification method | 704 |
| Health hazards identified | 49, 325M |
| Ignition temperatures | 49, 325M |
| Marking system for hazardous material | 704 |
| Melting points | 325M |
| Oxidizing materials | 49 |
| Personal protective equipment | 49 |
| Physical properties | 49 |
| Polymerization hazards identified | 49 |
| Propagation of flame | 49 |
| Protective clothing defined | 49 |
| Radioactivity hazard identification symbol | 704 |
| Reactions of two chemicals causing a hazard | 491M |
| Reactions with water, hazardous | 49, 325M |
| Reactions with water, marking symbol | 704 |
| Reactivity hazard identification method | 704 |
| Reactivity hazards identified | 49, 325M |
| Respiratory protective requirements | 49 |
| Shipping containers | 49 |
| Specific gravity | 325M |
| Storage recommendations | 49 |
| Toxicity | 49 |
| Vapor density | 49, 325M |
| Vapor-air density, defined | 49 |
| Water reactivity identification symbol | 704 |
| Water reaction of hazardous chemicals | 49 |
| Water solubility | 49, 325M |

SOURCE: From NFPA, *Fire Protection Guide on Hazardous Materials,* 9th ed. Quincy, Mass.: National Fire Protection Association, 1987.

**TABLE 3.2 Explosion Characteristics of Various Dusts**

| Type of dust | Explosibility index | Ignition sensitivity | Explosion severity | Maximum explosion pressure, psig* | Maximum rate of pressure rise, psi/s* | Ignition temperature† Cloud, °C | Ignition temperature† Layer, °C | Minimum cloud ignition energy, J | Minimum explosion concentration, oz/ft³‡ | Limiting oxygen percentages§ (spark ignition) |
|---|---|---|---|---|---|---|---|---|---|---|
| **Agricultural dusts** | | | | | | | | | | |
| Cellulose, alpha | >10 | 2.7 | 4.0 | 117 | 8,000 | 410 | 300 | 0.040 | 0.045 | — |
| Cornstarch commercial product | 9.5 | 2.8 | 3.4 | 106 | 7,500 | 400 | — | 0.04 | 0.045 | — |
| Lycopodium | 16.4 | 4.2 | 3.9 | 75 | 3,100 | 480 | 310 | 0.04 | 0.025 | C13 |
| Wheat starch, edible | 17.7 | 5.2 | 3.4 | 100 | 6,500 | 430 | — | 0.025 | 0.045 | C12 |
| Wood flour, white pine | 9.9 | 3.1 | 3.2 | 113 | 5,500 | 470 | 260 | 0.040 | 0.035 | — |
| **Carbonaceous dusts** | | | | | | | | | | |
| Charcoal, hardwood mixture | 1.3 | 1.4 | 0.9 | 83 | 1,300 | 530 | 180 | 0.020 | 0.140 | — |
| Coal, Pennsylvania, Pittsburgh (experimental mine coal) | 1.0 | 1.0 | 1.0 | 90 | 2,300 | 610 | 170 | 0.060 | 0.055 | — |
| **Chemicals** | | | | | | | | | | |
| Adipic acid | 1.9 | 1.7 | 1.1 | 84 | 2,700 | 550 | — | 0.060 | 0.035 | — |
| Bis-phenol A | >10 | 11.8 | 2.8 | 89 | 8,500 | 570 | — | 0.015 | 0.020 | C12 |
| Phthalic anhydride | 6.9 | 11.9 | 1.4 | 72 | 4,200 | 650 | — | 0.015 | 0.015 | C14 |
| Stearic acid, aluminum salt (aluminum tristearate) | >10 | 21.3 | 1.9 | 87 | 6,300 | 420 | 440 | 0.015 | 0.015 | — |
| Sulfur | >10 | 20.4 | 1.2 | 78 | 4,700 | 190 | 220 | 0.015 | 0.035 | C12 |
| **Drugs** | | | | | | | | | | |
| Aspirin (acetylsalicylic acid) $o\text{-}CH_3COOC_6H_4COOH$ | >10 | 2.4 | 4.3 | 88 | >10,000 | 660 | Melts | 0.025 | 0.050 | — |
| Vitamin C, ascorbic acid, $C_6H_8O_6$ | 2.2 | 1.0 | 2.2 | 88 | 4,800 | 460 | 280 | 0.060 | 0.070 | C15, N12 |
| **Metals** | | | | | | | | | | |
| Aluminum flake, A 422 extra fine lining, polished | >10 | 7.3 | 10.2 | 127 | 20,000+ | 610 | 326 | 0.010 | 0.045 | — |
| Magnesium, milled, grade B | >10 | 3.0 | 7.4 | 116 | 15,000 | 560 | 430 | 0.040 | 0.030 | — |

| | | | | | | | | | |
|---|---|---|---|---|---|---|---|---|---|
| Alloys and compounds | | | | | | | | | |
| Aluminum-cobalt alloy (60–40) | 0.4 | 0.1 | 3.5 | 92 | 11,000 | 950 | 570 | 0.100 | 0.180 | — |
| Thermoplastic resins and molding compounds | | | | | | | | | |
| Acrylamide polymer | 2.5 | 4.1 | 0.6 | 85 | 2,500 | 410 | 240 | 0.030 | 0.040 | — |
| Methyl methacrylate polymer | 6.3 | 7.0 | 0.9 | 84 | 2,000 | 480 | — | 0.020 | 0.030 | C11 |
| Cellulose acetate | >10 | 8.0 | 1.6 | 85 | 3,600 | 420 | — | 0.015 | 0.040 | C14 |
| Polycarbonate | 8.6 | 4.5 | 1.9 | 96 | 4,700 | .710 | — | 0.025 | 0.025 | C15 |
| Phenol formaldehyde molding compound, wood flour filler | >10 | 8.9 | 4.7 | 94 | 9,500 | 500 | — | 0.015 | 0.030 | C14 |

\* 1 psi = 6.894 kPa.

† °F = 9/5 (°C + 32).

‡ 0.1 oz/ft³ = 100 g/m³.

§ Numbers in this column indicate percentage, while the letter prefix indicates the diluent gas. For example, the entry C13 means dilution to an oxygen content of 13 percent with carbon dioxide as the diluent gas. The letter prefixes are: C = carbon dioxide and N = nitrogen.

SOURCE: From NFPA, *Fire Protection Handbook*, 9th ed., Quincy, Mass.: National Fire Protection Association, 1987.

explosibility indexes, ignition sensitivity, rate of pressure rise, ignition temperature of both a dust cloud and a dust layer, minimum ignition energy of a dust cloud, minimum explosion concentration, and limiting oxygen concentration in a spark chamber.

For new, unlisted dusts, NFPA 654, Chemical, Dye, Pharmaceutical and Plastics Industries, gives the requirements for testing the dust to determine the prevention techniques for its explosion hazard. Also see the U.S. Bureau of Mines publication (RI 5753), Explosibility of Agricultural Dusts, which contains data on the dust explosion hazard in air for 220 samples.

# Hazardous
# Process Equipment
# Safety Reviews

This chapter provides detailed information on the sources and use of recognized process safety review procedures required in the design of an industrial process that uses hazardous materials.

## Federal Regulations Governing Hazardous Materials

The following federal regulations have direct bearing on an industrial facility involved in the processing of hazardous materials:

1. The Toxic Substances Control Act (TSCA)

2. The Resource Recovery Act (RCRA)

3. Superfund (CERCLA, SARA)

4. U.S. Department of Transportation (DOT) Regulations

5. The Emergency Planning and Community-Right-to-Know Act

6. Local zoning ordinances

7. State building, fire, mechanical, electrical, and plumbing codes

8. The Occupational Safety and Health Act (OSHA)

9. The Clean Air Act amendments of 1990 (see Chap. 17)

See Chapter 2 for an outline of these regulations. Chapter 3 discussed the detailed information available from material safety data sheets for each hazardous material.

## Response and Reporting Requirements
## for Hazardous Material Spills

The Environmental Protection Agency (EPA) reports that 50 percent of the U.S. population takes drinking water from groundwater sources and therefore has established a number of regulations governing groundwater contamination. The Superfund Act (CERCLA) and the Superfund amendments and Reauthorization Act (SARA) establish controls for emergency responses to and reporting of incidents of hazardous materials spills for both industry and public safety agencies. SARA also requires OSHA to adopt regulations designed to protect hazardous materials emergency responders. In addition, the Clean Air Act amendments direct the EPA to take a larger role in process safety matters. As a result, the EPA has identified common elements in hazardous chemical accidents and is assisting state and local emergency planning officials in dealing with them. The Clean Air Act amendments also established a new Chemical Safety and Hazard Investigation Board to investigate accidents. This investigative agency is modeled after the National Transportation Safety Board.

**Emergency information.** Hazardous chemical spills or overfills that meet or exceed "reportable quantities" must be reported immediately to the National Response Center at 800-424-8802 or 202-267-2675. Chapters 17 through 20 provide more details. Information on what constitutes a "reportable quantity" in terms of leaks and spills is available from a RCRA/CERCLA hotline at 800-424-9346 or 202-382-3000.

### Site Considerations

**Environmental audits.** The first consideration when selecting a new site for an industrial facility is the completion of an environmental audit to avoid extensive cleanup costs from existing hazardous material contamination of the property and buildings. See Chapters 2 and 20 for detailed information.

**Hazardous operation spacing.** The second consideration is the safety of hazardous processing operations. Separation of operations is the most reliable way to protect life, health, and property. Explosions and fires in chemical plants cause two-thirds of the damage and most of the the lives in that industry, according to NFPA.

The site for a proposed industrial facility should be large enough to accommodate the following demands:

1. Adequate spacing of buildings and structures and other operations to afford exposure protection from adjacent explosions and fires

2. Adequate drainage runoff and containment space for accidental spills

3. Enough room for fire water supply tanks and a pumping service

4. Adequate fire department access

5. Facilities for containment of contaminated fire water in the event of a fire (Consideration should be given to the creation of settling and waste ponds or other forms of containment to prevent contamination of surface water or groundwater.)

6. Location of fire protection devices such as hydrants, hose houses, and water monitors, which need a minimum distance from buildings and structures (See NFPA 24 for minimum space requirements.)

Some of the more common potential site hazards found in industry that require proper spacing are tank truck and railcar tank loading or unloading facilities, tank farm storage facilities and their pump houses, drum rack storage facilities for flammable liquids, pulverized coal piles and conveyors, liquefied petroleum gas storage areas, ammonia storage tanks, underground fuel oil storage tanks, dust collectors, wood cooling towers, and electric substations.

Hazardous processes should be located in one-story buildings whenever possible. If this is not possible, such as when they are a part of a larger operation, they should, if possible, not be situated on upper floors or in basements, where codes often prohibit the location of hazardous or flammable materials because of restricted egress and poor access for fire fighting. Such processes also should not be located near building egresses or locations with high employee concentrations.

**Sources for minimum spacing requirements.**   Minimum spacing requirements are found in many sources. State building and fire codes, enforced NFPA standards, OSHA regulations, underwriters standards such as those of Industrial Risk Insurers (IRI),* Factory Mutual (FM), and American Petroleum Institute (API) standards all include distance requirements for various hazardous materials. However, when separation distances are specified in an enforced standard, they *must* be used. The applicable enforced NFPA standard for the specific hazardous material in question must be reviewed (see the NFPA list of over 250 standards in the Supplementary Sources).

---

*See Appendix A for IRI publication IM.2.5.2 on Plant Layout and Spacing for Oil and Chemical Plants for an example.

Also included in site considerations for exposure protection are adequate distances between hazardous processes and ignition sources,* control of spills, fire department equipment access for manual fire fighting, and security fences.

**Insufficient property for separation.**  When separation distances cannot be used, for whatever reasons, buildings codes require other means of protection. For example, NFPA 80A, A Recommended Practice for the Protection of Buildings from Exterior Fire Exposure, Chapter 3, "Means of Protection," presents three main methods for protecting buildings from exposure to fires from adjacent property:

1.  Separation distances

2.  Complete and continuous fire separation walls when buildings are up against each other

3.  Total automatic sprinkler protection

If two buildings must be up against each other and one or both require explosion-relief vents, then the common wall between them must be blast resistant, and no openings are permitted. The blast force such a wall must withstand can be calculated from NFPA 68, Explosion Venting. Moreover, explosion-relief vents must direct the discharge from an explosion in a safe direction or toward unoccupied areas with no activity or buildings. Other buildings in the direction of the explosion relief must be a minimum distance, as prescribed by the codes or enforced standards.

### Building Codes

The BOCA *National Building Code* states requirements for hazardous operations in Article 3, under use group H, High Hazard, Section 306 (see Chap. 8). These requirements include "all buildings and structures, or parts thereof, that are used for manufacturing, processing, generation or storage of corrosive, highly toxic, highly combustible, flammable or explosive materials that constitute a high fire or explosive hazard, including loose combustible fibers, dust and unstable materials." Table 306.2, "Use Group H, High Hazard Uses," provides a list of materials, processes, and manufacturers that are representative of use group H. It also refers to a number of NFPA standards that are enforced.

Section 306.2.1, "Exceptions," provides a list of buildings and rooms

---

*See Chapter 6 on 12 sources of ignition.

that should not be classified as use group H. Table 8.5 in this book lists different high-hazard materials and the amounts allowed in a building before a high-hazard use classification is required in part of or the entire building. Additional exceptions are indicated in the notes to Table 8.5.

Article 5, "General Area and Height Limitations," gives limits for use group H, high hazard; use group F, factory and industrial; and use group S, storage. (See Table 8.3; also see Table 8.2 for fire-resistance requirements.) In addition, Section 600.1 states in the second paragraph that "chemical plants, packing plants, grain elevators, refineries, flour mills and others shall be constructed in accordance with the recognized practice and requirements of the specific industry." Section 600.2, "Special High Hazards," also must be read. Section 600.3, "Means of Egress," sets out more restrictive requirements and modifies Article 8, "Means of Egress," for buildings with special uses and occupancies.

Section 617.0, "Combustible Dusts, Grain Processing and Storage, Section 618.0 "Explosion Hazards," Section 619.0, "Flammable and Combustible Liquids," Section 620.0, "Liquified Petroleum Gas Facilities," and Section 622.0, "Paint Spraying and Spray Booths," also must be reviewed. Section 603.0, "HPM Use Facilities," applies to the semiconductor industry, which also uses high-hazard materials (see Chap. 8 for more information).

## OSHA

The OSHA General Industry Safety and Health Standards (29 *CFR* 1910-106) Section H covers "processing plants" and Section I covers "refineries, chemical plants, and distilleries." Paragraph (H)(4)(iii) deals with the transfer of large quantities of flammable or combustible liquids, and paragraph (H)(4)(iv) deals with equipment and the escape of vapors and liquids. For further information on OSHA regulations, see Chapter 10 of this book.

## Regulations to Be Published

The Clean Air Act amendments direct the EPA to take a larger role in process safety matters. As a result, the EPA has collected chemical release data from industry and has issued reports assessing the present status of prevention activities. The EPA also has identified common elements in hazardous chemical accidents and is assisting state and local emergency planning officials. The amendments also establish an independent Chemical Safety and Hazard Investigation Board, which is modeled after the National Transportation Safety Board.

The 1990 Clean Air Act amendments require the EPA and OSHA to issue a report on November 15, 1992, recommending regulations for risk-management plans (RMPs) and hazard assessments (HAs). The regulations will cover each facility that produces, processes, handles, or stores any of the extremely hazardous substances listed in the 1990 amendments. Sixteen substances are listed at this time, and more are to be added by November 15, 1992, which will bring the list to about 100 substances. The recommended requirements must be consistent with standards established by ANSI, ASTM, and ASME. The EPA must publish the regulations by November 15, 1993, and compliance will be required within 3 years.

Hazard assessments must cover specific methodologies, techniques, parameters, and assumptions involved in simulating vapor and liquid/vapor releases. They must identify potential equipment and process failures and assess the magnitude of potential releases and the impact such releases would have on human health and the environment. Section 301 of Title III adds a new subsection to Section 112 of the Clean Air Act, Section 304, which directs OSHA to publish regulations for a chemical process safety standard to protect employees from the hazards of accidental releases of highly hazardous chemicals (HHCs) by using hazard assessments. A list of highly hazardous chemicals was published by the EPA on November 15, 1991.

## OSHA's New Process Safety Management Standard

On February 24, 1992, OSHA published its final standard covering process safety management of highly hazardous substances. The rule took effect May 26, 1992. It covers a wide variety of manufacturing industries. If workers are exposed in greater than threshold quantities to any of the 130 toxic and reactive chemicals listed in Table 10-2, the standard is enforced. The standard covers all flammable liquids and gases, except heating fuels, in quantities over 10,000 pounds.

The standard mandates one of the following methods or an equivalent recognized method:

1. What-if

2. Checklist

3. What-if/checklist

4. Hazard and operability study (HAZOP)

5. Failure mode and effects analysis (FMEA)

6. Fault tree analysis

The process hazard analysis must be updated and revalidated every 5 years.

## Recognized Hazardous Process Safety Reviews

Over the last two decades, regulators have moved toward greater formalization in the analysis of the hazards involved in processing dangerous chemicals. This was recently reinforced with passage of the 1990 Clean Air Act amendments, Section 301 of Title III for facility planning for the prevention of accidental releases of hazardous liquid or vapor contaminants (see Chap. 17). It also requires a systematic, detailed, and thorough safety analysis of every chemical process, including contributory and related events, in an effort to protect life, health, and property and to continue production and income uninterrupted. OSHA also enforces these formal analyses by reference.

This systematic approach examines the potential for fire, explosion, chemical reactivity, toxicity, corrosiveness, and temperature and environmental effects of every chemical process. Seven key modifiers—no, less, more, part of, as well as, reverse, and other than—are applied to every pipe, vessel, pump, valve, piece of process equipment, piece of materials handling equipment, and instrument in the process. The more complex the process, the more thorough is the review. Of necessity, therefore, such analyses are time-consuming and need to be done by experienced staffs.

Using all the relevant process flow and instrumentation diagrams, equipment plan drawings, and specifications, these recognized *process safety reviews* examine such operating deviations as (1) major operating limits (i.e., flow, temperature, pressure, levels, chemical reactivity, and mechanical stress), (2) chemical compositions of mixtures, and (3) reactions (e.g., unplanned reactions, explosions, equipment overpressure, exothermic reactions and overheating, and ignition of flammables). Therefore, process safety reviews must be conducted to prevent the accidental release of flammable, combustible, highly reactive, or toxic materials in sufficient amounts to endanger the life or safety of plant employees and neighbors and/or property and to continue productive operations. They also must be conducted to comply with the codes and regulations discussed earlier. These process safety reviews must be organized and recognized procedures to identify, evaluate, and control hazards associated with receiving, storing, processing/manufacturing, handling, and transporting hazardous materials. Their value is that they provide a systematic analysis that considers all possible occurrences in the process equipment and instrumentation so that no potential hazard is overlooked.

There are two accepted industrial approaches to ensuring the control of process hazards and the protection of life, property, and continuance of operations:

1. Dependable checklists

2. Recognized detailed process safety review procedures

A checklist is mandatory, and satisfies situations where hazardous materials are present to a minor extent. Both a checklist and a detailed process safety review are required when higher hazards are present or hazardous materials are processed, handled, or manufactured.

Checklists must be prepared by experienced engineers, but they require little experience to use and work with when the right questions are asked. They can be as detailed as necessary to satisfy the particular condition and have been known to be as long as 12 pages.

Process safety review procedures involve systematic, comprehensive, and precise analyses. They are selected and conducted by an experienced team of all the engineering disciplines required for the design, and the team should include an experienced safety engineer. Process safety reviews require considerable time and involve extensive reports. Five major methods have been developed to detect hazards, and these methods are listed in Table 4.1.

There are a number of sources for these procedures. One of the best is the *Guidelines for Hazard Evaluation Procedures,* published by the American Institute of Chemical Engineers (AIChE). It states in a summary in the foreword that "the purpose of this document is to make available the hazard evaluation procedures that are currently being used by many companies to reduce the risk of chemical process accidents."

This work was sponsored by the AIChE as a part of its continuing effort to improve safety performance in the chemical industry through

TABLE 4.1   Hazard Evaluation Procedures

| Procedure | Designation |
|---|---|
| 1. What-if analysis | WHAT-IF |
| 2. Hazard and operability study | HAZOP |
| 3. Failure mode and effect method | FMEA |
| 4. Fault-tree analysis | FAULT TREE |
| 5. Dow & Mond hazard indices | DMHI |

education of the engineers who design, start up, operate, and manage chemical and petrochemical process plants. The hazard evaluation procedures are described in detail in Chapter 2 for the most appropriate procedure(s) to be selected for a particular purpose with the help of the decision process described in Chapter 3. There is sufficient detail in Chapter 4 on how to use the procedures to enable many of these procedure to be put into practice by persons with little experience in hazards analysis. When particular expertise is required, it is so noted.

Selection of which major approach to use in hazards analysis depends on the size and degree of complexity of the process and equipment and the quantity and number of different hazardous materials present. To put this into perspective, Table 4.2 presents some examples of process accidents and how they can occur. Figure 4.1 is an example of a method in assessing a process hazard by reviewing the consequences and probability. Table 4.3 presents a matrix designed to help select an appropriate hazard evaluation procedure. Then Figure 4.2 presents an example of how to use process/system checklists, as well as examples of how to use the other hazard evaluation procedures.

### Information required for a what-if checklist

1. Process flow sheets
2. The heat and material balance
3. Process and instrumentation drawings and process flows diagrams
4. Plot plan
5. Equipment plan
6. Material safety data sheets for each chemical used listing the following essential data (see Chap. 3 for more information):
   a. Boiling points
   b. Freezing points
   c. Vapor pressures
   d. Flash points
   e. Combustion limits
   f. Ignition temperatures
   g. Thermal stability
   h. Reactivity
   i. Chronic and acute toxicity data
      (1) Oral
      (2) Inhalation
      (3) Skin
   j. Exposure limits

**TABLE 4.2 Elements of Accidents**

| Hazards | Initiating events/upsets | Intermediate events (system and operator responses to upsets) | | Accident consequences |
| --- | --- | --- | --- | --- |
| | | Propagating | Ameliorative | |
| | | Process-parameter deviations | Safety-system responses | |
| Significant inventories of | Machinery and equipment malfunctions: | Process-parameter deviations | Safety-system responses | Fires; explosions; impacts |
| a. Flammable materials | a. Pumps, valves | a. Pressure | a. Relief valves | |
| b. Combustible materials | b. Instruments, sensors | b. Temperature | b. Backup utilities | |
| c. Unstable materials | | c. Flow rate | c. Backup components | |
| d. Toxic materials | | d. Concentration | d. Backup systems | |
| e. Extremely hot or cold materials | | e. Phase/state change | | |
| f. Inerting gases (methane, carbon monoxide) | | | | |
| Highly reactive | Containment failures | Containment failures | Mitigation-system responses | Dispersion of toxic materials; dispersion of highly reactive materials |
| a. Reagents | a. Pipes | a. Pipes | a. Vents | |
| b. Products | b. Vessels | b. Vessels | b. Dikes | |
| c. Intermediate products | c. Storage tanks | c. Storage tanks | c. Flares | |
| d. By-products | d. Gaskets | d. Gaskets, bellows, etc. | d. Sprinklers | |
| | | e. Input/output or venting | | |

Reaction rates especially sensitive to

a. Impurities
b. Process parameters

Human errors

a. Operations
b. Maintenance
c. Testing

Loss of utilities

a. Electricity
b. Water
c. Air
d. Steam

External events

a. Floods
b. Earthquakes
c. Electrical storms
d. High winds
e. High-velocity impacts
f. Vandalism

Method/information errors

a. As designed
b. As communicated

Material releases

a. Combustibles
b. Explosive materials
c. Toxic materials
d. Reactive materials

Ignition/explosion operator errors

a. Omission
b. Commission
c. Diagnosis/decision making

External events

a. Delayed warning
b. Unwarned

Method/information failure

a. Amount
b. Usefulness
c. Timeliness

Control responses and operator responses

a. Planned
b. Ad hoc

Contingency operations

a. Alarms
b. Emergency procedures
c. Personnel safety equipment
d. Evacuations
e. Security

External events

a. Early detection
b. Early warning

Information flow

a. Routing
b. Methods
c. Timing

SOURCE: From AIChE, *Guidelines for Hazard Evaluation Procedures*. New York: AIChE, 1985, p. 1–3.

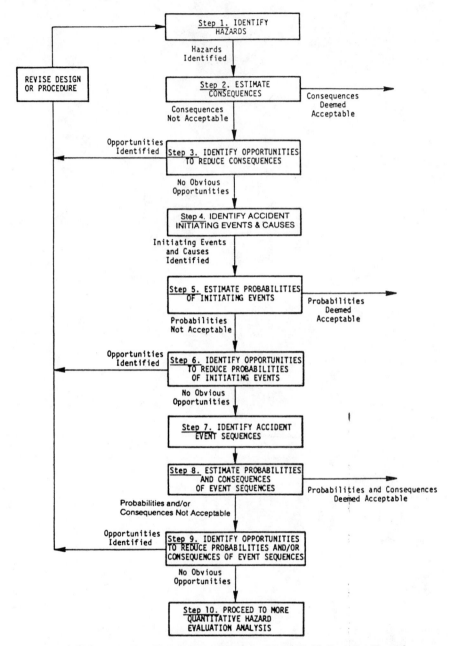

**Figure 4.1** Steps in predictive hazard evaluation. (*From Guidelines for Hazard Evaluation Procedures, © 1985 by the American Institute of Chemical Engineers. Reproduced by permission of the Center for Chemical Process Safety of AIChE.*)

**TABLE 4.3  Matrix Relating Hazard Evaluation Procedures to Hazard Evaluation Process Steps**

| Steps in hazard evaluation process | Process/ system checklists | Safety review | Relative ranking, Dow & Mond | Preliminary hazard analysis | What-if method | Hazard and operability study | Failure mode effects and criticality analysis | Fault-tree analysis | Event-tree analysis | Cause-consequence analysis | Human error analysis |
|---|---|---|---|---|---|---|---|---|---|---|---|
| Identify deviations from good practice | Primary purpose | Primary purpose | Primary purpose | | | | | | | | |
| Identify hazards | Primary purpose* | Primary purpose* | Primary purpose* | Primary purpose | Primary purpose | Primary purpose | Primary purpose | Provides context only | | | |
| Estimate "worst case" consequences | | | Primary purpose | | Primary purpose | Provides context only | Primary purpose | | | | |
| Identify opportunities to reduce consequences | | | Primary purpose | Secondary purpose | | Provides context only | Provides context only | | | | |
| Identify accident initiating events | | | | | Primary purpose | Primary purpose | Primary purpose | Primary purpose | | | Primary purpose |
| Estimate probabilities of initiating events | | | | | | Provides context only | Provides context only | Primary purpose | | | Primary purpose |
| Identify opportunities to reduce probabilities of initiating events | | | | | Primary purpose | | | Primary purpose | Primary purpose | Primary purpose | Primary purpose |
| Identify accident event sequences and consequences | | | | | | | | Primary purpose | Primary purpose | Primary purpose | |
| Estimate probabilities of event sequences | | | | | | | | Primary purpose | Primary purpose | Primary purpose | |

TABLE 4.3  Matrix Relating Hazard Evaluation Procedures to Hazard Evaluation Process Steps (Continued)

| Steps in hazard evaluation process | Hazard evaluation procedures | | | | | | | | | | |
|---|---|---|---|---|---|---|---|---|---|---|---|
| | Process/ system checklists | Safety review | Relative ranking, Dow & Mond | Prelimi- nary hazard analysis | What-if method | Hazard and operability study | Failure mode effects and criticality analysis | Fault-tree analysis | Event-tree analysis | Cause- consequence analysis | Human error analysis |
| Estimate magnitude of consequences of event sequences | | | | | | | | | Provides context only | Provides context only | |
| Identify opportuni- ties to reduce prob- abilities and/or con- sequences of event sequences | | | | | | | | | Primary purpose | Primary purpose | Primary purpose |
| Quantitative hazard evaluation | | | | | | | | Primary purpose | Primary purpose | Primary purpose | Primary purpose |

*Previously recognized hazards only.
SOURCE: From AIChE, *Guidelines for Hazard Evaluation Procedures.* New York: AIChE, 1985, p. 1–3.

**Figure 4.2**  Process/system checklists. (*From Guidelines for Hazard Evaluation Procedures,* © *1985 by the American Institute of Chemical Engineers. Reproduced by permission of the Center for Chemical Process Safety of AIChE.*)

# Process/System Checklists

### General Description

A process or system checklist can be applied to evaluating equipment, materials, or procedures. Also, the checklist can be used during any stage of a project to guide the user through common hazards by using standard procedures.

The checklist should be prepared by an experienced engineer who is familiar with the general plant operation and the company's standard procedures. Once the checklist has been prepared, it can then be applied by less experienced engineers and reviewed by a manager or staff engineer who has approval authority for the appropriate subsequent action.

A checklist will generally produce compliance with the minimal standards and identify areas that require further evaluation.

### Guidelines for Using Procedure

Examples of checklists for each of five phases of a project's life (design, construction, startup, operation, and shutdown) are provided below. These checklists are necessarily general, with a discussion of many of the elements to be checked. To be most useful, the checklists should be specifically tailored for an individual company, plant, or product.

These brief checklists are for illustrative purposes only. Examples of more complete checklists are shown in Appendix A [of the AIChE guidelines].

1. *Design*  During the design effort, the extent of hazard evaluation should be consistent with the preliminary or final design. The following discussion is appropriate for a final design and is more extensive than what would normally be needed for a preliminary design effort.

*Materials.*  Review the characteristics of all process materials—raw materials, catalysts, intermediate products, and final products. Obtain detailed data on these materials such as:

- Flammability
  What is the autoignition temperature?
  What is the flash point?
  How can a fire be extinguished?

- Explosivity
  What are the upper and lower explosive limits?
  Does the material decompose explosively?

- Toxicity
  What are the breathing exposure limits (e.g., Threshold Limit Values, Immediately Dangerous to Life and Health, etc.)?
  What personal protective equipment is needed?

- Corrosivity and Compatibility
  Is the material strongly acidic or basic?
  Are special materials required to contain it?
  What personal protective equipment is needed?

- Waste Disposal
  Can gases be released directly to the atmosphere?
  Can liquids be released directly to a sewer?
  Is a supply of inert gas available for purging equipment?
  How would a leak be detected?

(Continued)

Figure 4.2    Process/system checklists. (*Continued*)

- Storage
  Will any spill be contained?
  Is this material stable in storage?
- Static Electricity
  Is bonding or grounding of equipment needed?
  What is the conductivity of the materials, and how likely are they to accumulate static?
- Reactivity
  Critical temperature for auto reaction?
  Reactivity with other components including intermediates?
  Effect of impurities?

*Equipment.* Review the process flow sheet or equipment list to identify the hazards associated with each piece of equipment.

- Design Specifications
  Are design margins (or safety factors) clearly stated for temperature, pressure, flow, level, or other process variable?
  Are the materials of construction compatible with the process stream?
  Is the equipment subject to stress corrosion cracking (e.g., stainless steel)?
- Pressure Relief
  Have safety values been sized for all conditions (i.e., fire, loss of cooling, closed downstream valve)?
  Do pipelines need pressure relief for thermal expansion?
  Is there risk of the vents plugging?
- Plant Arrangement
  Has adequate spacing been provided between pieces of equipment?
  Are flame arrestors needed for equipment vents?
  Do any pieces of equipment need remotely operated valves?
- Electrical Equipment
  Does all equipment comply with the electrical classification?

*Procedures.* During the course of the design, the proper procedures for handling startup, shutdown, or emergency situations should be addressed.

- How should the plant operators and instrumentation and control systems react to the following contingencies?
  Fire
  Gas release
  Electrical power failure
  Cooling water failure
  Steam failure
  Loss of instrumentation (instrument air or electrical power)
  Loss of inert gas supply
- Do any plant interlocks have to be bypassed for plant startup or shutdown?
- Does the design consider a natural disaster such as earthquake, flood, or tornado?

2. *Construction*  During the construction period, several critical actions are required to avoid problems with adjacent facilities or in future operation.

*Materials*

- Has an authorized individual checked that the material received conforms to the design specifications?
- Have spare parts been ordered?

*Equipment*
- Has a hydrostatic test or other acceptance test been witnessed by an authorized individual?
- Are battery limit block valves accessible and clearly identified?

*Procedures*
- Are skilled craftsman being used?
- Is good housekeeping being practiced?
- Has an orderly transfer to Operations been planned?

3. *Startups*   Every possible effort should be made to simplify problems and actions during this hectic and critical period. This is an especially vulnerable time that requires thoughtful, deliberate action to avoid errors.

*Materials*
- Has there been prior planning for raw materials, utilities, and operating supplies to simplify any required action during startup?
- Have all suppliers been notified of startup plans?
- Have contingency plans been made for disposal of off-spec material?

*Equipment*
- Has all equipment been purged of air (if required)?
- Have all blinds been removed?
- Are all valves in their correct position?
- Have instrument/interlock checks been completed?
- Have all critical pieces of equipment been clearly identified
- Has the final inspection/acceptance of all equipment been completed?
- Does instrumentation fail safe?

*Procedures*
- Have startup and operating procedures been prepared in advance
- Is operator training complete
- Has a walk-through of the startup been completed?
- Have the startup plan and schedule been clearly communicated
- Are emergency procedures complete?

4. *Operation*   Once a plant has been operating for a long time, there is a tendency to become complacent about hazards. Plant operations staff must remain diligent to identify and minimize hazards.

*Materials*
- Do all raw materials continue to conform to specifications
- Is each receipt of material checked for identification
- What routine tests are needed to support plant operations
- Does the operating staff have access to Material Safety Data Sheets?
- Is fire fighting and safety equipment properly located and maintained?

*(Continued)*

**Figure 4.2**   Process/system checklists. (*Continued*)

---

*Equipment*

- Has all equipment been inspected as scheduled?
- Have pressure relief valves been inspected as scheduled?
- Have safety systems and interlocks been tested at appropriate times?
- Are the proper maintenance materials (spare parts) available?

*Procedures*

- Are the Operating Procedures current?
- Are the operators following the Operating Procedures?
- Are new operating staff trained properly?
- Are experienced operating staff kept up to date on all Operating Procedures?
- How are communications handled at shift change?
- Is the Operating Logbook being used properly?
- Is housekeeping acceptable?
- Are electrical tag-out procedures being used?
- Are work permits being used?
- Is gas testing being performed diligently?

5. *Shutdown*   This phase of a project or plant is usually neglected because people tend to look forward to the next project. Several hazards can be overlooked at this point unless diligence is maintained.

*Materials*

- Has the inventory of all chemicals been removed?
- Has all equipment been purged or flushed with inert material?

*Equipment*

- Is the equipment, including piping, gas-free?
- Have entry barriers been located at necessary points?

*Procedures*

- Has a shutdown plan or schedule been communicated to the appropriate staff?

---

7. Operating conditions (pressures and temperatures)
8. All equipment drawings and specifications, including the following data:
   a. Vessel sizes
   b. Materials of construction
   c. Pump specifications and characteristics
   d. Material and energy balances
   e. Agitation requirements
   f. Maximum allowable working pressures
   g. Vent sizing, basis and calculations
   h. Ventilation requirements
   i. Electrical diagrams

9. All controls and instrumentation

10. Plot plan

11. Operating procedures

References frequently used for these reviews are

1. Building and fire codes

2. NFPA standards that apply and are enforced

3. NEC (provides requirements for several hazardous classifications of electrical equipment plus guidance on when to use each class)

4. ASME Boiler and Pressure Vessel Code

5. API standards for equipment layout and process instruments

6. ISA standards for the manufacture, calibration, and application of process instruments.

**TABLE 4.4    What-If Checklist Form**

| Hazard | What-if item | Consequences | Recommended protection |
|---|---|---|---|
| Ammonia supply line to process in building | Valve A fails to open, with process disconnected | Ammonia is released into work area | Alarm/automatic safety valve B closes |

**TABLE 4.5    HAZOP Report Sheet**

| Item no. | Guide word* | Deviation | Possible causes | Consequence | Action required |
|---|---|---|---|---|---|
| 1 | No | Flow | | | |
| 2 | More | Flow | Operator error | Overflow | Overflow line is provided |
| 3 | Less | Flow | | | |
| 4 | Reverse | Flow | | | |
| 5 | No | Pressure | | | |
| 6 | More | Pressure | | | |
| 7 | Less | Pressure | | | |
| 8 | Negative | Pressure | | | |
| 9 | No | Temperature | | | |
| 10 | High | Temperature | | | |
| 11 | Low | Temperature | | | |
| 12 | Freezing | Temperature | | | |

*Results of deviation from normal operating procedures can be checked by systematically applying guide words.

Table 4.4 presents a sample what-if checklist form, and Table 4.5 presents a sample hazard and operability report sheet. See Chapter 5 for more information and enforced standards on hazardous processes confined in buildings.

# 5

# Hazardous
# Industrial Operations

This chapter summarizes some of the more common hazardous industrial operations conducted inside buildings and lists the related codes and enforced standards.

## Industrial Fire Records

Fire records show that most industrial fires that result in human injury and death are flash fires or explosions of highly flammable materials. Two factors responsible for such accidents were hazardous operations that were not isolated and lack of fire control systems—distinct modern code violations. In such situations, two major kinds of accidents can occur:

1. Accidental ignition of vapors during normal operations.
2. Uncontrolled release of flammable and combustible liquids or dusts, resulting in large volumes of vapors or dusts spreading throughout a building, with an increased probability that they will reach an ignition source.

Hazardous materials must be separated from other materials or isolated whenever possible, unless they are present in small quantities. When only small quantities are present, the codes require that hazardous materials be stored in storage cabinets approved by Underwriters Laboratories (UL). Table 8.5 lists the maximum amounts of hazardous materials that can be stored in a facility that has a rating other than high hazard. In addition, UL-approved small outside storage sheds that can be spaced the required minimum distances are also available.

## Codes and Regulations Governing Hazardous Materials

The following federal regulations directly govern the processing of hazardous materials:

1. The Toxic Substance Control Act (TSCA)
2. The Resource Recovery Act (RCRA)
3. Superfund (CERCLA, SARA)
4. U.S. Department of Transportation (DOT) Regulations
5. The Emergency Planning and Community-Right-to-Know Act
6. Local zoning ordinances
7. State building, fire, mechanical, electrical, and plumbing codes
8. The Occupational Safety and Health Act (OSHA)
9. The Clean Air Act Amendments of 1990

See Chapter 2 for an outline of these regulations.

## Accidental Spills

The Emergency Planning and Community-Right-to-Know Act requires the reporting of hazardous material releases. The EPA administers the section of the Superfund Amendments and Reauthorization Act (SARA) legislation that requires industry to report releases of hazardous substances. SARA also requires OSHA to adopt regulations designed to project emergency responders. In addition, the DOT has issued regulations governing the movement of hazardous materials by air, water, rail, road, and pipeline. See Chapter 2 for more information.

Superfund legislation establishes controls for emergency responses to and the reporting of incidents of spills for industry. For more detailed information on these codes, regulations, and enforced standards, see Chapter 2.

## Site Hazards

Tank truck and railcar tank unloading, tank farm storage facilities and their pump houses, drum rack storage facilities for flammable liquids, pulverized coal piles and their conveyors, liquefied petroleum gas storage facilities, ammonia storage tanks, underground fuel oil storage tanks, dust collectors, wood cooling towers, and electric sub-stations are some of the more common site hazards found in industry. All these facilities are covered by one or more of the codes, regulations, or standards. Such facilities are required to be spaced a minimum distance from an industrial building and each other unless other approved precautions are taken. See the section Site Considerations in Chapter 4 for more information.

## Hazardous Processes Confined in Buildings

Hazardous processes confined in buildings pose a more serious threat to life safety and property than those installed outdoors with the required spacing. Gases, vapors, and/or dusts released from outside process equipment are not confined by walls and roofs and are therefore less likely to reach the lower explosive limit (LEL) for vapors or the minimum explosion concentration (MEC) for dust than when the process is installed inside. Gases, vapors, and/or dusts from outside process equipment are more likely to be dispersed, even in mild breezes, and are less likely to reach an ignition source. Obviously, for reasons such as weather and seasonal changes of climate, among others, locating some processes outside cannot be done.

When hazardous materials are accidentally released from process equipment located inside buildings and/or an accidental spill occurs and the hazardous gas, vapor, and/or dust begins to fill the building interior, they are much more likely to reach the LEL for vapors or MEC for dust. With the more sources of ignition (see Chap. 6) and generally greater concentration of workers inside buildings, there is a much greater threat to life and safety.

### Large-volume buildings are a greater hazard

Large-volume buildings pose a more severe threat than small buildings because they can accumulate larger vapor/dust clouds with more fuel and generate more severe explosive forces and/or larger fires and larger clouds of dangerous toxic smoke. Further, there are likely more sources of ignition and more employees in larger facilities. Also, there are probably more combustibles and the fire that generally follows an explosion will be more difficult to extinguish. Building codes recognize this and reduce the allowable area and height for high-hazard occupancy classifications. See Chapter 8 for further discussion.

### Greater hazard after ignition

After ignition of a gas, vapor, or dust fire, the walls and roof of a building will restrict dispersion and dilution and prevent dissipation of the heat, toxic gases, and smoke from the fire. This allows the ignition temperatures of the surrounding materials to be reached more rapidly and results in faster fire growth. Although fire walls do restrict the spread of fire, they also can slow attempts by employees to escape a fire. The volume of smoke can increase rapidly to three times that of the original room air. Smoke that can be inhaled and that conceals pathways to exits poses a threat, and the physical danger is also increased from collapsing walls and roofs.

### High-hazard classifications

For these reasons, industrial buildings in which hazardous materials are processed are frequently classified as high-hazard occupancies under state building codes and as a result become very expensive to construct with compliance. The building codes, regulations, and enforced standards written for these high-hazard classifications are extensive, complex, confusing, and often conflict with each other. See Chapter 7 for occupancy descriptions and risk factors for various contents.

### Comprehensive, organized approach required

As a consequence of these increased regulations, a lengthy, thorough, and extensive code review is a must if one is to comply with the requirements of the many volumes, chapters, sections, and paragraphs that address in detail the issues of life safety, property and environment protection, and production continuance. (See the section Early Comprehensive Reviews in Chapter 1 for further discussion.)

### Prevention of vapor/dust releases

Table 5.1 lists some of the many safeguards to prevent the escape of hazardous gases, vapors, liquids, and dusts from a process into an in-

**TABLE 5.1   Methods to Prevent Vapor/Dust Releases and Ignition**

| | |
|---|---|
| 1. Process vessel containment or closed systems housing hazardous materials | Chaps. 4 and 14 |
| 2. Exhaust hoods enclosing materials handling transfer points | Chap. 13 |
| 3. Separation of hazardous materials operations | Chap. 8 |
| 4. General building ventilation | Chap. 13 |
| 5. Pneumatic conveyor systems | Chap. 5 |
| 6. Isolation of grinding mills, mixers, blenders, dryers, etc., and dust collectors in smaller rooms | Chap. 8 |
| 7. Control of ignition sources | Chaps. 6 and 15 |
| 8. Isolating electrical devices in pressurized cabinets or rooms | Chap. 15 |

TABLE 5.2   NFPA Special Hazardous Operations Standards

| Number | Title |
|---|---|
| NFPA 30 | Flammable and Combustible Code |
| NFPA 31 | Installation of Oil Burning Equipment |
| NFPA 33 | Spray Applications Using Flammable and Combustible Materials |
| NFPA 34 | Dipping and Coating Processes Using Flammable or Combustible Liquids |
| NFPA 35 | Manufacture of Organic Coatings |
| NFPA 36 | Solvent Extraction Plants |
| NFPA 37 | Installation and Use of Stationary Combustion Engines and Gas Turbines |
| NFPA 40E | Storage of Pyroxylin Plastic |
| NFPA 43A | Storage of Liquid and Solid Oxidizing Materials |
| NFPA 43B | Organic Peroxide Formulations |
| NFPA 43C | Storage of Gaseous Oxidizing Materials |
| NFPA 43D | Storage of Pesticides in Portable Containers |
| NFPA 45 | Fire Protection for Laboratories Using Chemicals |
| NFPA 46 | Storage of Forest Products |
| NFPA 49 | Hazardous Chemicals Data |
| NFPA 50 | Bulk Oxygen Systems at Consumer Sites |
| NFPA 50A | Gases: Hydrogen Systems at Consumer Sites |
| NFPA 50B | Liquefied Hydrogen Systems at Consumer Sites |
| NFPA 51 | Design and Installation of Oxygen–Fuel Gas Systems for Welding, Cutting and Allied Processes |
| NFPA 51A | Acetylene Cylinder Charging Plants |
| NFPA 51B | Cutting and Welding Processes |
| NFPA 52 | Compressed Natural Gas (CNG) Vehicular Fuel Systems |
| NFPA 54 | National Fuel Gas Code |
| NFPA 58 | Liquefied Petroleum Gases, Storage and Handling |
| NFPA 61A | Starch Manufacturing and Handling |
| NFPA 61B | Grain Elevators and Bulk Handling |
| NFPA 61C | Fire and Dust Explosions in Feed Mills |
| NFPA 61D | Fire and Dust Explosions in Milling of Agriculture Commodities for Human Consumption |
| NFPA 65 | Aluminum Processing, Finishing |
| NFPA 68 | Venting of Deflagrations |
| NFPA 69 | Explosion Prevention Systems (Inerting and Suppression) |
| NFPA 75 | Protection of Electronic Computer/Data Processing Equipment |
| NFPA 82 | Incinerators |
| NFPA 85A | Prevention of Furnace Explosions in Fuel Oil and Natural Gas Single-Burner Boiler Furnaces |

dustrial building. Also see Table 5.2 for a list of hazardous operations standards and Tables 6.1, 9.10, 12.3, 15.1, and 15.2 for further applicable standards.

**Process vessel containment.**   When hazardous materials can be completely contained in the process equipment, such as vessels, piping, and materials handling enclosures, during normal operations, without open transfer points, and the presence of hazardous materials can be

TABLE 5.2  NFPA Special Hazardous Operations Standards (*Continued*)

| Number | Title |
|---|---|
| NFPA 85B | Furnace Explosions in Natural Gas–Fired Multiple-Burner Boiler Furnaces |
| NFPA 85D | Prevention of Furnace Explosions in Fuel Oil–Fired Multiple-Burner Boiler Furnaces |
| NFPA 85E | Furnace Explosions in Pulverized Coal–Fired Multiple-Burner Boiler Furnaces |
| NFPA 85F | Pulverized Fuel Systems |
| NFPA 85G | Furnaces Implosions in Multiple-Burner Boiler Furnaces |
| NFPA 85H | Combustion Hazards in Atmospheric Fluidized Bed Combustion System Boilers |
| NFPA 85I | Stoker Operation |
| NFPA 86 | Ovens and Furnaces, Design, Location and Equipment |
| NFPA 86C | Industrial Furnaces Using a Special Processing Atmosphere |
| NFPA 86D | Industrial Furnaces Using Vacuum as an Atmosphere |
| NFPA 211 | Chimneys, Vents, and Solid Fuel–Burning Appliances |
| NFPA 231 | General Storage |
| NFPA 231C | Rack Storage of Materials |
| NFPA 231D | Storage of Rubber Tires |
| NFPA 231E | Storage of Baled Cotton |
| NFPA 231F | Rolled Paper Storage |
| NFPA 321 | Basic Classification of Flammable and Combustible Liquids |
| NFPA 325M | Fire Hazard Properties of Flammable Liquids, Gases, and Volatile Solids |
| NFPA 480 | Magnesium, Storage and Handling |
| NFPA 481 | Titanium, Handling and Storage |
| NFPA 482 | Production, Processing, Handling and Storage of Zirconium |
| NFPA 490 | Storage of Ammonium Nitrate |
| NFPA 491M | Hazardous Chemical Reactions |
| NFPA 650 | Pneumatic Conveying Systems for Handling Combustible Materials |
| NFPA 651 | Manufacture of Aluminum or Magnesium Powder |
| NFPA 654 | Chemical, Dye, Pharmaceutical and Plastics Industries, Prevention of Fire and Dust Explosions |
| NFPA 655 | Prevention of Sulfur Fires and Explosions |
| NFPA 664 | Fires and Explosions in Wood Processing and Woodworking Facilities |

avoided in the building, this provides a much safer working environment and can be a great source of cost savings in building construction. The costs of building code high-hazard occupancy classifications, hazardous electrical (classified) locations, extensive fire suppression systems, and complex fire alarm systems all can be reduced.

For example, when hazardous explosive materials are completely enclosed in process equipment designed to resist and contain the maximum pressures the materials could generate in an explosion or the process equipment is installed with adequately designed explosion venting routed to outdoors as required by codes, an approved explosion suppression system, or an approved inerting system, a number of costly building design parameters can be avoided. Generally, building, fire, OSHA, or other enforced standards such as NFPA 654 require explosion containment, explosion venting to outdoors, vessel inerting, or explosion suppression. These regulations also require explosion isolation in the process equipment in the form of chokes, rotary valves, instant-acting dampers, or flame snuffers. (Some of these items operate with a small explosive cartridge.)

Explosion suppression systems for flammable gases, vapors, or suspended flammable dusts are specified under NFPA 69, Chapter 4. These systems can be used to protect certain kinds of processing equipment, storage tanks, materials handling equipment, and laboratory and pilot plant equipment. NFPA 654, Chemical, Dye, Pharmaceutical, and Plastic Industry, provides valuable information on what to consider and what test data are required to determine if these systems can be effective.

The codes still require designers to address safety issues during those periods when completely enclosed equipment is opened for cleaning and servicing and there is a potential for hazardous materials to escape into the building on an infrequent or short-term basis.

**Exhaust hoods enclosing materials handling transfer points.** Enclosing liquid and granular materials transfer points within ventilating hoods with sufficient inward airflow to prevent vapors or dusts from escaping into a building is common practice. General ventilation, as well as makeup air to maintain positive air pressures with respect to process vessels and enclosures is also a common practice. Many codes and standards address this. They give minimum distances from outside the hood inlet where more expensive classified electrical service (explosion-proof) is mandatory. Frequently, however, the electrical service for the rest of the building can be a lower-cost system. See Chapter 15 for more information on locations that require hazardous electrical (classified) location designations and Table 15.1 for a list of enforced standards. Table 13.1 also provides more information.

Paint spraying is a common example of this kind of situation. If it is done without a spray-booth enclosure in an area that is not very large, which is sometimes the case, the code requires the use of classified electric devices and wiring throughout the entire area to prevent ignition of the vapors in the area. This can be a costly requirement. However, if the paint-spraying operation is performed in a spray booth that is installed in compliance with NFPA 33, Spray Application Using Flammable and Combustible Materials, then only the interior of the booth and the space within a few feet of its opening(s) are required to use classified electrical devices and wiring. Obviously, the added cost of the spray booth must be compared with the savings in room construction costs. In a large factory with a lot more equipment and operations, the cost of the booth is a great deal less than the room costs. More important, the hazard to workers in the large factory is reduced as well.

There are a number of excellent references that give detailed criteria for designing hoods and enclosures and specifying air inlet velocity. Two are *Air Pollution Engineering Manual,* 2d edition, published by the EPA (see Chap. 13 for more details on the contents of this manual) and *Industrial Ventilation Guide,* published by American Governmental Industrial Hygienists.

**Separation of hazardous materials operations.** Separating operations that generate hazardous vapors and/or dusts from larger areas and isolating them in small, cutoff rooms enclosed within fire-rated walls, attached buildings separated by a fire- or blast-resistant wall, or small, remote buildings frequently can avoid an expensive high-hazard occupancy classification for the larger area. A single, enclosed bag-slitting operation within a large warehouse and an enclosed liquid-adding operation to small finished paint containers within a large paint warehouse are common examples of this.

**General building ventilation.** General building ventilation is required by code in two specific situations. The first is when an enclosed process vessel door is opened for inspection or maintenance. In this situation, the process vessel is maintained under negative pressure or pressure that is lower than the room pressure, to reduce the dust or vapor release into the room. Positive room air pressure is maintained by makeup air. The second is when an enclosed process system is extensive and leakage into the room from rotating seal points or other points is significant. NFPA 30, Flammable and Combustible Code, for example, requires general building ventilation for the storage of containers inside a building because of leakage and possible accidents resulting in spills.

**Pneumatic conveyor systems.** Pneumatic conveyor systems offer greater safety from explosions and fire than any other type of bulk conveyors (see NFPA 650, Pneumatic Conveying Systems).

**Isolation of grinding mills, mixers, blenders, dryers, etc., and dust collectors.** As we have seen, processing equipment can be a frequent source of explosions and/or fires. The codes governing such equipment, such as building codes, NFPA standards for specific hazards, and OSHA specify spacing, explosion barriers, and/or blast-resistant walls for the protection of nearby personnel. The safest location for such equipment is generally remote and outside, with explosion suppression systems and chokes to block flame fronts from traveling back to operator stations through ducts or pipes. However, when equipment such as dust collectors, for example, are installed inside, they must be located near an outside wall for explosion venting, enclosed by fire walls, and have varying degrees of fire and explosion and protection. For more information, see NFPA 654 and other standards.

**Control of ignition sources.** For 12 sources of ignition that must be avoided, see Chapter 6. Also see Chapter 15 for electrical hazardous (classified) locations and NFPA standards for bonding and grounding.

**Isolating electrical devices in pressurized cabinets or rooms.** Isolating electrical spark- and heat-producing devices in separate pressurized enclosures or rooms when hazardous vapors and dusts cannot be contained in process vessels and ventilating hood enclosures is another option the codes allow (see Table 9.9). NFPA 496 gives design details for this option.

**Some typical hazardous operations and applicable codes (see Table 5.2)**

**Flammable and combustible liquids.** The safest and, in most instances, the cheapest method of transferring, dispensing, and storing flammable and combustible liquids is to keep them confined in approved vessels, containers, and piping. The most frequently enforced standard for these operations is NFPA 30, Flammable and Combustible Liquids Code. This standard provides detail requirements in terms of locations, equipment and piping specifications, ventilation, fire control, sources of ignition, and other details for

1. Outside tank storage
2. Inside tank storage
3. Small-container storage
4. Liquid handling, transfer, and use

Floor drainage is also needed when flammable liquids are present (1) to minimize the spread of fire and (2) to help extinguish a fire by removing the fuel. See the Appendix of NFPA 15 for drainage system design in areas containing flammable liquids. In addition, the codes mandate containment of contaminated fire water runoff to protect surface and groundwaters in the event of a fire.

For dipping and coating operations, local ventilation is a must whenever these materials are exposed to the room to keep the escaping vapors below the lower explosive limits. The rate of ventilation is specified by code or reference. See NFPA 34, for example. This enforced standard specifies a safe location, confining the vapor area to within 5 ft (1.52 m) of the operation with an approved ventilation method, construction of the equipment, temperature control of the liquid, control of electrical and other sources of ignition, and a local automatic fire suppression system.

Building or room automatic fire suppression systems are always required by building codes in places where flammable or combustible liquids are used or stored because these operations are classified as high hazard unless the amounts of these hazardous materials are small. Flammable liquids (see definition in NFPA 321, Basic Classification of Flammable and Combustible Liquids) form flammable vapors at temperatures below 100°F and can become a major threat. Any spilled liquid spreads rapidly [each gallon of liquid will cover 20 ft$^2$ (1.86 m$^2$) of floor space] and also evaporates rapidly to form vapors that can quickly and easily reach ignition sources (see Chap. 6). Code requirements are covered in the building codes, the fire codes, OSHA documents, and enforced NFPA standards.

**Spray finishing.** Spray finishing using flammable materials is common in the fabrication of many products. Overspray of the hazardous materials needs to be controlled and confined, and sources of ignition also need to be controlled, as defined in NFPA 70, Article 5-16.

**Explosive dusts.** Explosive dusts are created in many industrial operations. Reduction or elimination of these dusts generally requires the use of enclosing exhaust hoods and dust collectors. However, dust collectors are a frequent source of dust explosions followed by fires. Codes and standards frequently specify locations and explosion venting or suppression for these devices depending on the potential hazard of the dust (see Table 3.2). A U.S. Bureau of Mines publication, *Explosibility of Agricultural Dusts,* also contains data on dust explosion hazards in air for 220 different substances. (See also Chap. 12.) Code requirements for dust explosion protection are almost always found in the building codes, the fire codes, OSHA documents, and enforced NFPA standards.

**Chemical processes.** Chemical processes generally involve some form of mixing, high-temperature reactions, distilling, evaporating, filtering, absorption or adsorption, crushing, grinding, and/or drying. Because of their high degree of hazard, these processes require a great deal of safety expertise and are usually reviewed by a team of safety experts that always includes experienced safety personnel from the underwriter's staff and chemical, process, and instrumentation engineers (see Table 4.1). Chapter 4 should be consulted for recognized safety review procedures for all hazardous materials processing, whether large or small.

Again, whenever possible, the best and, in most instances, the least expensive way to ensure the safety of these processes is to keep them confined in approved vessels, containers, and piping, with pressure-relief devices vented to the outside of the building. Of course, explosions and fires can occur inside these vessels, and when this potential exists, enforced standards specify one of four safeguards: additional containment, venting to the outside, suppression systems, or inerting systems (see Chap. 12).

**Plastic products.** Plastics production generally involves the use of polymers, hazardous additives, and dusts. Therefore, facilities involved in plastics production also must be designed in accordance with the regulations governing chemical processes (preceding section).

**Boilers, furnaces, ovens, dryers, and incinerators.** The degree of hazard of these kinds of equipment varies with the type of fuel, the size of equipment, the quantity of fuel stored, and in the case of the furnaces and dryers, the product being heated. Locating equipment such as this inside buildings often requires separate rooms with fire walls and some form of fire suppression. Particular attention also must be paid to adjacent operations that may contain hazardous materials. It is equally important to avoid locations near code-required egresses and large quantities of stored explosive, flammable, or combustible materials. In addition, fire wall separation is generally required for adjacent office, computer, or other populated areas.

Explosion venting and exhaust of combustion products and of vapors from drying processes to outdoors are also frequently required. Moreover, overheat protection is a must, and makeup air supply and general ventilation are frequently mandated.

Code requirements for protection are almost always found in the building codes, the fire codes, OSHA, and enforced NFPA standards. (For a list of enforced standards specifying ovens, boilers, and furnaces see Table 5.2.)

**Welding and cutting.** Approximately 6 percent of fires in industrial properties have been caused by welding and cutting operations. Cutting and certain arc welding operations produce literally thousands of sparks that can spread as far as 35 ft (10.67 m), igniting nearby combustible materials. State fire codes and NFPA 51, "Oxygen-Fuel Gas Systems for Welding, Cutting and Allied Processes," govern this.

**Commercial cooking.**    Heated oils for food processing and similar operations are also a frequent hazard and have specific code and standard requirements. Cooking in a plant cafeteria is also a potentially hazardous situation. NFPA 96 covers the basic requirements for the installation of hoods, grease removal devices, exhaust ducts, dampers, air moving devices, auxiliary equipment, and fire protection for the exhaust systems and the cooking equipment used in industrial applications. Overhead sprinklers also prevent the spread of the local fire and are often required. Protection of the heated oil from the sprinkler water is also necessary and can be provided by an overhead hood. Code requirements are almost always found in the building codes, the fire codes, OSHA documents, and enforced NFPA standards.

**Heated oils.**    Heated oils for quenching operations also constitute a potential hazard. Special local automatic fire suppression systems are frequently required. Overhead sprinklers also prevent the spread of a local fire and are often required. Protection of the heated oil from the sprinkler water is also necessary and can be provided by an overhead hood. Code requirements are almost always found in the building codes, the fire codes, OSHA documents, and enforced NFPA standards.

**Other hazardous operations.**    Many other operations are potentially hazardous and are too numerous to list. Code officials, underwriters, and NFPA personnel are valuable sources of information, since they deal with these matters on a continuing basis.

## Other National Fire Protection Association Special Hazards Standards

The NFPA has a number of standards governing various hazardous materials that are enforced by state codes and that must be complied with in industrial facilities. Some of the more frequently used standards are listed in Table 5.2.

Each NFPA standard should be checked in the state building code appendix, the state fire code appendix, the state mechanical code appendix, the state electric code appendix, and the referenced standards listed in the OSHA regulations to see if they are legally enforced. However, good safety judgment must always prevail. Local officials can insist on the enforcement of any general industry standard not listed in the state codes under a catchall phrase in the codes whenever they have reason to believe a hazard exists to life, health, or property (see Chap. 1 for more information).

Another source of governing hazardous industrial operations is

NFPA's *Industrial Fire Hazards Handbook,* 3d edition. This handbook comprises 50 chapters, including complete chapters on bulk grain handling, vegetable and animal oil processing, paint and coatings manufacturing, rubber products, aluminum and nonferrous metals processing, wood products, furniture manufacturing, pulp and paper manufacturing, paper products manufacturing, printing and publishing, textile manufacturing, clay products plants, plastic products, motor vehicle assembly, shipyards, food processing, semiconductor manufacturing, chemical processing, storage and filling of aerosols products, radioactive materials, and many others.

# Twelve Sources
# of Ignition

There are 12 different sources of ignition for combustible or explosive vapor/dust clouds that can be found in an industrial facility. These are listed in Table 6.1.

All these sources must be examined when a small or large building or room has hazardous or ignitable materials present. The flash points and ignition energies of the materials are important to know when reviewing potential industrial hazards because the flash points of some liquids are actually below room temperature. (See Chapter 3 for sources of information on ignition characteristics.)

Table 6.2 lists various NFPA standards that govern control of ignition sources in specific industries.

**TABLE 6.1  Twelve Sources of Ignition**

| | |
|---|---|
| 1 | Electrical (see Chap. 15) |
| 2 | Open flames |
| 3 | Frictional heat (bearings or others) |
| 4 | Hot surfaces (ovens or furnaces) (see Chap. 5) |
| 5 | Cutting and welding (see Chap. 5) |
| 6 | Mechanical sparks |
| 7 | Static electricity (see Chap. 15) |
| 8 | Radiant heat (infrared heaters) |
| 9 | Heat-producing chemical reactions (see Chap. 3) |
| 10 | Smoking |
| 11 | Lightning (see Chap. 15) |
| 12 | Spontaneous ignition |

TABLE 6.2  NFPA Standards Governing Sources of Ignition in Various Industries

| Item | NFPA standard |
|---|---|
| Aluminum processing and finishing | 65:3-4 |
| Chemicals, dyes, pharmaceuticals, and plastics | 654:chap. 5; 654:A-5-1.1 |
| Combustible fiber storage | 1:3-8.2.2 |
| Dipping and coating processes | 34:chap. 6; 34:A-6 |
| Dusts | 1:3-8.3.3 |
| Electrical | 907M:2-3 |
| Flammable and combustible liquids | 30:2-6; 30:4-7.2; 30:5-5.2 |
| Gas | 54:1.6 |
| Hyperbaric facilities | 99:C-1.2.4 |
| LP-gas systems | 58:3-3.8; 58:3-8; 58:1-7; 59:1-3; 58:3-8.2; 58:table 3-8.2.2; 59:1-9 |
| Manholes, sewers, and underground structures | 328:1-2; 328:2-1.2 |
| Organic coating operations | 35:7-1 |
| Solvent extraction plants | 36:2-1-5; 36:3-3 |
| Spray application | 33:chap. 3; 33:13-4; 33:A-4 |
| Static electricity | 77:1-4.2; 77:2-1 |
| Sulfur crushing, grinding, and pulverizing | 655:2-6; 655:A-2-6.1 |
| Wastewater treatment plants | 820:6-3 |
| Wood processing and woodworking facilities | 664: chap 6; 664:A-6-2.1 |

# The *Life Safety Code*

## Origin

The National Fire Protection Association's (NFPA) *Life Safety Code* was developed as a result of work by the NFPA Committee on Safety to Life begun in 1913. The committee drafted the *Life Safety Code* after lengthy reviews of notable fires involving loss of life and analyses of their causes. This work led to the adoption of standards for the construction of stairways and exit facilities for factories and other buildings. At first, the committee published pamphlets such as "Outside Stairs for Fire Exits" in 1916 and "Safeguarding Factory Workers from Fire" in 1918. The *Building Exits Code* was first published by the NFPA in 1927. In 1977, the committee had grown to 11 subcommittees responsible for various chapters. The NFPA committees receive reports from the teams investigating major or significant fires. In addition, the NFPA is also active in laboratory fire research.

## Where Enforced

Since all states do not enforce the NFPA *Life Safety Code* for industrial buildings, you must check the applicable local building codes or contact the local authorities to see if the code is enforced in your locale. Nevertheless, when industrial buildings house processes that use hazardous materials, state building codes frequently enforce other NFPA standards that may, in turn, refer to and enforce various chapters, sections, and, paragraphs of the *Life Safety Code*. (See the section Interlocking Maze of Enforced Codes, Regulations, and Standards in Chapter 1.)

## Scope of the *Life Safety Code*

The NFPA *Life Safety Code* applies to all types of buildings, including industrial facilities. It has separate chapters for each building occupancy classification and for new and existing structures. The *Life Safety Code* is concerned with life safety alone, whereas national and state building codes are written to protect life, property (including adjacent buildings), and the continuance of profitable use of the facility.

## NFPA *Life Safety Code* Content

The NFPA states, "when fully incorporated, the measures in the NFPA *Life Safety Code* are sufficient to insure against major loss of life." The code addresses construction, protection, and occupancy features designed to minimize danger to life from fire, smoke, and panic. The code also identifies design criteria for egress facilities that allow prompt escape from buildings.

### Occupancy descriptions

Chapter 4 of the *Life Safety Code* classifies occupancies and defines content hazards. It describes low-hazard, ordinary-hazard, and high-hazard contents. Occupancy classifications are dependent on the burning characteristics, not on the quantity, of the contents.

*Low-hazard contents* are defined as those materials with such low combustibility that no self-propagating fire can occur and the only possible danger is from panic, fumes, smoke, or fire from adjacent sources that would require emergency exits. *Ordinary-hazard contents* are defined as those materials which are liable to burn with moderate rapidity or give off considerable volumes of smoke. *High-hazard contents* are defined as those materials which are liable to burn with extreme rapidity or which develop poisonous fumes or explosions.

### Risk of contents

The basic purpose in classifying contents is to delineate their risk. The classification is based on the rate of fire spread and the development of toxic fumes, both of which affect the time available for occupants to safely evacuate the facility. High-hazard occupancy classifications include occupancies where gasoline and other flammable liquids are used, which might result in the release of flammable and explosive vapors; where explosive dust materials may be produced; where toxic hazardous chemicals are manufactured; where combustible fibers are processed; and other similar hazardous occupancies.

A high-hazard occupancy classification is limited to those industrial buildings housing extremely hazardous operations. Incidental use of small quantities of flammable liquids in a building does not constitute a high-hazard occupancy, although some extra life safety precautions may be required during the limited period of use. Refer to Chapter 5 of NFPA 30, Flammable and Combustible Liquids Code, for guidance. Storage of flammable liquids such as paint in sealed containers, for example, does not normally require a high-hazard occupancy classification unless the operation includes opening of the containers. Such operations could be conducted in a separate room with a fire barrier between the storage and mixing areas. See the *Life Safety Handbook* for further discussion.

### Means of egress, construction, and fire protection

Chapter 5 of the *Life Safety Code* specifies egress requirements in detail in 19 pages. Chapter 6 of the code covers fire protection, including construction, compartmentalization, smoke barriers, special hazards protection, and interior finishes. Chapter 7 of the code covers building service and fire protection equipment, including utilities, HVAC equipment, smoke control, elevators and dumbwaiters, vertical conveyors, incinerators, detection and alarm systems, and sprinklers and other extinguishing systems.

### Office buildings and manufacturing buildings

Chapters 26 and 27 of the *Life Safety Code* cover new and existing business (office buildings) occupancies, respectively. They include requirements for special means of egress and fire protection systems. Chapter 28 of the code covers industrial occupancies, and it applies to both new and existing facilities. The requirements outlined in this chapter include factories making products of all kinds and properties used for such operations as processing, assembling, mixing, packaging, finishing or decorating, and repairing various products and materials. Included are requirements governing special means of egress and fire protection.

### Warehouses and open structures

Chapter 29 of the *Life Safety Code* covers both new and existing storage occupancies, establishing requirements for special means of egress and fire protection. Chapter 30, Section 30-1.3.7, of the code covers unusual structures, including operations conducted in open structures (such as refining and chemical processing) and operations conducted under roofs or canopies that provide shelter without enclosing walls.

This chapter also sets requirements for special means of egress and fire protection.

### Life Safety Code Handbook

In 1978, the NFPA published its first edition of the *Life Safety Code Handbook,* which essentially explains the *Life Safety Code* and offers commentaries on its content. This handbook is presently in its fifth edition. Readers are cautioned, however, to look on the commentaries in the handbook only as views expressed by contributors to the book.

### Industrial Life Safety Mission Largely Achieved by Automatic Sprinkler Systems

The *Life Safety Code Handbook* states, "Automatic sprinkler protection in industrial occupancies has been a principal factor in ensuring life safety through the control of fire spread. Limiting the size of the fire by the operation of sprinklers provides sufficient time for the safe evacuation of people exposed to the fire."

Moreover, today's industrial facilities are safer than those in the past because processes have been automated and are not as labor intensive. Instead of many operators working on the floor with the hazardous process, some operators are now stationed in automated process control rooms that often have fire protection and are located away from any danger. Another advantage of this arrangement is that operators are able to activate manual fire alarms more quickly. As a result, the fire department responds more quickly and the potential to loss of life and damage to the production facility are reduced.

### Alternatives to the Life Safety Code

In 1988, NFPA published its first edition of NFPA 101M, Alternate Approaches to Life Safety. The NFPA states that this document is intended to be used *with* the *Life Safety Code, not* as a substitute. Section 1-5 of the *Life Safety Code* allows alternative compliance and construction cost savings with the code under equivalency concepts when such equivalency is approved by the authority having jurisdiction. The methodology in NFPA 101M can be used to help determine equivalency by being part of the technical documentation submitted to the authority having jurisdiction.

NFPA 101M, Chapter 7, "Fire Safety Evaluation System for Business Occupancies," presents a measuring system to compare the level of safety provided by alternatives to the *Life Safety Code* and an arrangement of safeguards that differ from those specified in the *Life*

*Safety Code.* This chapter evaluates 13 safety parameters starting with construction and includes comparisons of hazards, fire extinguishing, fire detection and alarms, smoke control, and egress requirements. It provides a rating system by which to assign numerical values to these parameters, which are then totaled and compared with the measures prescribed in the *Life Safety Code* (see Fig. 8.1). Some state building codes also have chapters that allow fire safety evaluations for some occupancies.

# 8

# Building Codes Made User Friendly

This chapter attempts to make building codes *user friendly* by outlining a typical building code in order to simplify it, to illustrate how to save review time, and to remove some of the mystery the novice code reader confronts. The code used for this purpose in this chapter is the BOCA *National Building Code,* one of the three model building codes adopted by many states.

## Origin of Building Codes

The first building code was published in England in 1189. In Colonial America, the first building code was published in New York in 1625. It was not until the twentieth century, however, that the massive industrialization and population growth of the United States prompted a greater concern for loss of life and property that resulted in the creation of enforced building codes and fire regulations. Early in the twentieth century, the National Board of Fire Underwriters, in an attempt to protect their interests, wrote the Model Building Law, and in 1905 this law was published as a national building code.

## What Are Building Codes?

Building codes are laws that mandate minimum requirements for the design and construction of buildings and structures in an attempt to protect life safety and property. These laws generally are enforced by local municipalities, who are responsible for responding to building fires that threaten occupants and property. State legislatures generally delegate this power to enact and enforce building codes to local governments. This is especially true with large municipalities, but in less populated rural areas, the states often retain the authority to review proposed building drawings for code compliance because such reviews require a great deal of expertise with today's complex codes, regulations, and enforced standards.

## Model Codes

Today, most states have adopted one of the three model codes used across the country. The Building Officials and Code Administrators (BOCA) *National Building Code* were first published in 1950 and are used primarily in northern and eastern states. The *Southern Standard Building Code* (SSBC) was first published in 1945 and is used predominantly in the South. And the *Uniform Building Code* (UBC) was first published in 1927 and is generally enforced in western states. The Council of American Building Officials (CABO) makes an effort to coordinate the many codes through their Board for the Coordination of the Model Building Codes.

All three model codes are composed of multiple volumes. Each separate volume covers a different design discipline or construction trade. For example, BOCA publishes a separate *National Building Code, National Fire Code, National Mechanical Code, National Plumbing Code, National Energy Code,* and miscellaneous others. The state electrical code is usually a copy of NFPA 70, National Electric Code. The state building code will have requirements regarding permits, procedures, etc. Rather than adopt one of the model codes, some states write their own codes. Frequently, however, these state codes are essentially amended versions of one of the three model codes. In addition, many local governments pass ordinances that address conditions specific to their particular region that become part of the building code.

The National Conference of States on Building Codes and Standards, Inc. (NCSBCS), publishes the "Directory of State Building Codes and Regulations." (See the Supplemental Sources for the address.) Local ordinances are available at the local government offices.

This directory provides complete information for each state on

1. Titles of codes and years of the latest editions
2. Technical basis for the codes
3. Titles of latest administrative rules and the years of the latest and original editions
4. Preemptive applications

5. Occupancy classification

6. Level of enforcement

7. Full contract information for administrating and enforcing the codes

## Permits and Certified Local Building Departments

Many states allow the local governments to establish state-certified building departments, which include a plans review staff and building inspection personnel. These building departments must hire and/or train qualified people, who then must pass examinations to become certified before the state will authorize them to review and approve building plans. In such situations, the building code is enforced by review of a complete set of building documents by the building department, which then may issue a *building permit*. Further enforcement is ensured by a building inspector, who examines the building to be sure that it was constructed in accordance with the approved plans. Only then will the building inspector issue an *occupancy permit*, which allows the building to be occupied.

## Local Ordinances

Local or municipal ordinances are supplements to state building codes that generally serve to adjust the state codes to local conditions. Typical local ordinances include the following:

1. Street and public services code

2. Planning and zoning code

3. Building code

4. Fire prevention code

The zoning code must be reviewed for restrictions to industry before one selects a site for an industrial facility. The zoning code will show the business districts and industrial districts on a zoning map.

Local ordinances generally reference the state codes, contain requirements for flood control, mandate restrictions for high-hazard facilities (e.g., preventing their construction in densely populated areas), provide requirements for building appearances, and contain provisions for all the local building, plumbing, electrical, and other inspections.

Local fire codes generally enforce state fire codes and other standards, mandate fire limits (which often include type of construction, number of stories, and local standards for fire hydrants), and provide for fire inspections, etc.

## Building Code Outline

The balance of this chapter will be taken up with an outline of a typical building code (the Boca *National Building Code*). This outline will assist industrial planners in choosing the most economical building site, in determining the most efficient building area and number of floors, and in establishing the most appropriate occupancy classification, which is sometimes confusing in industrial buildings. This outline will also save considerable time and spare industrial planners some of the frustration that accompanies hunting for elusive but important details, details that are not found in an organized sequence but rather are scattered sporadically among multiple chapters with some interlocking but incomplete and random cross-references. (See the section Interlocking Maze of Enforced Codes, Regulations, and Standards in Chapter 1 for further discussion.)

## Typical State Building Code

### General administrative content, permits, and plan submission

Article 1 of virtually all building codes covers administration. Section 101 of the BOCA *National Building Code,* for example, addresses the applicability of codes and includes the following: It requires builders to apply for a permit to build. The application can be submitted by either the owner or the owner's agent. The application must be accompanied by detailed building plans, as well as a site plan and structural, mechanical, and electrical plans, including calculations. The building drawings and proposed materials and equipment are either approved and a building permit is granted, or rejected for noncompliance. Building materials and equipment must be in accordance with enforced testing standards.

Sections 101.5 of the BOCA code states: "When the provisions herein specified for health, safety and welfare are more restrictive than other regulations, this code shall control; but in any case, the most rigid requirements of either the building code or other regulations shall apply whenever they conflict."

### Existing buildings: alterations and repairs

Section 103 of the BOCA *National Building Code* applies to existing structures and covers changes in use, additions, alterations, and repairs. Section 104 distinguishes between repairs that require permits and ordinary repairs that do not require a permit.

Changes in use of existing buildings are also covered in Sections 103, 104, and 505 and Article 32 of the BOCA *National Building Code*. Article 32 allows for repair, alterations, addition, and/or change of use without requiring full compliance with Articles 2 through 31, except where compliance with other provisions in the code is specifically stated. New code provisions for proposed changes of occupancy for an existing building can be complex, and the codes must be reviewed carefully and the local authorities should be consulted.

The code recognizes that many existing buildings do not comply with the latest revisions in the codes but were in compliance at the time they were built. When upgrading these buildings to the latest code is cost prohibitive, the code allows for a controlled departure from full compliance without compromising the safety of the building. Article 32 evaluates 16 different items on an overall safety basis, including building height, area, fire area, space division, corridors, vertical openings, automatic fire suppression systems, mechanical systems, fire alarms and communication, smoke control, egresses, elevators, lighting, and mixed uses. NFPA 101M, Alternate Approaches to Life Safety, also does a similar evaluation (see Fig. 8.1 and Chap. 7).

### Maintenance of safe conditions in existing buildings

Most codes do not require or authorize local building inspectors to conduct periodic inspections. However, after an addition or alteration to an existing building under a building permit, an inspector may discover a noncomplying condition in another part of the building. Although the condition may not be in the addition or alteration, the code still considers it a violation, and the inspector has the authority to revoke the initial occupancy permit of the entire building; operations would have to stop. However, if the new addition or alteration is in compliance and separate, it may be granted an occupancy permit.

This paragraph of the code should be studied carefully. The building inspector in such situations normally must have permission of the owner or a search warrant for probable cause, except when he or she is inspecting for an occupancy permit after the construction has just been completed.

Section 2503 requires the maintenance of all existing mechanical equipment and systems in safe operating condition.

**Table 3205.1**
**SUMMARY SHEET - BUILDING SCORE**

Existing use _____   Proposed use _____

Year building was constructed _____   No. of stories ____ Height in ft. _____

Type of construction _____   Area per floor _____

Percentage of open perimeter _____%   Percentage of height reduction _____ %

Completely suppressed:   Yes ___ No ___   Corridor wall rating _____

Compartmentation:   Yes ___ No ___   Required door closers: Yes ___ No ___

Fireresistance rating of vertical opening enclosures _____

Type of HVAC system _____, serving number of floors _____

Automatic fire detection:   Yes ___ No ___, type and location _____

Fire protective signaling
  system:   Yes ___ No ___, type _____

Smoke control:   Yes ___ No ___, type _____

Adequate exit routes:   Yes ___ No ___   Dead ends:   Yes ___ No ___

Maximum exit access travel distance _____   Elevator controls:   Yes ___ No ___

Means of egress emergency
  lighting:   Yes ___ No ___   Mixed uses:   Yes ___ No ___

| Safety parameters | Fire safety (FS) | Means of egress (ME) | General safety (GS) |
|---|---|---|---|
| 3204.2.1 Building height | | | |
| 3204.2.2 Building area | | | |
| 3204.2.3 Fire area | | | |
| 3204.2.4 Space division | | | |
| 3204.2.5 Corridor walls | | | |
| 3204.2.6 Vertical openings | | | |
| 3204.2.7 HVAC systems | | | |
| 3204.2.8 Automatic fire detection | | | |
| 3204.2.9 Fire protective signaling system | | | |
| 3204.2.10 Smoke control | * * * * | | |
| 3204.2.11 Exit capacity | * * * * | | |
| 3204.2.12 Dead ends | * * * * | | |
| 3204.2.13 Max. exit access travel distance | * * * * | | |
| 3204.2.14 Elevator control | | | |
| 3204.2.15 Means of egress emergency lighting | * * * * | | |
| 3204.2.16 Mixed uses | | * * * * | |
| 3204.2.17 Automatic sprinklers | | ÷ 2 = | |
| Building score — total value | | | |

* * * * No applicable value to be inserted.

**Figure 8.1**  Summary sheet—building scores. (*Reprinted from BOCA National Building Code/1990, Building Officials and Code Administrators International, Inc. Published by arrangement with author. All rights reserved.*)

## New building location and site requirements

Included in the building code are site considerations for exposure protection from fire in adjacent buildings and fire department equipment access for manual fire fighting. Paragraph 502.2, "Street Frontage Increase," Table 504.2, "Minimum Fire Resistance Rating of Exterior Walls," and Table 906.2, "Exterior Wall Resistance Ratings," must be reviewed when selecting the location of a building on a piece of property. These requirements are designed to prevent the spread of fire between buildings and from floor to floor through window openings. Section 906.1 has an exception that deletes the exterior wall fire rating when the combined areas and height of two buildings on a piece of property comply with Table 501.

When separation distances are not feasible for any of a number of reasons, such as insufficient property area, the building code requires other means of protection. For example, NFPA 80A, A Recommended Practice for the Protection of Buildings from Exterior Fire Exposure, Chapter 3, "Means of Protection," permits a number of methods for protecting buildings from exposure to fires from adjacent buildings. These methods are listed in Table 8.1. (See NFPA 80A for more details.)

The first item generally needed from the building code is the minimum distances required from property lines and adjacent buildings. In addition, the local zoning ordinances also must be reviewed for setbacks. Fire department access is also an economic consideration here, for fire extinguishing system costs can increase when fire department access is limited.

Table 906.2 of the BOCA code provides exterior fire wall ratings based on separation distances and use groups. This table must be used in conjunction with Table 401 (see Table 8.2). Section 906.2.2 allows for a reduction in exterior wall fire rating in a non-load-bearing wall when the building is protected throughout with an automatic sprinkler system.

The code generally specifies separation distances from a common line between buildings. Therefore, care must be exercised to ensure that the distance is twice that given in the table. The enforced NFPA standards applicable to any hazardous materials used in the facility

**TABLE 8.1  Methods to Protect from Exposure to Fires**

1. Separation distances
2. Complete, continuous, and structurally independent fire separation walls when buildings are up against each other
3. Total automatic sprinkler protection
4. Deluge system that provides a water curtain on exterior wall

**TABLE 8.2  Fire-Resistance Ratings of Structure Elements (In hours)**

| Structure element[a] | | Noncombustible | | | | | Noncombustible/combustible | | | Combustible | |
|---|---|---|---|---|---|---|---|---|---|---|---|
| | | Type 1 Section 402.0 | | Type 2 Section 403.0 | | | Type 3 Section 404.0 | | Type 4 Section 405.0 | Type 5 Section 406.0 | |
| | | Protected | | Protected | | Unprotected | Protected | Unprotected | Heavy timber[e] | Protected | Unprotected |
| | | 1A | 1B | 2A | 2B | 2C | 3A | 3B | 4 | 5A | 5B |
| 1 Exterior walls | Load-bearing[j] | 4 | 3 | 2 | 1 | 0 | 2 | 2 | 2 | 1 | 0 |
| | Non-load-bearing[j] | | | | | | | | | | |
| 2 Fire walls and party walls (Section 907.0)[m] | | 4 | 3 | 2 | 2 | 2 | 2 | 2 | 2 | 2 | 2 |
| | Fire enclosure of exits (Sections 817.11, 909.0)[b] | 2 | 2 | 2 | 2 | 2 | 2 | 2 | 2 | 2 | 2 |
| 3 Fire separation assemblies (Section 909.0) | Shafts (other than exits) and elevator hoistways (Sections 909.0, 915.0)[b] | 2 | 2 | 2 | 2 | 2 | 2 | 2 | 2 | 1 | 1 |
| | Mixed use separation (Section 313.0)[n] | | | | | | | | | | |
| 4 Fire partitions (Section 910.0) | Other separation assemblies[i] | 1[d] | 1[d] | 1[d] | 1[d] | 1[d] | 1 | 1 | 1 | 1 | 1 |
| | Exit access corridors[f,g] | 1[d] | 1[d] | 1[d] | 1[d] | 1[d] | 1 | 1 | 1 | 1 | 1 |
| | Tenant spaces separations[f] | 1[d] | 1[d] | 1[d] | 1[d] | 0[d] | 1 | 0 | 1 | 1 | 0 |
| 5 Dwelling unit separations (Sections 910.0, 913.0)[f,j] | | 1[d] | 1[d] | 1[d] | 1[d] | 1[d] | 1 | 1 | 1 | 1 | 1 |
| 6 Smoke barriers (Section 911.0)[g] | | 1 | 1 | 1 | 1 | 1 | 1 | 1 | 1 | 1 | 1 |
| 7 Other nonbearing partitions | | 0[d] | 0[d] | 0[d] | 0[d] | 0[d] | 0 | 0 | 0 | 0 | 0 |

| | | | | | | | | | | |
|---|---|---|---|---|---|---|---|---|---|---|
| 8 Interior bearing walls, bearing partitions, columns, girders, trusses (other than roof trusses) and framing (Section 912.0) — Supporting more than one floor | 4 | 3 | 2 | 1 | 0 | 1 | 0 | see Sec. 405.0 | 1 | 0 |
| Supporting one floor only or a roof only | 3 | 2 | 1½ | 1 | 0 | 1 | 0 | see Sec. 405.0 | 1 | 0 |
| 9 Structural members supporting wall (Section 912.0)[g,o] | 3 | 2 | 1½ | 1 | 0 | 1 | 0 | 1 | 1 | 0 |
| 10 Floor construction including beams (Section 913.0)[h] | 3 | 2 | 1½ | 1 | 0 | 1 | 0 | see Sec. 405.0[e] | 1 | 0 |
| 11 Roof construction, including beams, trusses and framing, arches, and roof deck (Section 914.0)[e,j] — 15' or less in height to lowest member[k] | 2 | 1½ | 1[d] | 1[d] | 0[d] | 1 | 0[d] | see Sec. 405.0[e] | 1 | 0 |
| More than 15' but less than 20' in height to lowest member | 1[d] | 1[d] | 1[d] | 0[d] | 0[d] | 0 | 0[d] | see Sec. 405.0 | 1 | 0 |
| 20' or more in height to lowest member | 0[d] | 0[d] | 0[d] | 0[d] | 0[d] | 0 | 0[d] | see Sec. 405.0 | 0 | 0 |

[a] For fire-resistance rating requirements for structural members and assemblies which support other fire-resistance rated members or assemblies, see Section 912.1.

[b] For reductions in the required fire-resistance rating of exit and shaft enclosures, see Sections 817.11 and 915.3.

[c] For substitution of other structural materials for timber in Type 4 construction, see Section 1703.1.1.

[d] Fire-retardant-treated wood permitted, see Sections 904.3 and 1702.4.

[e] For permitted uses of heavy timber in roof construction in buildings of Types 1 and 2 construction, see Section 914.4.

[f] For reductions in required fire-resistance ratings of exit access corridors, tenant separations and dwelling unit separations, see Section 810.4 and 810.4.1.

[g] For exceptions to the required fire-resistance rating of construction supporting exit access corridor walls, tenant separation walls in covered mall buildings, and smoke barriers, see Sections 911.4 and 912.2.

[h] For buildings having habitable or occupiable stories or basements below grade, see Section 807.3.1.

[i] Not less than the rating required by code.

[j] For Use Group R-3, see Section 309.4.

[k] 1 foot = 304.8 mm.

[l] Not less than the rating based on fire separation distance (see Section 905.2).

[m] Not less than the rating required by Table 907.1

[n] Fire-resistance rating corresponding to the rating required by Table 313.12.

[o] Not less than fire-resistance rating of wall supported.

also must be reviewed, for many of them mandate minimum separation distances. (See the NFC Alphabetical Listing in the Supplemental Sources in the back of this book and the discussion in Chap. 4 for more information.)

### General building requirements

**Occupancy classifications.**  Since different buildings vary in their use, number of occupants, amounts and kinds of hazardous contents, construction materials, and configuration, the building code classifies them by *use groups* or *occupancy classifications* to identify the degree of threat to life safety and the degree of fire hazard.

Article 3 of the BOCA code defines use-group classifications. Use groups that apply to industry are B, office buildings; F, factory buildings or ordinary hazard; and H, high-hazard factory buildings and storage or warehouses. There is also a "doubtful use" paragraph that allows the building inspector discretion as to which use group he or she would assign the building. Some codes break use-group classifications into subgroups, such as F-1 and F-2 for factory uses, depending on the combustibility of the contents. Currently, subgroup classifications are under consideration for use group H. Whenever the operations or contents of a factory present some risk, the owner should be prepared to furnish as much detail as possible about the contents or operations, the number of operators normally present, exit paths or an egress plan, and other fire-protection information with the building construction drawings to be certain that the occupancy classification is not too severe and costly. Use classifications for the processing of hazardous materials are frequently very complicated and require a detailed analysis (see Chap. 4).

**Fire-resistant construction.**  Article 4 of the BOCA code mandates the minimum fire resistance required in building construction materials. Building materials are rated by fire grading classifications. *Fire grading* is the number of hours that a building resists a fire. Table 8.2 is Table 401 from the BOCA code; and it lists the five construction types allowed and defines the different materials permitted. Table 902, "Fire Grading of Use Groups," in the BOCA code lists the specific fire gradings for each use group. These gradings are based on the time the occupants need to exit a building given the amount of combustible contents and their burn times. NFPA 220, Types of Building Construction, also covers this material and presents a table similar to Table 8.2.

**Maximum allowable area and height.**  Article 5 of the BOCA code contains requirements for the sizes of buildings and their locations on the property relative to streets, lot lines, and other buildings on the same property. Section 501 specifies the area and height limitations for the different use groups and types of construction and lists a number of exceptions (see Table 8.3). The code reduces the fire hazards of different occupancy classifications by limiting floor area and building height. With industrial buildings, the contents are the most important factor in determining fire hazard. Article 5 mandates limits for use group H, high-hazard occupancies, use group F, factory and industrial occupancies, use group S, storage occupancies, and use group B, office occupancies.

**Allowable increases in area and height.**    Section 502.2 allows increases in area for increased street frontage because of immediate fire department access. Section 502.3 allows considerable increases in area for fully sprinklered buildings, except in use group H. Section 503.1 allows increases in height or number of floors for fully sprinklered buildings, again except in use group H.

Therefore, the fire resistance classifications in Table 8.2 and the use-group classifications in Table 8.3 balance the combustible contents of a building with the combustible building materials by reducing the building size when necessary for safety. See Chapters 3, 4, 5, and 7 for discussions of the contents of industrial buildings and the *Life Safety Code.* Also see Chapter 9 for a checklist of code-allowed trade-offs and possible cost-saving items.

**Options for multiple occupancy classifications.**    Often an industrial operation will involve multiple occupancies, such as business (office), factory, and storage. The code allows as many as five options in this situation, which are listed in Table 8.4. In the first option, the manufacturing operation and storage occupancies can be combined in one building. In this arrangement, the code requires that the more strict occupancy classification apply to both occupancies. In the second option, the two occupancies must be horizontally and vertically separated by fire separation walls having a resistance rating equal to the highest rating of the two occupancies (found in Table 902).

The third option is a building completely separated by a structurally independent fire (separation) wall that allows collapse of construction on either side without collapse of the wall. (*Note:* The reader is cautioned to check the definition in the applicable code of the term *fire separation wall,* because the codes are not consistent on the use of this term.)

The fourth option is incidental use. When the second use merely supports the first or main use of the building, will not occupy more than generally 10 percent of the floor area, and does have a higher fire rating, then the total building can be classified according to the main use.

**TABLE 8.3  Height and Area Limitations of Buildings[a]**

| | Type of construction | | | | | | | | | |
| | Noncombustible | | | | | Noncombustible/combustible[k] | | | Combustible | |
| | Type 1 Protected[b] | | Type 2 | | | Type 3 | | Type 4 Heavy timber | Type 5 | |
| | | | Protected | | Unprotected | Protected | Unprotected | | Protected | Unprotected[j] |
| Use group[a] | 1A | 1B | 2A | 2B | 2C | 3A | 3B | 4 | 5A | 5B |
|---|---|---|---|---|---|---|---|---|---|---|
| A-1 Assembly, theaters | NL | NL | 5 St. 65' 19,950 | 3 St. 30' 13,125 | 2 St. 30' 8,400 | 3 St. 40' 11,550 | 2 St. 30' 8,400 | 3 St. 40' 12,600 | 1 St. 20' 8,925 | 1 St. 20' 4,200 |
| A-2 Assembly, nightclubs, and similar uses | NL | NL 7,200 | 3 St. 40' 5,700 | 2 St. 30' 3,750 | 1 St. 20' 2,400 | 2 St. 30' 3,300 | 1 St. 20' 2,400 | 3 St. 30' 3,600 | 1 St. 20' 2,550 | 1 St. 20' 1,200 |
| A-3 Assembly, lecture halls, recreation centers, terminals, restaurants other than nightclubs | NL | NL | 5 St. 65' 19,950 | 3 St. 40' 13,125 | 2 St. 30' 8,400 | 3 St. 40' 11,550 | 2 St. 30' 8,400 | 3 St. 40' 12,600 | 1 St. 20' 8,925 | 1 St. 20' 4,200 |
| A-4 Assembly, churches[d] | NL | NL | 5 St. 65' 34,200 | 3 St. 40' 22,500 | 2 St. 30' 14,400 | 3 St. 40' 19,800 | 2 St. 30' 14,400 | 3 St. 40' 21,600 | 1 St. 20' 15,300 | 1 St. 20' 7,200 |
| B Business | NL | NL | 7 St. 85' 34,200 | 5 St. 65' 22,500 | 3 St. 40' 14,400 | 4 St. 50' 19,800 | 3 St. 40' 14,400 | 5 St. 65' 21,600 | 3 St. 40' 15,300 | 2 St. 30' 7,200 |
| E Educational[e,d] | NL | NL | 5 St. 65' 34,200 | 3 St. 40' 22,500 | 2 St. 30' 14,400 | 3 St. 40' 19,800 | 2 St. 30' 14,400 | 3 St. 40' 21,600 | 1 St. 20' 15,300[e] | 1 St. 20' 7,200[e] |
| F-1 Factory and industrial, moderate[i] | NL | NL | 6 St. 75' 22,800 | 4 St. 50' 15,000 | 2 St. 30' 9,600 | 3 St. 40' 13,200 | 2 St. 30' 9,600 | 4 St. 50' 14,400 | 2 St. 30' 10,200 | 1 St. 20' 4,800 |
| F-2 Factory and industrial, low[i] | NL | NL | 7 St. 85' 34,200 | 5 St. 65' 22,500 | 3 St. 40' 14,400 | 4 St. 50' 19,800 | 3 St. 40' 14,400 | 5 St. 65' 21,600 | 3 St. 40' 15,300 | 2 St. 30' 7,200 |
| H High hazard[f] | 5 St. 65' 16,800 | 3 St. 40' 14,400 | 2 St. 30' 11,400 | 2 St. 30' 7,500 | 1 St. 20' 4,800 | 2 St. 30' 6,600 | 1 St. 20' 4,800 | 2 St. 30' 7,200 | 1 St. 20' 5,100 | NP |
| I-1 Institutional, residential care | NL | NL | 9 St. 100' 19,950 | 4 St. 50' 13,125 | 3 St. 40' 8,400 | 4 St. 50' 11,550 | 3 St. 40' 8,400 | 4 St. 50' 12,600 | 3 St. 40' 8,925 | 2 St. 35' 4,200 |
| I-2 Institutional, incapacitated | NL | 8 St. 90' 21,600 | 4 St. 50' 17,100 | 2 St. 30' 11,250 | 1 St. 20' 7,200 | 1 St. 20' 9,900 | NP | 1 St. 20' 10,800 | 1 St. 20' 7,650 | NP |
| I-3 Institutional, restrained | NL | 6 St. 75' 18,000 | 4 St. 50' 14,250 | 2 St. 30' 9,375 | 1 St. 20' 6,000 | 2 St. 30' 8,250 | 1 St. 20' 6,000 | 2 St. 30' 9,000 | 1 St. 20' 6,375 | NP |

| | | | | | | | | | |
|---|---|---|---|---|---|---|---|---|---|
| M Mercantile | NL | NL | 6 St. 75' 22,800 | 4 St. 50' 15,000 | 2 St. 30' 9,600 | 3 St. 40' 13,200 | 2 St. 30' 9,600 | 4 St. 50' 14,400 | 2 St. 30' 10,200 | 1 St. 20' 4,800 |
| R-1 Residential, hotels | NL | NL | 9 St. 100' 22,800 | 4 St. 50' 15,000 | 3 St. 40' 9,600 | 4 St. 50' 13,200 | 3 St. 40' 9,600 | 4 St. 50' 14,400 | 3 St. 40' 10,200 | 2 St. 35' 4,800 |
| R-2 Residential, multiple-family | NL | NL | 9 St. 100' 22,800 | 4 St. 50'g 15,000g | 3 St. 40' 9,600 | 4 St. 50'g 13,200g | 3 St. 40' 9,600 | 4 St. 50' 14,400 | 3 St. 40' 10,200 | 2 St. 35' 4,800 |
| R-3 Residential, one- and two-family | NL | NL | 4 St. 50' 22,800 | 4 St. 50' 15,000 | 3 St. 40' 9,600 | 4 St. 50' 13,200 | 3 St. 40' 9,600 | 4 St. 50' 14,400 | 3 St. 40' 10,200 | 2 St. 35' 4,800 |
| S-1 Storage, moderate | NL | NL | 5 St. 65' 19,950 | 4 St. 50' 13,125 | 2 St. 30' 8,400 | 3 St. 40' 11,500 | 2 St. 30' 8,400 | 4 St. 50' 12,600 | 2 St. 30' 8,925 | 1 St. 20' 4,200 |
| S-2 Storage, low[h] | NL | NL | 7 St. 85' 34,200 | 5 St. 65' 22,500 | 3 St. 40' 14,400 | 4 St. 50' 19,800 | 3 St. 40' 14,400 | 5 St. 65' 21,600 | 3 St. 40' 15,300 | 2 St. 30' 7,200 |
| U Utility, miscellaneous | NL | NL | | | | | | | | |

[a]Height limitations of buildings are shown in upper figure as stories and feet above grade. Area limitations of one- and two-story buildings facing on one street or a public space not less than 30 feet wide are shown in lower figure as area in square feet per floor.

See the following sections for general exceptions to Table 501; Section 501.4 Allowable area reduction for multistory buildings; Section 502.2 Allowable area increase due to street frontage; Section 502.3 Allowable area increase due to automatic sprinkler system installation; Section 503.1 Allowable height increase due to automatic sprinkler system installation; Section 504.0 Unlimited area one-story buildings.

1 foot = 304.8 mm; 1 square foot = 0.093 m².

[b]Buildings of Type 1 construction permitted to be of unlimited tabular heights and areas are not subject to special requirements that allow increased heights and areas for other types of construction (see Section 501.5); NL = not limited.

[c]For tabular area increase in buildings of Use Group E, see Section 502.4.

[d]For height exceptions for auditoriums in buildings of Use Groups A-4 and E, see Section 503.2.

[e]For height exceptions for day care centers of Type 5 construction, see Section 503.3.

[f]For exceptions to height and area limitations for buildings of Use Group H, see Article 6 governing the specific use. For other special fire-resistive requirements governing specific uses, see Section 904.0.

[g]For exceptions to height of buildings for Use Group R-2 of Types 2B and 3A construction, see Section 904.2.

[g]For exceptions to height of buildings for Use Group R-2 of Types 2B and 3A construction, see Section 904.2.

[h]For height and area exceptions for open parking structures, see Section 607.0.

[i]For exceptions to height and area limitations for special industrial uses, see Section 501.1.1.

[j]NP = not permitted.

TABLE 8.4  Building Code Options for Multiple Occupancies

---

*Option 1:* Combine into one building using the stricter occupancy
*Option 2:* One building using fire walls
*Option 3:* Two separate buildings with a combined total not exceeding the table maximum
*Option 4:* One occupancy with incidental use of a second occupancy
*Option 5:* Two buildings separated the minimum distance
*Option 6:* Unlimited area one-story buildings with automatic sprinklers
*Option 7:* Special industrial use building with fire walls

---

The fifth option is buildings separated to at least the minimum distance prescribed in Table 504.2, "Minimum Fire Resistance Rating of Exterior Walls," and Table 906.2, "Exterior Wall Fire Resistance Ratings," based on the separation distances and use groups. There is also a "mixed occupancy" paragraph that must be read when this condition exists.

Option six involves unlimited area one-story buildings. Section 504 allows unlimited areas for ordinary-hazard industrial facilities, use groups B, F, and S, which are often found in industrial facilities. The building must be one story, all above grade, with adequate egresses, construction types 1, 2, 3, or 4, fully sprinklered, not exceed 85 ft in height, and have exterior separation and special protection for exterior wall openings.

The code also has a special industrial use classification (option 7) in paragraph 501.1.1.1 for buildings and structures designed to house low-hazard industrial processes, including, among others, electric-, gas-, or steam-powered rolling mills and structural metal fabrication shops and foundries requiring large and unusual heights to accommodate craneways or special machinery and equipment. The code exempts these buildings from the height and area limitations of Table 501. There are other examples of buildings that exceed the height limitation of Table 8.3 with a number of elevated working platforms that are normally classified as one-story buildings.

Exemptions such as this are allowed, as explained elsewhere, when the application of Table 501 is impractical. It is the responsibility of the code official to determine when the application of this section is appropriate.

NFPA 101, the *Life Safety Code,* allows the maximum egress travel distance to be increased to 400 ft (122 m) in low- or ordinary-hazard occupancies if the following additional conditions are met:

1. One-story building

2. Smoke and heat vents

3. Automatic fire protection

Article 6 of the BOCA code lists additional requirements for protecting special uses and occupancies. It may revise the requirements specified in other articles. In addition, it includes additional requirements for the use, handling, and storage of hazardous materials.

**Two buildings considered as one and high-rise processes.**    Two buildings on the same lot that do not exceed the area and height limits in Table 8.3 when added together can be classified as one.

Occasionally, a process design requires considerable height for gravity feed, may have multiple solid floors, and may require operators to be located more than 75 ft above grade or fire department access. This extends the building into the high-rise occupancy classification. Although the code generally specifies this classification for occupancies other than industrial, it can and has been applied to industrial buildings. The high-rise occupancy classification can become very expensive owing to additional requirements to protect people above the fire department access height of municipal fire ladder trucks. Sprinklers, compartmentation, added fire walls, enclosed stairways, and added fire alarms can all increase construction costs. When the process building is normally unoccupied, with the possible exception of hazardous production materials (HPM) facilities, which are covered separately under Section 603 (which generally applies to semiconductor facilities and areas of comparable research and development), this becomes an unnecessary expense. A second review of the process to reduce the height and avoid this may be advisable.

**Mezzanines.**    Section 605 of the BOCA code covers mezzanines, which can be a complex issue in an industrial facility. Many processes require great height, and small platforms that will not normally be occupied are needed at various levels for servicing the equipment. Most codes state that these platforms are not considered floors until they exceed one-third the area of the floor below. Moreover, these platforms do not often contribute significantly to the fire hazard. Both the building code under mezzanines and OSHA regulations need to be reviewed for egress requirements, however, because mezzanines can be required to have two means of egress. Also, particular attention should be paid to the reach of fire hoses when standpipes are required. It should be pointed out, though, that allowable mezzanine areas are sometimes increased under the special industrial use classification in the code.

**Egresses.**    Article 8 in the BOCA code presents, in great detail, the minimum requirements for means of egress and the maximum distances occupants must travel to exit a building in the event of a fire. Section 814 details horizontal exits through a common fire wall into adjacent buildings which sometimes can be used to provide some of the code-required egresses. Section 818 specifies smokeproof stair towers for buildings with occupants located more than 75 ft above fire department access.

NFPA 101, the *Life Safety Code,* which is enforced in some states for industry, also has an extensive chapter on means of egress. OSHA's General Industry Standards, found in Title 29 of the *Code of Federal Regulations (CFR),* Part 1910, Subpart E, also has extensive requirements for egresses that have been picked up from NFPA 101. Some states enforce all three of these standards and require egresses to conform to the most strict of the three.

The complexity of these compound codes soon becomes apparent, for these codes were written by different committees at different times and therefore are not identical. They are, however, similar in their minimum requirements, because they were developed from real fire incidents.

**Hazardous operations.**   The BOCA code defines hazardous operations in Article 3 under use group H, high hazard (Section 306), to include "all buildings and structures, or parts thereof, that are used for manufacturing, processing, generation or storage of corrosive, highly toxic, highly combustible, flammable or explosive materials that constitute a high fire or explosive hazard, including loose combustible fibers, dust and unstable materials." Table 306.2, "Use Group H, High-Hazard Uses," lists the materials, processes, and manufacturing operations that are indicative of use group H. It also refers to a number of NFPA standards that are enforced.

Section 306.2.1 lists exceptions to use group H. Table 8.5, which is BOCA Table 306.2.1, lists the maximum amount of hazardous materials allowed in a building classified as ordinary-hazard or factory occupancy. Additional exceptions are indicated in the table notes.

Also, Section 600.1 states in the second paragraph that "chemical plants, packing plants, grain elevators, refineries, flour mills and others shall be constructed in accordance with the recognized practice and requirements of the specific industry." Section 600.2, "Special High Hazards," must be read. And Section 600.3, "Means of Egress," mandates more restrictive requirements and modifications to Article 8, "Means of Egress," for buildings with special uses and occupancies.

Section 600.2 covers additional fire-resistance requirements for special high-hazard occupancies that exceed five stories or 65 ft. Section 617.0, "Combustible Dusts, Grain Processing and Storage," Section 618.0, "Explosion Hazards," Section 619.0, "Flammable and Combustible Liquids," Section 620.0, "Liquefied Petroleum Gas Facilities," and Section 622.0, "Paint Spraying and Spray Booths," must be re-

TABLE 8.5 Exempt Amounts of Hazardous Materials, Liquids, and Chemicals

| Material | Maximum quantities |
|---|---|
| 1. Flammable liquids | |
| Class I-A | 30 gal* |
| Class I-B | 60 gal* |
| Class I-C | 90 gal* |
| 2. Combustible liquids† | |
| Class II | 120 gal* |
| Class III-A | 250 gal* |
| 3. Combination flammable liquids‡ | 120 gal* |
| 4. Flammable gases | 3000 ft³ at 1 atm of pressure at 70°F |
| 5. Liquefied flammable gases | 60 gal |
| 6. Combustible fibers—loose | 100 ft³ |
| 7. Combustible fibers—baled | 1000 ft³ |
| 8. Flammable solids | 500 lbs |
| 9. Unstable materials | No exemptions |
| 10. Corrosive materials | 55 gal |
| 11. Oxidizing materials—gases | 6000 ft³ |
| 12. Oxidizing materials—liquids | 50 gal |
| 13. Oxidizing materials—solids | |
| Class 1 | 4000 lbs |
| Class 2 | 1000 lbs |
| Class 3 | 200 lbs |
| Class 4 | 10 lbs§ |
| 14. Organic peroxides | 10 lbs |
| Class 1 | No exemptions |
| Class 2 and 3 | 10 lbs |
| 15. Nitromethane (unstable materials) | No exemptions |
| 16. Ammonium nitrate | 1000 lbs |
| 17. Ammonium nitrate compound mixtures containing more than 60% nitrate by weight | 1000 lbs |
| 18. Highly toxic material and poisonous gas | No exemptions |
| 19. Irritants | 5000 lbs |
| 20. Sensitizers | 5000 lbs |
| 21. Smokeless powder | 20 lbs¶ |
| 22. Black sporting powder | 5 lbs¶ |

*The maximum quantities shall be increased by 100 percent in areas not accessible to the public. In buildings equipped throughout with an automatic sprinkler system in accordance with Section 1004.2.1, the maximum quantities shall be increased 100 percent in the areas accessible to the public.

†Tank storage up to 660 gallons for oil piping systems meeting the requirements of the mechanical code or the fire prevention code listed in Appendix A shall be permitted.

‡Containing not more than the exempt amounts of Class 1-A, 1-B, or 1-C flammable liquids.

§The maximum quantity shall be 50 pounds when stored in magazines in accordance with NFiPA 495 listed in Appendix A.

¶Maximum quantities in the amount specified by NFiPA 495 shall be permitted when stored in accordance with NFiPA 495 listed in Appendix A.

SOURCE: From BOCA. *National Building Code.* Table 306.2.1.

viewed when these hazards are present. Section 603.0, "HPM Use Facilities," applies to the semiconductor industry, which also uses high-hazard materials.

A high-hazard occupancy classification is limited to industrial buildings that house extremely hazardous operations. Incidental use of restricted quantities of flammable liquids in a building does not constitute a high-hazard occupancy, although some extra life safety precautions may be required during the limited period of use. (See Chaps. 4 and 5; also see the sections Occupancy Descriptions and Risk of Contents in Chap. 7.)

**Special rooms.**  Special rooms such as mechanical equipment rooms, drying rooms, and so on are covered in Article 25 of the BOCA code, which includes the approval, construction, and operation of mechanical appliances, equipment, and systems. This article also sets requirements for room construction, for additional fire walls, for the location of equipment, for automatic fire protection systems for some rooms, and for other important items, such as explosion vents, spark protection, and so on.

**Structural requirements and fireproofing.**  Articles 11 through 23 of the BOCA code cover building structural requirements. Article 11 specifies minimum design loads for buildings, towers, chimneys, and tanks. It specifies dead loads, live loads, and concentrated loads, and includes minimum design loads for snow, wind, and earthquakes. It also references ANSI standard A58.1. Article 12 sets out minimum design loads for foundations and allowed soil loads.

Table 8.2 presented the requirements for fire resistance of structural elements as buildings increase in height. Options to fireproofing steel are given in Table 8.6.

Increased costly fireproofing can sometimes be avoided by the careful arrangement of multiple occupancies. For example, locating an office on an upper floor above an industrial activity may require the addition of fireproofing to all the steel supporting the upper office floor

---

**TABLE 8.6   Fireproofing Options**

*Option 1:* Multiple occupancy arrangements
*Option 2:* Avoid multiple floors when possible
*Option 3:* Avoid locating office occupancies above hazards
*Option 4:* Review lower-cost fireproofing options
*Option 5:* Avoid high-hazard occupancies over 5 stories
*Option 6:* Substitute class II for class I materials when sprinklers are available

---

as well as the first floor columns, as set out in Tables 8.2 and 8.3. Table 8.2 sets out the increased requirements for fireproofing structural elements when they support more than one floor for any occupancy. Early consideration should be given to this in the building planning. Section 905.2.3 of the code requires special fire-resistive construction for use group B, or offices, in types 2C, 3B, and 5B construction. Sections 903.2 and 912.2 of the code allow alternatives to expensive fireproofing through the use of heat shields, approved membrane or ceiling protection, separation, or other means approved by the building inspector. Section 600.2 of the code covers additional fire-resistance requirements for special high-hazard occupancies that exceed 5 stories or 65 ft. Section 922.7.1 allows the substitution of class II materials for class I materials when an approved automatic fire suppression system is provided.

**Automatic and manual fire suppression systems.** Article 10 of the BOCA code specifies *where* fixed manual extinguishing systems (standpipes), automatic extinguishing systems, fire alarm and detection systems, smoke control systems, and portable extinguishers are required. Design details for fire protection and fire alarm systems (manual or automatic) are found in the *National Fire Code* and enforced referenced standards. (See Table 12.2 for information on fire extinguishing systems; see Chap. 13 for smoke control systems; and see Chap. 16 for information on fire alarm systems.)

Industrial building occupancies are often confused with sprinkler system water density flow requirements for light hazard, ordinary-hazard groups 1, 2, and 3, and extra-hazard groups 1 and 2 found in NFPA 13, Installation of Sprinkler Systems. The intent of these classifications is to establish the rate of sprinkler system water flow (that is, gallons per minute per square foot of space) to enable the system to apply sufficient water on a fire to extinguish it. These classifications are not building occupancy classifications. The sprinkler system water flow is based on the British thermal unit (Btu) production of the burning material.

## Mechanical code and energy conservation

Article 7 of the BOCA code covers general lighting and ventilation. Articles 24 through 31 cover other miscellaneous building items, including mechanical systems, elevators, electrical service, plumbing systems, and energy conservation. Mechanical equipment such as boilers and other pressure vessels, dryers, incinerators, heating, ventilating, and air conditioning are covered in Article 25, which, in turn, enforces the more detailed BOCA *National Mechanical Code*. Article 31 covers energy conservation. See Chapters 13 and 14 for more information on these subjects.

**Elevators and electrical systems.**   Article 26 covers elevators. Article 27 covers the electrical systems and enforces NFPA 20, the *National Electrical Code* (see Chap. 15).

**Plumbing and process piping.**   Plumbing is covered in Article 28. Plumbing includes the potable water supply, sanitary drainage, venting, storm drainage, plumbing fixtures, and private sewage disposal. Article 28 enforces the BOCA *National Plumbing Code* (see Chap. 14). Process piping is covered in Article 25, which enforces the BOCA *National Mechanical Code* (see Chap. 14).

**State code example**

The first item on any design agenda must be to contact the local or state building authority to record and obtain copies of all the codes that are enforced. Local ordinances are available at the local government offices. Large metropolitan areas have their own building departments. Rural areas generally use county or state building departments. The National Conference of States on Building Codes and Standards, Inc. (NCSBCS), publishes a directory of state building codes and regulations. (See the description of contents in the beginning of this chapter.)

The State of Ohio Building Code, for example, which is an amended version of the BOCA model code, refers to approximately 370 documents published by about 50 national organizations. In addition, the State of Ohio Fire Code refers to another 100 documents published by 10 national organizations (see Chap. 11 for a discussion of references).

Although many of these reference documents specify minimum materials specifications and are merely listed in a project's specifications, some need to be read and incorporated into project design drawings. An example of this is the ANSI elevator standard, which prohibits the routing of sprinkler piping through an elevator shaft because such pipes present a hazard to the electrical controls. This prohibition is not found in the fire codes or NFPA 13, but local authorities have required contractors to relocate such piping when it was incorrectly installed in an elevator shaft.

There are over 250 National Fire Protection Association (NFPA) standards (see Alphabetical Listing in Supplemental Sources at the end of the book) written by over 150 committees. Many of these are directly referenced in the building, fire, mechanical, and other codes and are therefore enforceable by local authorities. About 70 of these are referenced and enforced by the BOCA *National Fire Code.* Included are NFPA 70, better known as the *National Electric Code,* and NFPA 101, better known as the *Life Safety Code.* The American National Standards Institute (ANSI), the American Society for Testing and Materials (ASTM), and several other organizations also have written enforced standards (see Chap. 11).

Further cross-references are found within the standards themselves, and these also can be enforced. Details specified in these standards have been developed over almost a century of fire investigations and research by a number of organizations. More than 2400 individuals participate on these code-writing committees. The standards are reviewed and developed by consensus agreements as to the fairest and best methods to achieve life safety and protection of property and the environment.

## Extensive Code Reviews and Plan Checklists

Chapter 1 discussed the major reasons to undertake an early and comprehensive review of the codes, regulations, and enforced standards governing industrial facilities. In addition to those reasons, many statements in the enforced standards are more strict than the building code. For example, a 1½-hour–rated fire door was required by a state building code, whereas NFPA 30 required a 3-hour–rated fire door for a flammable liquids storage warehouse. The fire marshall insisted on the more stringent requirement in his final inspection before issuing the occupancy permit. Fire wall requirements are also repeated in this standard.

Today, some suburban building authorities require a letter from the owner or planner in charge of an industrial project stating that all applicable codes, regulations, and standards have been complied with in the preparation of the construction documents. This represents another reason for early, comprehensive review.

### Plan review checklist

An outline for a cursory review of the building codes, regulations, and enforced standards that can be used at the beginning but must be followed by a more detailed review as the design progresses is given in Table 8.7.

TABLE 8.7  Code Review Checklist

---

*Step 1:* Determine the use-group occupancy classification of the building, or determine how many use-groups occupancy classification(s) are needed.

*Step 2:* Review fire district zoning limitations.

*Step 3:* Determine minimum type of construction required (see table similar to Table 8.3 in most codes):

    a. Determine maximum floor area and height allowed by type of construction (see second table similar to Table 8.3 in most codes).

    b. Check allowable area increases (found in Table 8.3 in most codes).

*Step 4:* Check detailed occupancy requirements.

*Step 5:* Check detailed construction requirements:

    a. Fire resistance of structural members (Table 8.2).

    b. Fire extinguishing system requirements.

    c. Fire alarm system requirements.

    d. Means of egress requirements.

*Step 6:* Review related fire, mechanical, energy, plumbing, and electrical codes requirements.

*Step 7:* Check all the enforced standards (see appendix in most codes).

---

## Insurance Underwriters' Standards

Various insurance organizations such as the American Insurance Association, Factory Mutual Systems, Industrial Risk Insurers, Insurance Services Offices, and others investigate fires, issue detailed reports, and develop standards. Fire research and testing are conducted by laboratories such as Underwriters Laboratories, Inc. (UL), Factory Mutual Research Corporation (FM), and others. Government agencies such as the U.S. Fire Administration (USFA), National Bureau of Standards Center for Fire Research, and other federal agencies develop data for reports and standards.

Although many of these standards are not legally enforceable by code, they are recognized as good practice. Occasionally, there will arise a conflict between one of these standards and the building code. These conflicts are usually resolved through separate discussions with the underwriters and local officials.

The codes require the use of approved materials and equipment which must be followed whenever a test has been conducted on a specific material or piece of equipment, approval for use has been granted, and a listing is published by a laboratory such as UL or FM. These laboratories publish these listings in book form and use enforced standards.

## Code Variances

All building codes allow requests for variances and have appeal procedures. A variance is normally requested through the building inspector and generally requires a written request with justifications. The appeal procedure is a formal, written request to either the building inspector or directly to a building board when the appeal is to review an inspector's interpretation of the code (see Chap. 9 for more information).

# Economical Code Options Checklist

This chapter provides a code options checklist for economical planning to avoid some of the needless construction cost pitfalls that are unwittingly formatted into so many projects in the planning stages. The checklist itemizes options in four major areas (Table 9.1). These options, which are allowed by most codes, can *save thousands and thousands of dollars*. Subheadings in the list will serve to expedite your review for your particular project.

### Need for a Planning Checklist

Too often project leaders discover too late that overlooked code requirements add construction costs that could have been avoided. These added costs too often cause the project to exceed the original, approved construction budget. Often such projects are overcommitted to the original design because the final construction documents are complete and the calendar time to redesign is not available. On other projects, construction has already begun, and it is too late to make changes or too late to extend the completion schedule. This situation occurs even more frequently in the fast-track construction methods that are used so often in industry today to expedite production startup and the income on the investment in the facility.

**TABLE 9.1  Four Major Areas of Code Cost Trade-Offs**

| | |
|---|---|
| *Area 1:* Site planning trade-offs | See Chaps. 4, 8, 12, and 14 |
| *Area 2:* Building code trade-offs | See Chaps. 5 and 8 |
| *Area 3:* Process versus building cost trade-offs | See Chaps. 4, 5, 8, and 12 |
| *Area 4:* Environmental regulations | See Chaps. 17 through 21 |

Many of these situations result from the fact that today's complex and extensive building codes, regulations, and enforced standards are not user friendly. They require a great deal of experience and familiarity on the part of the designers or simply demand sufficient calendar time to plod through each significant paragraph with its multitude of incomplete cross-references to other documents and standards for compliance (see Chap. 1).

To expedite project planning and to allow economical compliance with the codes, the project leader can, through the use of this checklist, guide the project through planning the building location on a proposed site, deciding on the area and the number of floors, establishing the least costly occupancy classification, and so on in the most economical manner possible while still maintaining compliance with the codes. The reviewer must remember to read the local enforced codes, when using this checklist in the initial planning or preparation of the final construction drawings, because they are necessarily extensive and vary with each locality. In addition, many communities issue legally enforced and frequent amendments to model and/or state codes.

## Economic Options in Codes

A number of economical options are allowed by building codes, and they are frequently overlooked, resulting in needless construction costs. Table 9.2 lists the reasons for overlooked cost savings.

1. *Options not clear in the codes:*   Sometimes options, alternatives, or exceptions are scattered throughout the chapters, and finding them requires familiarity and expertise.

2. *Nonfamiliarity and infrequent use of codes:*   Many building designers merely spot-check the codes on an intermittent basis because they do not have the time to review them thoroughly.

3. *Some trade-offs are interdisciplinary:*   Since some designers are scheduled to participate in planning on a staggered basis, poor communication and coordination result.

---

**TABLE 9.2   Reasons for Frequently Overlooked Cost Savings**

1. Options not clear in the codes.
2. Nonfamiliarity and infrequent use of codes.
3. Some trade-offs are interdisciplinary and sometimes are not discussed.
4. Preliminary meetings involving all disciplines are not held.
5. Design time is often too short.
6. Conscientious professionals sometimes get bogged down and use overkill.

---

4. *Lack of preliminary meetings involving all disciplines:* Sound economic decisions for industrial facilities that use hazardous materials can only be made if all disciplines are involved in the early planning stages.

5. *Design time is too short:* Because of committed investments, interest payments, and the income that the facility will bring as soon as production is started, design time is often abbreviated, and therefore, comprehensive code reviews are often not done.

6. *Overkill:* Because of item 5, conscientious professionals use overkill and include items in the building design that are not always mandated by the building codes, regulations, and enforced standards.

## Economical Code Options Checklist

The reader is cautioned that the code options given herein are allowed by most codes. However, one should always seek final approval from the local authorities.

### I   Site trade-offs

**A   Environmental audits.**   Environmental audits to assess for contamination must be performed for both new sites and existing property and buildings to avoid extensive costs of cleanup. Superfund liability can be inherited in the purchase of a previously contaminated site and/or building. Hazardous waste contamination is seldom apparent and requires the review of experienced environmental engineers (see Chap. 20).

**B   Location of building(s) and site operations.**   Significant cost savings can result from studies that are reviewed by all concerned of the location of building(s), tank farms, rail car and truck unloading stations, and so on on a property. Maintaining the minimum separation distances required by the codes and the enforced standards is often the least expensive option. When the property does not allow adequate space for such separations, the costs of automatic fire extinguishing systems and fire- and blast-resistant walls or barriers must be added in to project costs (see Chap. 4).

**C   Single buildings.**   The first item generally needed from the building code is the minimum distances required from property lines or any existing nearby structures. In addition, the local zoning ordinances also must be reviewed for building set-backs from streets. Fire department

TABLE 9.3    Economical Reasons for Using Separation Distances*

1. Egress distances are generally shorter and therefore there is less threat to life safety.
2. Building construction materials can be less expensive.
3. The codes are less likely to require interior fire suppression systems.
4. With sufficient separation distances, the codes are less likely to require fire-resistant outside walls to protect from fire exposure from adjacent buildings.
5. The codes will not require exterior automatic deluge sprinklers to protect from fire exposure from adjacent buildings.

*When separation distances cannot be used for any of a number of reasons, buildings codes require other means of protection.
*Note:* Obviously, the cost differences among these options are not always as apparent as we would like them to be, and estimates must be made for comparisons. Costs will vary from project to project for the same code-allowed trade-off.

access is also a consideration here, for automatic fire extinguishing systems costs can increase when fire department access is obstructed.

Section 502 of the BOCA *National Building Code,* for example, allows area increases for street frontage increases. When a building with windows or structure has more than 25 percent of its perimeter fronting on a street or unoccupied space of 30 ft (9.14 m) or more, the allowed building area increases proportionately with the frontage increase because of the added access for the fire department. See also "Windowless Story" in Section 1002.15 of the BOCA code.

Either fire department access or an automatic sprinkler system is generally required for buildings of less than three or four stories and less than 24,000 ft$^2$ (2229.6 m$^2$) in total area on all floors. The required access must generally be 20 ft (6.10 m) wide and paved. Separation distances, when feasible, are probably the cheapest form of fire protection for the reasons listed in Table 9.3.

## D  Multiple new buildings

1. When there are two or more buildings on the same lot, Section 501.2.1 mandates that they have exterior fire wall ratings, or twice the separation distances specified in Table 906.2, or be treated as one building with a total area of the two added together.

2. NFPA 80A, A Recommended Practice for the Protection of Buildings from Exterior Fire Exposure, Chapter 3, "Means of Protection," also permits a number of methods for protecting buildings from exposure to fires from adjacent buildings and property. These methods are listed in Table 9.4. See NFPA 80A for more details.

3. Section 906.1 of the BOCA code, for example, has an exception that deletes the exterior wall fire rating when the combined areas and heights of the two buildings comply with Table 501.

**TABLE 9.4   Methods for Protecting Buildings from Exposure Fires**

1. Separation distances
2. Complete, continuous, and structurally independent fire separation walls when buildings are up against each other
3. Total automatic sprinkler protection
4. Deluge system providing a water curtain on exterior wall

4. Section 906.2.2 allows a reduction in the fire rating of a non-load-bearing exterior wall when the building is protected throughout with an automatic sprinkler system, except in use group H classifications.

5. Section 906.3.1 allows an increase in the area of unprotected openings in an exterior wall when the building is protected throughout with a sprinkler system, again except in use group H classifications.

6. Section 906.5 deletes the requirement for protection of openings less than 15 ft above an adjacent roof or an adjacent building that runs less than 15 ft horizontally when the roof has a fire rating of 1 hour.

### E   Other site trade-offs

1. Cooling towers: Cost of combustible cooling towers with fire protection versus noncombustible cooling towers. Combustible cooling towers over a specified size require open-head fire protection sprinklers. Noncombustible towers are exempt from this. See NFPA 214.

2. Flammable liquids storage: Cost of underground storage tanks complying with new EPA regulations (see Chap. 20) versus aboveground storage with approved vaults and/or fire and explosion protection.

3. Options in the selection of pipe materials for underground fire protection water supplies (see Chap. 12).

## II   Building trade-offs

### A   Single building and single occupancy (see Table 9.5)

1. The first economical decision involves a comparison of the *materials of construction versus the size of the building.* Use-group classifications (Table 8.3) and fire-resistance classifications (Table 8.2) vary with all changes in building size based on the types and amounts of combustible materials present. Table 8.2 indicates that building costs increase as the type of construction goes from 5 to 1. Table 8.3 shows that the costs of construction increase as the area and height or num-

**TABLE 9.5   Some Single-Building Trade-Offs**

1. Materials of construction versus size of the building.
2. Allowable increases in area and height. (See notes to Table 8.3.)
3. Two buildings do not exceed the area and height limits of one. (See BOCA commentary volume.)
4. Egress distances can be increased if additional criteria are met.
5. Use of horizontal exits.
6. Automatic fire alarm systems are not required if the building is sprinklered.
7. Smokeproof enclosures are not required if the building is sprinklered.
8. Fire rating of exit corridors is not required if the building is sprinklered and has an automatic alarm system.

ber of floors increase. Table 8.3 also reflects higher building costs when the hazard of the building contents increases. Table 902 of the code also increases the demand for fire resistance in a building in terms of occupancy.

2. *Allowable increases in area and height:*   Section 502.3 of the BOCA code allows considerable increases in area for a fully sprinklered building, except in use group H. Section 503.1 allows increases in height or number of floors for fully sprinklered buildings, again except in use group H. Cost comparisons of sprinklers versus subdividing the building with fire walls can be made.

3. Costs can be reduced when *two buildings on the same lot do not exceed the area and height limits in Table 8.3* when added together and, therefore, can be classified as one. Both exterior wall fire resistance ratings and opening protection can be reduced.

4. NFPA 101, *Life Safety Code,* allows the egress travel distance to be increased to 400 ft (122 m) in low- or ordinary-hazard occupancies if the following additional criteria are met: (a) it is a one- story building, (b) smoke and heat vents are installed, and (c) automatic fire-extinguishing protection is provided. (The *Life Safety Code* sometimes can be used to justify a variance.)

5. Use of horizontal exits into adjacent building areas, which generally are separated by a 2-hour firewall, is often overlooked and can be a cost savings. Section 807.5.1 of the code increases the exit travel distance for ordinary- or low-hazard factory and storage buildings when they are equipped with both automatic heat and smoke roof vents installed in accordance with Section 930 and an automatic sprinkler system.

6. Section 1018.4 deletes the requirement for an automatic fire alarm system and allows only a manual fire alarm system when the building is equipped throughout with an approved automatic fire suppression system.

7. Section 818.2.1 allows the substitution of sprinklers for smokeproof enclosures in multistory buildings if the stairwells are pressurized.

8. Section 810.4.1 deletes the requirement for fire rating for exit access corridors when the building has a sprinkler system with an automatic alarm connected to a central station.

## B  Multiple occupancies and multiple buildings

1. Often an industrial operation will involve multiple occupancies, such as business (office), factory, and storage. The code allows the designer a number of options in this situation, as shown in Table 9.6.

2. In addition to the options listed in the table, Section 906.2.2 allows a reduction in the exterior fire wall rating when it is non-load-bearing and the building is protected throughout with an automatic sprinkler system.

3. The often overlooked use of horizontal exits through fire walls into an adjacent new or existing building with a properly rated fire door at all floor levels is common in many industrial occupancies and can be substituted for a percentage of the code-required egresses.

## C  High-hazard occupancies.  High-hazard occupancy classifications are very expensive to construct. Tables 9.7 and 9.9 list some ways to reduce costs.

1. *Avoid high-hazard occupancy classifications:*  If the hazardous materials can be kept to small amounts, they can be stored in fire-rated or UL-listed metal cabinets to avoid a high-hazard building occupancy classification. See Table 8.5 for an example of typical maximum quantities of hazardous materials allowed in use group F-1, moderate-hazard factory and industrial uses, if a sprinkler system is installed.

---

**TABLE 9.6  Building Code Options for Multiple Occupancies**

*Option 1.* Combine into one building using the stricter occupancy
*Option 2.* One building using fire walls
*Option 3.* Two separate buildings with a combined total not exceeding the table maximum
*Option 4.* One occupancy with incidental use of a second occupancy
*Option 5.* Two buildings separated by the minimum distance
*Option 6.* Unlimited area one-story buildings with automatic sprinklers
*Option 7.* Special industrial use building with fire wall

---

*Note:* See Chapter 8 for explanations of the items listed.

TABLE 9.7    Reducing High-Hazard Classifications

| | |
|---|---|
| 1. Avoid high-hazard classifications | See Chap. 5 |
| 2. Reduce high-hazard area | See Chap. 8 |
| 3. Enclose release points of hazardous materials | See Chap. 5 |
| 4. Substitute mechanical ventilation | See Chaps. 5 and 8 |
| 5. Twelve exceptions to high-hazard building occupancy classifications | See Chap. 8 |

2. *Reduce the high-hazard occupancy area:*    Isolate the hazardous material operations or storage in a building, when they exceed the maximum amounts allowed in ordinary-hazard occupancies, with the proper fire walls or blast-resistant walls. This allows the major part of the building to be built to the less costly ordinary-hazard or factory classification (see also Table 5.1).

3. *Enclose the release point of the operation with capture hoods*: Prevent the release of hazardous vapors or dusts into the building area from a single hazardous materials operation such as bag splitting or from a materials handling transfer point or any other operation such as paint spraying or coating with the use of ventilating hoods (see Chaps. 5 and 13).

4. *Substitute mechanical ventilation for building explosion vents*: Section 617.3 allows the substitution of reliable mechanical ventilation for explosion-relief vents. The ventilation must be adequate to prevent the building room from reaching the minimum explosive concentrations of the dust(s) as determined by test. All pockets of stagnant air must be avoided. Reliability must be designed into the ventilation system. Interlock the ventilating fan(s) with the dust-producing operation so that it cannot operate without the simultaneous operation of the ventilating system. This can result in costs savings in those locations where outside roofs and/or walls are too remote or are not sufficiently large to provide the minimum of square footage of relief vents required by the codes.

5. *Twelve exceptions to high-hazard building occupancy classifications*:    Section 306.2.1 of the BOCA code lists 12 exceptions to high-hazard building construction that were developed by the Council of American Building Officials (CABO) Board for the Coordination of the Model Building Codes. These exceptions are sometimes missed.

D    **Existing building safety analysis.**    Article 32 of the BOCA code covers repairs, alterations, and additions to existing buildings without requiring full compliance with Articles 2 through 31 and allows the designer to evaluate the building based on 16 life safety items of the building for many occupancies, but not for use group H. (See Figure 8.1.)

**E  High-rise added costs.**  When a process design requires consider-able height for gravity feed through a number of process vessels and requires operators to be located more than 75 ft (22.86 m) above grade (fire department access by ladder) building officials and fire marshals can and have exercised the high-rise occupancy classification in the code. This is very expensive because of the additional code require-ments to protect people above the maximum fire department access height. Some of these requirements are sprinklers, compartmentaliza-tion, added fire walls, enclosed stairways, and added fire alarm sys-tems. Smoke detectors or automatic sprinkler protection is required in all mechanical, electrical, transformer, and telephone equipment rooms. Often a less costly revision to the process can save considerable building construction costs.

**F  Fireproofing costs.**  Early planning decisions can be made to reduce the need for more costly fireproofing construction and provide for the lower-cost construction, such as type 2C unprotected steel. Table 9.8 lists fireproofing options.

**G  Asbestos removal options.**  Compare the cost of encapsulating noncriterial locations with the cost of removal, and confirm your deci-sion with the local enforcing agency. The U.S. EPA now issues litera-ture on approved methods for doing this.

## III  Economic trade-offs in hazardous process equipment and buildings

**A  Avoid high-hazard classifications.**  Avoiding high-hazard classifica-tions can result in tremendous construction cost savings and can re-duce risks to life safety as well. Although this is not always possible (see Chap. 8), the first step is careful planning of the process equip-ment plus some comparative costs studies. For example, Table 9.9 lists eight options in the prevention of vapor/dust releases.

Table 8.3 shows that less costly building construction is permitted and more building area and height are allowed when the fire hazard of

**TABLE 9.8  Fireproofing Options**

1. Economical multiple-occupancy arrangement.
2. Avoid multiple floors when the option exists.
3. Avoid locating offices or highly populated worker areas above hazards.
4. Review lower-cost fireproofing options.
5. Avoid high-hazard occupancies in more than 5 stories.
6. Substitute class II for class I materials when the building is sprinklered.

*Note:* For items 1 through 6, see Structural Requirements and Fireproofing in Chap. 8.

**TABLE 9.9   Methods to Prevent Vapor/Dust Releases**

| | |
|---|---|
| 1. Process vessel containment or closed process systems | See Chaps. 4, 5, and 14 |
| 2. Exhaust hoods enclosing materials handling transfer points | See Chap. 13 |
| 3. Separation of hazardous materials operations | See Chap. 8 |
| 4. General building ventilation | See Chap. 13 |
| 5. Pneumatic conveyor systems | See Chap. 5 |
| 6. Isolation of grinding mills, mixers, blenders, dryers, etc., and dust collectors in smaller rooms | See Chap. 8 |
| 7. Control of 12 ignition sources | See Chaps. 6 and 15 |
| 8. Isolating electrical devices in pressurized cabinets or rooms | See Chap. 15 |

the contents and/or process is reduced. Early in the design process, large building cost reductions can be achieved if the process and equipment are designed with this in mind. Isolating a hazardous operation in small fire-rated rooms whenever possible and confining hazardous materials in process vessels and piping so that it will not escape into the building and come into contact with ignition sources are not only safer but also may be less costly. Many times these factors are ignored in process design. However, attention to these details early in the design process can result in a reduction in risk to workers, the building, the equipment, and production.

In addition, process equipment often is specified to contain internal explosions. Most maximum pressure rises resulting from explosions contained in vessels, as listed by NFPA for explosion-tested materials, do not reach 150 lb/in$^2$ (10.56 kg/cm$^2$). ASME-rated pressure vessels can easily contain this force. Process equipment that is too large to fabricate to ASME ratings can be designed to resist a lower explosion pressure, with the excess pressure relieved through an explosion vent and routed through the roof of the building. NFPA 68 provides a reliable formula to determine the size of the vent and the backpressure on the vessel. When the vent area is increased, the backpressure is reduced (see Chap. 5).

Separating operations that generate hazardous vapors and/or dusts from large areas and isolating them into small rooms enclosed with fire-rated walls, attached buildings separated with a fire-rated wall or a blast-resistant wall, or small, remote buildings frequently allows one to avoid an expensive high-hazard occupancy classification for the entire facility. A single bag-slitting operation separately enclosed for a large warehouse and a liquid mixing operation for small finished paint containers separated from a large paint warehouse are common examples of this. See NFPA's *Life Safety Code Handbook* for more detailed discussion of this.

TABLE 9.10    Options for Reducing Electrical Costs

1. Purged and pressurized enclosures for instrumentation
2. Purged and pressurized enclosures for small electrical enclosures
3. Purged and pressurized control rooms
4. Purged power equipment enclosures
5. Intrinsically safe equipment and wiring

Note: See Chapter 15 and NFPA 70 for more information.

When high-hazard occupancy classifications cannot be avoided, options do exist for reduction of the costs of safe installation of electrical systems by eliminating or reducing the expensive electrical hazardous (classified) locations. Table 9.10 lists these options.

## B    Intercode or interdisciplinary trade-offs

1. The BOCA *National Mechanical Code* specifies local ventilating hood designs and minimum air inlet velocities in enforced references standards that can be installed to reduce the area required for costly electrical hazardous (classified) locations (see Chaps. 5, 13, and 15).

2. Section 1018.4 of the BOCA *National Fire Code* allows the deletion of an automatic fire detection system when a building is equipped with a fire suppression system; then only a manual fire alarm system is required.

3. Compare the cost of a foam-water sprinkler with that of a clear-water sprinkler. Foam-water demand can be one-half to one-third that of clear-water systems and may reduce costs of pipe, pumps, and fire water storage tanks (see Chap. 12).

4. Check the fire code for allowed substitutions of other, less expensive extinguishing agents and systems.

5. Codes sometimes allow the substitution of reliable mechanical ventilation complying with the mechanical code for explosion relief for combustible dusts.

6. See Chapter 13 for various options and cost ratings for new chiller plants in relation to the CFCs.

## C    Plumbing

1. *Water supply backflow prevention:*   Two options or more often present themselves in an industrial facility that requires process water and domestic supply. The first option is a common water supply for the building serving both the drinking water and the process water

demand with backflow preventers at every process connection to the common water main in the building. The second option is separate domestic and process water supply systems originating at the valve pit or municipal water main with suitable protection. This obviously requires an economic review when the water supply system becomes complex. (See Chap. 14 for further discussion.)

2. *Central versus local hot water heating:*  Domestic or process water heating can be either from a central or a local hot water heater. Small and remote hot water demands are generally less costly to supply with a locally installed unit.

3. *Process waste and vent systems:*  Process areas with many floor drains can sometimes use combination waste and vent systems, which are permitted by most plumbing codes. The savings are realized by eliminating the many individual vents required by each floor drain trap. However, some special design considerations are required, such as oversizing and others, as specified in the plumbing codes. (See Chap. 14.)

**D  Electrical**  There are several cost-saving options in terms of transformer location, such as outdoors with minimum spacing, indoors with fire protection, or on roof with structural reinforcement and fire protection (see Chap. 15 for tables showing minimum requirements for each location).

## IV  Environmental regulation trade-offs

### A  With air pollution-control equipment

1. Substitution of toxic materials, process changes, pollution controls, or sometimes special operator training can be used to reach required emission reductions.

2. Review inlet air hood design(s) for efficiency to eliminate any excess volume above that required by the codes before sizing costly pollution-control equipment (see Chap. 13).

3. Review air pollution with the local EPA office to determine which level of control is required in your region. The requirements for the degree of control vary with attainment or nonattainment area, the toxic material, and potential emissions (see Chap. 17).

4. Review cost benefits of early hazardous air pollutants (HAP) emission reductions (90 percent) and the 6-year extension allowed for compliance to new maximum achievable control technology (MACT) or greatest achievable control technology (GACT) standards by 1990

Clean Air Act (CAA) amendments if the source is subject to MACT prior to 1994.

5. Review the possibility of grouping emission sources to obtain an extension on compliance.

6. An industrial facility may reduce the emissions from one source below the requirements of the EPA standard and earn credits for other sources that are above the EPA standards.

7. Review opportunities for "banking" emission reductions or trading with other facilities.

8. Review the potential for eliminating any of the about 100 extremely hazardous substances listed by the CAA amendments of 1990.

9. When volatile industrial emissions are involved, careful review of the requirements of both Title I and Title III of the CAA amendments of 1990 is recommended. They include creditable offsets that involve reasonably available control technology (RACT), lowest achievable emission rates (LEAR), and MACT for compliance and cost (see Chap. 17).

**B  With water pollution-control equipment.**  Review inlet wastes sources and quantities for efficiency to eliminate any unpolluted miscellaneous water source before sizing control equipment. Also eliminate any storm water runoff from entering water pollution-control equipment (see Chap. 18).

**V  Code variances**

We all recognize the commendable intent of codes, regulations, and enforced standards. However, codes, regulations, and enforced standards should not always and unquestionably be applied without analysis. Keeping in mind their intent, a cost/benefit eye should scan the requirements for situations where large construction costs are required with little benefit. When confronted with such situations, one should conduct a safety analysis, and if it indicates that the requirement is indeed excessive, a variance can be requested from the local authority, with evidence of the analysis as support (see Chap. 10 for an OSHA model variance application).

All building codes allow requests for variances and have appeal procedures. A variance is normally requested through the building official and generally requires a written request with justifiable reasons. The appeal procedure is a formal written process made either through the building official or directly to a building board when the appeal is to review an official's interpretation of the code.

Many state-credited plan review staffs will review a decision when they are challenged about a complex code interpretation or an overly costly code requirement and that challenge is supported with recognized data based on the purpose of life safety and property loss prevention. These staffs have sources available to advise them on the merits of the proposed variance.

## VI  Other comparisons normally made

Many other cost comparisons that are normally made in building design by each of the disciplines are not the intent of this list. For example, the HVAC system for an office building must be selected from a broad number of systems that are available on the basis of performance and cost.

# Occupational Safety and Health Act

The Occupational Safety and Health Act was passed in 1970 and amended in 1982; it is known as Title 29 of the *Code of Federal Regulations (CFR)*, Parts 1900 to 1999. It extends to all employers and their employees in the United States. Workplaces covered by other federal agencies under other federal laws are not covered; if the laws do not apply in a specific area, then OSHA applies. The act states that each employer "shall furnish...a place of employment which is free from recognized hazards that are causing or are likely to cause death or serious physical harm to his [or her] employees."

## Scope of OSHA Regulations

OSHA develops safety and health standards. These standards supersede the Walsh-Healey Act, the Service Contract Act, the Construction Safety Act, the Arts and Humanities Act, and the Longshoremen's and Harbor Workers' Compensation Act. Employers of 11 or more workers must maintain records of occupational injuries and illnesses as they occur. OSHA is concerned primarily with employee safety and health and does not emphasize property protection as much as the building codes do.

OSHA standards fall into four major categories:

- General industry
- Maritime
- Construction
- Agriculture

TABLE 10.1    OSHA Subparts Affecting Industry

| | |
|---|---|
| Subpart B: | Adoption and extension of established federal standards (see Fig. 11.1) |
| Subpart D: | Walking-working surfaces |
| Subpart E: | Means of egress |
| Subpart F: | Powered vehicles and work platforms |
| Subpart G: | Occupational health and environmental control |
| Subpart H: | Hazardous materials (See also Table 10.2.) |
| Subpart L: | Fire protection |
| Subpart M: | Compressed gases |
| | |
| Subpart N: | Materials handling |
| Subpart O: | Machinery guarding |
| Subpart O: | Welding, cutting, and brazing |
| Subpart R: | Special industries |
| Subpart S: | Electrical |
| Subpart Z: | Toxic and hazardous substance (OSHA regulations devote hundreds of pages to hazardous materials under subpart H and subpart Z that have extensive detail. See also Table 10.2.) |

Note: Requirements for different industrial operations are found under the specific industries described throughout the regulations.

In the design of new industrial facilities or alterations to existing buildings and industrial processes, it is necessary to review OSHA, Part 1910, for subparts that affect industry (Table 10.1).

Section 1910.1001, under subpart Z, "Toxic and Hazardous Substances," covers asbestos. For more extensive detail, see Chapter 21. Table Z-1-A, "Limits for Air Contaminants," lists over 500 substances and includes approved sampling and analytical methods for each substance. Table Z-3 lists mineral dusts.

## Processing Hazardous Materials

OSHA's Hazard Communication Standard (29 *CFR* 1910.1200) was promulgated in 1975. In 1991 the Laboratory Standard (29 *CFR* 1910.1450) was passed for chemicals in laboratories. Section (g)(1) requires a legal document for every hazardous material manufactured. Therefore, in an industrial facility, a materials safety data sheet (MSDS) must be used for every hazardous material that is received, stored, used, processed, and shipped.

The Clean Air Act amendments passed in November 1990 direct the EPA to take a larger role in process safety matters. As a result, the EPA has collected chemical release data from industry and has issued reports assessing the present status of prevention activities. In addition, the EPA has identified common elements in hazardous chemical accidents and is assisting state and local emergency officials in prevention and cleanup planning. The amendments also establish a new

Chemical Safety and Hazard Investigation Board, an independent safety board modeled after the National Transportation Safety Board.

The 1990 amendments also require that a report be issued by the EPA and OSHA on November 15, 1992, recommending regulations for risk management plans (RMPs) and hazard assessments (HAs). The report will cover each facility that produces, processes, handles, or stores any of the extremely hazardous substances (EHSs) listed in the 1990 amendments. Sixteen substances were initially listed, and more are to be added by November 15, 1992, which will bring the list to about 100 substances. Procedures recommended will be consistent with standards established by ANSI, ASTM, and ASME. The EPA must publish the regulations by November 15, 1993, and compliance is required within 3 years.

Hazard assessments must cover specific methodologies, techniques, parameters, and assumptions for simulating vapor and liquid/vapor releases. They must identify potential equipment and processes failures and assess the magnitude of releases and their impacts on the health of people and the environment. Section 301 of Title III adds a new subsection to Section 112 of the Clean Air Act, section 304. It directs OSHA to publish regulations for a chemical process safety standard to protect employees from the hazards of accidental releases of highly hazardous chemicals (HHCs) using hazard assessments. A list of highly hazardous chemicals was published by the EPA on November 15, 1991 (see Chap. 17).

## OSHA's New Process Safety Management Standard

On February 24, 1992, OSHA published (in the *Federal Register*) its final standard covering process safety management of highly hazardous substances. The standard, which took effect May 26, 1992, covers a wide variety of manufacturing industries. If workers are exposed in greater than threshold quantities, to any of the 130 toxic and reactive chemicals listed in Table 10.2, the standard is enforced. In addition, all flammable liquids and gases, except heating fuels, in quantities over 10,000 pounds are covered.

The standards mandate one of the following methods or an equivalent recognized method:

1. What-if
2. Checklist
3. What-if/checklist
4. Hazard and operability study (HAZOP)

TABLE 10.2    List of Toxic and Reactive Chemicals

| CAS | Chemical Name | TQ |
|---|---|---|
| 75-07-0 | Acetaldehyde | 2500 |
| 107-02-8 | Acrolein (2-propenal) | 150 |
| 814-68-6 | Acrylyl chloride | 250 |
| 107-05-1 | Allyl chloride | 1000 |
| 107-11-9 | Allylamine | 1000 |
| varies | Alkylaluminums | 5000 |
| 7664-41-7 | Ammonia, anhydrous | 10000 |
| 7664-41-7 | Ammonia solutions (>44 percent ammonia by weight) | 15000 |
| 7790-98-9 | Ammonium perchlorate | 7500 |
| 7787-36-2 | Ammonium permaganate | 7500 |
| 7784-42-1 | Arsine (also called arsenic hydride) | 100 |
| 542-88-1 | Bis(chloromethyl) ether | 100 |
| 10294-34-5 | Boron trichloride | 2500 |
| 7637-07-2 | Boron trifluoride | 250 |
| 7726-95-0 | Bromine | 1500 |
| 13863-41-7 | Bromine chloride | 1500 |
| 7789-30-2 | Bromine pentafluoride | 2500 |
| 7787-71-5 | Bromine trifluoride | 15000 |
| 106-96-7 | 3-Bromopropyne (also called propargyl bromide) | 100 |
| 75-91-2 | Butyl hydroperoxide (tertiary) | 5000 |
| 614-45-9 | Butyl perbenzoate (tertiary) | 7500 |
| 75-44-5 | Carbonyl chloride (see phosgene) | 100 |
| 353-50-4 | Carbonyl fluoride | 2500 |
| 9004-70-0 | Cellulose nitrate (concentration >12.6 percent nitrogen) | 2500 |
| 7782-50-5 | Chlorine | 1500 |
| 10049-04-4 | Chlorine dioxide | 1000 |
| 13637-63-3 | Chlorine pentrafluoride | 1000 |
| 7790-91-2 | Chlorine trifluoride | 1000 |
| 96-10-6 | Chlorodiethylaluminum (also called diethylaluminum chloride) | 5000 |
| 97-00-7 | 1-Chloro-2,4-dinitrobenzene | 5000 |
| 107-30-2 | Chloromethyl methyl | 500 |
| 76-06-2 | Chloropicrin | 500 |
| none | Chloropicrin and methyl bromide mixture | 1500 |
| none | Chloropicrin and methyl chloride mixture | 1500 |
| 80-15-9 | Cumene hydroperoxide | 5000 |
| 460-19-5 | Cyanogen | 2500 |
| 506-77-4 | Cyanogen chloride | 500 |
| 675-14-9 | Cyanuric fluoride | 100 |
| 110-22-5 | Diacetyle peroxide (concentration >70 percent) | 5000 |
| 334-88-3 | Diazomethane | 500 |
| 94-36-0 | Dibenzoyl peroxide | 7500 |
| 19287-45-7 | Diborane | 100 |
| 110-05-4 | Dibutyl peroxide (tertiary) | 5000 |
| 7527-29-4 | Dichloro acetylene | 250 |
| 4901-96-0 | Dichlorosilane | 2500 |
| 557-20-0 | Diethylzinc | 10000 |
| 105-64-6 | Diisopropyl peroxydicarbonate | 7500 |
| 105-74-8 | Dilauroyl peroxide | 7500 |
| 75-78-5 | Dimethyldichlorosilane | 1000 |
| 57-14-7 | 1,1-Dimethyl hydrazine | 1000 |
| 124-40-3 | Dimethylamine, anhydrous | 2500 |
| 97-02-9 | 2,4-Dinitroaniline | 5000 |

TABLE 10.2   List of Toxic and Reactive Chemicals (*Continued*)

| CAS | Chemical Name | TQ |
|---|---|---|
| 1338-23-4 | Ethyl methyl ketone peroxide | 5000 |
| 109-95-5 | Ethyl nitrite | 5000 |
| 75-04-7 | Ethylamine | 7500 |
| 371-62-0 | Ethylene fluorohydrin | 100 |
| 75-21-8 | Ethylene oxide | 5000 |
| 151-56-4 | Ethyleneimine | 1000 |
| 7782-41-4 | Fluorine | 1000 |
| 50-00-0 | Formaldehyde | 1000 |
| 110-00-9 | Furan | 500 |
| 684-16-2 | Hexafluoroacetone | 5000 |
| 7647-01-0 | Hydrochloric acid | 5000 |
| 7681-39-3 | Hydrofluoric acid | 1000 |
| 10035-10-6 | Hydrogen bromide | 5000 |
| 7647-01-0 | Hydrogen chloride | 5000 |
| 74-90-8 | Hydrogen cyanide | 1000 |
| 7664-39-3 | Hydrogen fluoride | 1000 |
| 7722-84-1 | Hydrogen peroxide (52 percent by weight or greater) | 7500 |
| 7783-07-5 | Hydrogen selenide | 150 |
| 7783-06-4 | Hydrogen sulfide | 1500 |
| 7803-49-8 | Hydroxylamine | 2500 |
| 13463-40-6 | Iron, pentacarbonyl- | 250 |
| 75-31-0 | Isopropylamine | 5000 |
| 463-51-4 | Ketene | 100 |
| 78-85-3 | Methacryladehyde | 1000 |
| 920-46-7 | Methacryloyl chloride | 150 |
| 30674-80-7 | Methacryloyloxyethyl isocyanate | 100 |
| 126-98-7 | Methyl acrylonitrile | 250 |
| 74-89-5 | Methylamine, anhydrous | 1000 |
| 74-83-9 | Methyl bromide | 2500 |
| 74-87-3 | Methyl chloride | 15000 |
| 79-22-1 | Methyl chloroformate | 500 |
| 1338-23-4 | Methyl ethyl ketone peroxide (concentration >60 percent) | 5000 |
| 453-18-9 | Methyl fluoroacetate | 100 |
| 421-20-5 | Methyl fluorosulfate | 100 |
| 60-34-4 | Methyl hydrazine | 100 |
| 74-88-4 | Methyl iodide | 7500 |
| 624-83-9 | Methyl isocyanate | 250 |
| 74-93-1 | Methyl mercaptan | 5000 |
| 79-84-4 | Methyl vinyl ketone | 100 |
| 75-79-6 | Methyltrichlorosilane | 500 |
| 13463-39-3 | Nickel carbonyl (nickel tetracarbonyl) | 150 |
| 7697-37-2 | Nitric acid | 500 |
| 10102-43-9 | Nitric acid | 250 |
| 100-01-6 | p-Nitroaniline | 5000 |
| 75-52-5 | Nitromethane | 2500 |
| 10102-44-0 | Nitrogen dioxide | 250 |
| 10102-44-0 | Nitrogen oxides (NO; NO2; N204; N203) | 250 |
| 10544-72-6 | Nitrogen tetroxide | 250 |
| 7783-54-2 | Nitrogen trifluoride | 5000 |
| 10544-73-7 | Nitrogen trioxide | 250 |
| 8014-94-7 | Oleum (65 to 80 percent by weight; also called fuming sulfuric acid) | 1000 |

TABLE 10.2   List of Toxic and Reactive Chemicals (*Continued*)

| CAS | Chemical Name | TQ |
|---|---|---|
| 20816-12-0 | Osmium tetroxide | 100 |
| 7783-41-7 | Oxygen difluoride (fluorine monoxide) | 100 |
| 10028-15-6 | Ozone | 100 |
| 19624-22-7 | Pentaborane | 100 |
| 79-21-0 | Peracetic acid (concentration >60 percent acetic acid; also peracetic acid) | 1000 |
| 7601-90-3 | Perchloric acid (concentration >60 percent by weight) | 5000 |
| 594-42-3 | Perchioromethyl-mercaptan | 150 |
| 7616-94-6 | Perchloryl fluoride | 5000 |
| 75-44-5 | Phosgene | 100 |
| 7803-51-2 | Phosphine | 100 |
| 10025-87-3 | Phosphorus oxychloride (also called phosphoryl chloride) | 1000 |
| 7719-12-2 | Phosphorus trichloride | 1000 |
| 106-96-7 | Propargyl bromide | 100 |
| 627-3-4 | Propyl nitrate | 2500 |
| 107-44-8 | Sarin | 100 |
| 7783-79-1 | Selenium hexafluoride | 1000 |
| 7803-52-3 | Stibine (antimony hydride) | 500 |
| 7446-09-5 | Sulfur dioxide | 1000 |
| 5714-22-7 | Sulfur pentafluoride | 250 |
| 7783-60-0 | Sulfur tetrafluoride | 250 |
| 7446-11-9 | Sulfur trioxide (also called sulfuric anhydride) | 1000 |
| 7783-80-4 | Tellurium hexafluoride | 250 |
| 116-14-3 | Tetrafluoroethylene | 5000 |
| 10036-47-2 | Tetrafluorohydrazine | 5000 |
| 75-74-1 | Tetramethyllead | 1000 |
| 7719-09-7 | Thionyl chloride | 250 |
| 1558-25-4 | Trichloro(chloro-methyl)silane | 100 |
| 27137-85-5 | Trichloro(dichloro-phenyl)silane | 2500 |
| 10025-78-2 | Trichlorosilane | 5000 |
| 79-38-9 | Trifluorochloroethylene | 10000 |
| 2487-90-3 | Trimethoxysilane | 1500 |

5. Failure mode and effects analysis (FMEA)

6. Fault tree analysis

The process hazard analysis must be updated and revalidated every five years. (See Chapter 4 for more details.)

## Enforcement

Section 8(a) of the Occupational Safety and Health Act gives compliance officers the right to enter without delay any place of employment to inspect for violations of the act, although the Supreme Court has ruled employers may require a search warrant. However, OSHA can obtain a search warrant on the basis of a complaint, a history of violations, a high-hazard industry, a fatality or catastrophe, or a random selection basis. OSHA inspections are, with few exceptions, conducted without advance notice. Imminent-danger situations are given top priority; next are accidents resulting in fatalities or injuries resulting in the hospitalization of five or more employees; then comes high-hazard industries. If OSHA violations are found, citations are issued with penalties for each infraction.

## OSHA Inspections

OSHA conducts two types of inspections/investigations: programmed and unprogrammed. Programmed inspections are the more common and frequent. Unprogrammed investigations are those arising from employee complaints, reports of imminent danger, or reports of fatalities or catastrophes (five or more employees hospitalized for more than 24 hours). Accidents involving extensive property damage are treated as complaints.

Since 1981, OSHA has been using a targeting system designed to concentrate programmed safety inspections on manufacturers with high injury rates. Workplaces with lost workday injury rates below 4.2 per 100 would not be subject to a programmed inspection. However, companies that do not keep accurate safety records are frequently inspected. Limited inspections are done in industries whose records indicate problems with specific processes or areas. See the OSHA *Field Manual* for more information. Reports of imminent danger result in an investigation within 24 hours. Employee complaints of serious hazards are investigated within 5 days. Nonserious complaints are investigated within 30 days.

## State OSHA Laws

An individual state can sign agreements with OSHA to formally take over all enforcement activity if it submits a plan that is at least as effective as the federal program and is certified. All state standards are available from the Office of Federal and State Operations, Occupational Safety and Health Administration, U.S. Department of Labor, Room 305, Railway Labor Building, 400 First Street NW, Washington, D.C. 20210.

## Variance Procedures

Variances may be requested from a specific OSHA standard or regulation if it can be proved that a facility or a method of operation provides employee protection "at least as effective as" that required by OSHA. A permanent variance (alternative to a particular requirement or standard) may be granted to employers who prove that their conditions, practices, means, methods, operations, or processes provide a safe and healthful workplace as effectively as would compliance with the standard.

In making the determination, OSHA weighs the employer's evidence and arranges a variance inspection and hearing, where appropriate. If OSHA finds the request valid, it prescribes a permanent variance detailing the employer's specific exceptions and responsibilities under the ruling. When applying for a permanent variance, an employer must inform employees of the application and of their right to request a hearing. Within 6 months after a permanent variance has been issued, the employer or employees may petition OSHA to modify or revoke the variance. OSHA also may do this of its own accord.

An employer may apply for a variance from a safety standard when that employer's practice does not follow the letter of the standard but provides safety equal to or better than the OSHA requirement. There are four types of variances:

*Temporary,* which are issued for limited periods.

*Permanent,* which can remain in effect indefinitely.

*National defense,* to avoid serious impairment of defense.

*Research,* to try improvement experiments for safety.

There is no standard form for an application, but OSHA has published a model letter that may be followed in an application (Fig. 10.1). Before a variance is granted, OSHA or the state conducts a single-purpose, preannounced noncompliance inspection.

### Subpart B: Adoption and Extension of Established Federal Standards

The provisions of this part adopt and extend the applicability of established federal standards. The standards of agencies of the U.S. government and of organizations that are not agencies of the U.S. government that are legally incorporated by reference in this part have the same force and effect as other standards in this part (see Fig. 11.1).

### Subpart D: Walking-Working Surfaces

This part covers definitions, general requirements, guarding floor and wall openings, fixed industrial stairs, portable wood and metal ladders, fixed ladders, safety requirements for scaffolding, manually pro-

## MODEL VARIANCE APPLICATION

**Model variance application.** The Office of Standards has released the following informal model variance application for use by companies in applying for a variance from standards:

Assistant Secretary for Occupational Safety and Health
U.S. Department of Labor
Washington, D.C. 20210

Dear Sir:

Pursuant to Section 6(d) of the Williams-Steiger Occupational Safety and Health Act of 1970 (84 Stat. 1596: 29 U.S.C. 655),..................respectfully requests a permanent variance from the requirements of 29 CFR 1910.179(b)(4), concerning wind indicator on the outdoor bridge of a Gantry Crane.

(1) Applicant—....................

(2) Place of employment—Same as (1)................................

(3)...................... has a Gantry Crane which operates beside a slip for unloading shallow draft barges. It currently is used only for unloading salt barges, usually about twice a year. Because of the location of our operation and the experience we have had with high wind conditions,..................recognizes the importance for monitoring wind conditions. As a result, our plant has two wind indicating devices with visual and automatic recording devices. We have a well established plan for monitoring Federal Weather Bureau reports and emergency plans of action for pending high winds. The key wind indicating device is located in the Shift Superintendent's office. A

Shift Superintendent is on duty around the clock, seven days a week and is responsible for the plant. He keeps a close watch on the wind conditions and also monitors weather forecasts at least three times during each eight-hour period. A written record is kept of the weather conditions. If there are any changes in wind conditions or anticipated changes due to approaching bad weather, the wind indicators and weather forecast are monitored continuously. Because of these well established policies and the limited use of the Gantry, we feel that our plan would offer a safer operation. In addition, we feel that the installation of a wind indicating device on the Gantry Crane would not be feasible because of conditions which tend to cause malfunction. Our past experience has verified this consistently. The Gantry Crane is very close to the molten sulfur pits and salt water. The close proximity to these agents creates a corrosive condition which would make the wind indicator inoperative soon after installation. We feel our monitoring and early warning system is more effective and safe than is the use of an infrequently used and difficult to maintain wind velocity instrument on the crane.

(4) Due to the corrosive conditions present around the Gantry Crane,..................feels that our established procedures would give more reliable information than an indicator on the crane. Therefore, we feel that this would insure the safety of the crane and operator better by following our procedures.

Respectfully submitted,

....................

Manager.

(5) This is to certify that a copy of the variance from Standard 1910.179(b)(4) requested by.............................., has been posted in an appropriate place for employees to examine. Also, an explanation of their right to send comments or petition for a hearing is explained on an attached sheet.

Posted on......................, 19...

....................
Manager.

..............................................Witness—Member of ICWU, Local (6)

### To All Employees

The attached form is a copy of the variance application submitted for a variance from Standard 1910.179(b)(4). This is to inform you that you may request a hearing with the Assistant Secretary for Occupational Safety and Health, U.S. Department of Labor, according to Standard 1905.15, Request for Hearing, if you object to the variance requested. This request must be filed in writing.

....................
Manager.

(7).................... also respectfully requests that an interim order be granted to allow operation of the Gantry Crane without the indicator until action is taken on the variance application. We feel that the safety of the employees will be guaranteed because we do have wind indicators being monitored at our plant and the Gantry operator would be promptly informed before wind velocities rose or approached a dangerous level.

....................
Manager.

**Figure 10.1** Model variance request letter.

pelled mobile ladder stands and scaffolds (towers), other working surfaces, sources of standards, and standards organizations.

## Subpart E: Means of Egress

As in the building, fire, and life safety codes, maximum distances for exiting a workplace are given. Although the distances specified compare with those in state building codes, there are differences that must be reviewed. OSHA also includes egress requirements from working platforms.

## Detailed Scope of Regulations

Table 10.3 presents the Table of Contents and Index from the OSHA Regulations to illustrate the extensive scope of these regulations and to allow readers to determine if a specific item is regulated.

In 1972, OSHA published a booklet entitled, *Guide for Applying Safety and Health Standards* (29 *CFR* 1910), in the form of

**TABLE 10.3 OSHA Table of Contents**

**TABLE 10.3 OSHA Table of Contents (Continued)**

**TABLE 10.3   OSHA Table of Contents (*Continued*)**

## MEANS OF EGRESS

| | Reference |
|---|---|
| General Requirements | 1910.36 |

**To Be Checked**

| | | Reference |
|---|---|---|
| ☐ | Exit Components | 1910.37 |
| ☐ | Protective Enclosure of Exits | 1910.37 |
| ☐ | Width and Capacity | 1910.37 |
| ☐ | Egress Capacity and Occupant Load | 1910.37 |
| ☐ | Arrangement of Exits | 1910.37 |
| ☐ | Access to Exits | 1910.37 |
| ☐ | Exterior Ways of Exit Access | 1910.37 |
| ☐ | Discharge from Exits | 1910.37 |
| ☐ | Headroom | 1910.37 |
| ☐ | Changes in Elevation | 1910.37 |
| ☐ | Maintenance and Workmanship | 1910.37 |
| ☐ | Furnishings and Decorations | 1910.37 |
| ☐ | Automatic Sprinkler Systems | 1910.37 |
| ☐ | Alarm and Fire Protection Systems | 1910.37 |
| ☐ | Fire Retardant Paints | 1910.37 |
| ☐ | Exit Markings | 1910.37 |

## HAZARDOUS MATERIALS

| | Material | Reference |
|---|---|---|
| ☐ | Compressed Gas | 1910.101 |
| ☐ | Acetylene | 1910.102 |
| ☐ | Hydrogen | 1910.103 |
| ☐ | Oxygen | 1910.104 |
| ☐ | Nitrous Oxide | 1910.105 |
| ☐ | Flammable and Combustible Liquids | 1910.106 |
| ☐ | Spray Finishing Using Flammable and Combustible Liquids | 1910.107 |
| ☐ | Dip Tanks Containing Flammable or Combustible Liquids | 1910.108 |
| ☐ | Explosives and Blasting Agents | 1910.109 |
| ☐ | Liquid Petroleum Gases | 1910.110 |
| ☐ | Anhydrous Ammonia | 1910.111 |

## FIRE PROTECTION

| To Be Checked | | Reference |
|---|---|---|
| ☐ | Portable Fire Extinguishers | 1910.157 |
| ☐ | Standpipe and Hose Systems | 1910.158 |
| ☐ | Automatic Sprinkler Systems | 1910.159 |
| ☐ | Fixed Dry Chemical Extinguishing Systems | 1910.160 |
| ☐ | Carbon Dioxide Extinguishing Systems | 1910.161 |
| ☐ | Local Fire Alarm Signaling Systems | 1910.163 |

## GENERAL ENVIRONMENTAL CONTROLS

| To Be Checked | | Reference |
|---|---|---|
| ☐ | Sanitation | 1910.141 |
| ☐ | Nonwater Carriage Disposal Systems | 1910.143 |
| ☐ | Marking of Physical Hazards | 1910.144 |
| ☐ | Accident Prevention Signs and Tags | 1910.145 |

## WALKING — WORKING SURFACES

| To Be Checked | | Reference |
|---|---|---|
| ☐ | Floor and Wall Openings and Holes | 1910.23 |
| ☐ | Fixed Industrial Stairs | 1910.24 |
| ☐ | Portable Wood Ladders | 1910.25 |
| ☐ | Portable Metal Ladders | 1910.26 |
| ☐ | Fixed Ladders | 1910.27 |
| ☐ | Scaffolding | 1910.28 |
| ☐ | Manually Propelled Mobile Ladder Stands and Scaffolds | 1910.29 |
| ☐ | Other Working Surfaces | 1910.30 |

## MATERIALS HANDLING AND STORAGE

| To Be Checked | | Reference |
|---|---|---|
| ☐ | Handling Materials-General | 1910.176 |
| ☐ | Indoor General Storage | 1910.177 |
| ☐ | Powered Industrial Trucks | 1910.178 |

**Figure 10.2** Compliance checklist. (*From OSHA Compliance Checklist, August 1976, Union Carbide Coatings Materials, 270 Park Avenue, New York, N.Y. 10017*)

# OCCUPATIONAL NOISE EXPOSURE

Reference: 1910.95
Permissible Noise Exposures[1] (Table G-16)

| Duration per day (hours) | Sound level dBA slow response |
|---|---|
| 8 | 90 |
| 6 | 92 |
| 4 | 95 |
| 3 | 97 |
| 2 | 100 |
| 1½ | 102 |
| 1 | 105 |
| ½ | 110 |
| ¼ or less | 115 |

[1]When the daily noise exposure is composed of two or more periods of noise exposure of different levels, their combined effect should be considered, rather than the individual effect of each. If the sum of the following fractions: $C1/T1 + C2/T2 \ldots Cn/Tn$ exceeds unity, then, the mixed exposure should be considered to exceed the limit value. $Cn$ indicates the total time of exposure at a specified noise level, and $Tn$ indicates the total time of exposure permitted at that level.

Exposure to impulsive or impact noise should not exceed 140 dB peak sound pressure level.

# PERSONAL PROTECTIVE EQUIPMENT

| To Be Checked | Reference |
|---|---|
| ☐ Eye and Face Protection | 1910.133 |
| ☐ Respiratory Protection | 1910.134 |
| ☐ Occupational Head Protection | 1910.135 |
| ☐ Occupational Foot Protection | 1910.136 |
| ☐ Electrical Protective Devices | 1910.137 |

# MACHINERY AND MACHINE GUARDING

| | Reference |
|---|---|
| General Requirements | 1910.212 |

| To Be Checked | |
|---|---|
| ☐ Types of Guarding | 1910.212 |
| ☐ Point of Operation Guarding | 1910.212 |
| ☐ Barrels, Containers, Drums | 1910.212 |
| ☐ Exposure of Blades | 1910.212 |
| ☐ Anchoring of Fixed Machinery | 1910.212 |

# ELECTRICAL REQUIREMENTS

Reference: 1910.309

(a) The requirements contained in the following articles and sections of the National Electrical Code, NFPA No. 70-1971; ANSI C1-1971 (Rev. of C1-1968) shall apply to all electrical installations and utilization equipment:

Articles:

| | |
|---|---|
| 500 | Hazardous Locations. |
| 501 | Class I Installations (Hazardous Locations). |
| 502 | Class II Installations (Hazardous Locations). |
| 503 | Class III Installations (Hazardous Locations). |

Sections:

| | |
|---|---|
| 250-58 (a)-(b). | Equipment on Structural Metal. |
| 250-59 (a), (b). and (c). | Portable and/or Cord Connected and Plug Connected Equipment, Grounding Method. |
| 400-3 (a)-(b). | Flexible Cords and Cable, Uses. |
| 400-4 | Flexible Cords and Cable Prohibited. |
| 400-5 | Flexible Cords and Cables, Splices. |
| 400-9 | Overcurrent Protection and Ampacities of Flexible Cords. |
| 410-10 | Pull at Joints and Terminals of Flexible Cords and Cables. |
| 422-8 | Installation, Appliances w/Flexible Cords. |
| 422-9 | Installation, Portable Immersion Heaters. |
| 422-10 | Installation, Appliances Adjacent to Combustible Material. |
| 422-11 | Stands for Portable Appliances. |
| 422-12 | Signals for Heated Appliances. |
| 422-14 | Water Heaters. |
| 422-15 (a), (b). | Installation of Infrared Lamp and Industrial Heating Appliances. |
| 110-14 (a)-(b). | Electric Connection. |
| 110-17 (a)-(c). | Guarding Live Part. |
| 110-18 | Arcing Parts. |
| 110-21 | Marking. |
| 110-22 | Identification. |
| 240-16 (a), (b). (c), and (d). | Location in Premises (for Overcurrent Protection Devices). |
| 240-19 (a) and (b). | Guarding of Arcing or Suddenly Moving Parts of Overcurrent Protection Devices. |
| 250-3 (a)-(b). | D.C. System Grounding. |
| 250-5 (a)-(c). | A.C. Circuits & Systems To Be Grounded. |
| 250-7 | Circuits Not To Be Grounded. |
| 250-42 (a)-(d). | Fixed Equipment Grounding, General. |
| 250-43 (a)-(i). | Fixed Equipment Grounding, Specific. |
| 250-44 (a)-(e). | Nonelectrical Equipment Grounding. |
| 250-45 (a), (b). (c), and (d). | Equipment Connected by Cord and Plug, Grounding. |
| 430-142 (a)-(d). | Stationary Motor, Grounding. |
| 430-143 | Portable Motors, Grounding. |
| 250-50 (a)-(b). | Equipment Grounding Connections. |
| 250-51 | Effective Grounding |
| 250-57 (a)-(b). | Fixed Equipment Method of Grounding. |
| 422-16 | Appliance Grounding. |
| 422-17 | Installation of Wall-mounted Ovens and Counter-mounted Cooking Units. |

(b) Every new electrical installation and all new utilization equipment installed after March 15, 1972, and every replacement, modification, or repair or rehabilitation, after March 15, 1972, of any part of any electrical installation or utilization equipment installed before March 15, 1972, shall be installed or made, and maintained, in accordance with the Provisions of the 1971 National Electrical Code, NFPA No. 70-1971; ANSI C1-1971 (Rev. of C1-1968).

(c) Notwithstanding the provisions of paragraphs (a) and (b) of this section, the effective date of the requirement in section 210-7 of the National Electrical Code, that all 15- and 20-ampere receptacle outlets on single-phase circuits for construction sites shall have approved ground-fault circuit protection for personnel, is postponed pending reconsideration of the requirement.

Figure 10.2   Compliance checklist. (*Continued*)

OSHA Standard 2072. This 30-page guide presents 16 technical subparts and lists the specific subjects covered along with references to specific paragraphs. It is a handy reference to OSHA's regulations for any operation in any industry.

OSHA published its final standard for air contamination in all industries, including grain-handling operations, in January of 1989, but this was challenged by the National Grain and Feed Association and the AFL-CIO. In 1990, OSHA reached a settlement that includes five steps to meet the standard.

For a quick reference to frequently used sections of OSHA, see Fig. 10.2. For material approved for incorporation by reference, see Fig. 11.1.

# Enforced Standards of Codes and Regulations

## Origin

Codes and standards had their origin in this country in the late 1800s. Standards are primarily written by nonprofit national technical organizations who develop codes and standards as one of their activities.

*Standards* are technical documents that can consist of a few paragraphs or hundreds of pages. They are written by the committees of technical organizations, which are made up of professionals and specialists who are proficient in various technical fields. Initially, standards are voluntary rules and guidelines for the construction and installation of numerous materials and equipment. They are enforced when the local, state, or federal government writes and legally adopts a code and the standard is listed as part of the code. When this occurs, the standard is known as an *enforced standard,* and compliance is required.

## *Code of Federal Regulations (CFR)*

The *Code of Federal Regulations (CFR)* is the source of all federal regulations. Federal laws passed by Congress are called *legislative law. Regulations* are usually written by federal agencies and are law because they are authorized by congressional legislation.

The *CFR* is organized by title and section. For example, Title 40 is "Protection of Environment," Title 29 is "Occupational Safety and Health Standards," and Title 10 is "Energy." The *CFR* is kept up to date by individual issues of the *Federal Register.* These two publications must be reviewed together to determine the latest version of a federal code, regulation, or standard.

## State and Local Laws and Regulations

State laws and their subsequent regulations are published in state administrative codes and regulations. Local municipalities also pass local ordinances, which are generally authorized by state charters.

## Sources of National Standards

### ANSI

The American National Standards Institute (ANSI) is a private-sector standards-coordinating center. It was established as the American Standards Association (ASA) in 1918 and was reconstituted in 1966 as the United States of America Standards Institute. Its name was changed in 1969 to the American National Standards Institute.

ANSI consists of 200 voluntary member organizations of preeminent professional-technical societies. It coordinates the activities of its members for codes and standards in this country. ANSI does not write standards itself but serves as an organization that validates the general acceptability of the work of technical experts. It guarantees that the standard-writing group used democratic procedures that gave everyone who will be directly and materially involved by the use of the standard an opportunity to participate in the development by commenting on the proposed standard before it was adopted.

When the need for a standard arises, ANSI determines which of its member organizations is best qualified to develop it. ANSI provides interface with and advice to departments and agencies of governments at all levels on standards-related issues. It serves as the recognized U.S. member of major nontreaty standards-developing bodies. ANSI publishes an extensive catalog listing all its standards and includes standards adopted from 94 member organizations.

### ASTM

The American Society for Testing and Materials (ASTM), as one of the ANSI member organizations, publishes 68 volumes or 16 separate books of standards, many of which apply to the construction industry. ASTM standards in building codes consist of 7080 pages containing 1300 standards in four volumes.

### ASME

The American Society of Mechanical Engineers (ASME) is another of the many member organizations of ANSI. By itself, it consists of

The Director of the Federal Register has approved under 5 U.S.C. 552(a) and 1 CFR Part 51 the incorporation by reference of the following publications. This list contains only those incorporations by reference effective as of the revision date of this volume. Incorporations by reference found within a regulation are effective upon the effective date of that regulation. For more information on incorporation by reference, see the preliminary pages of this volume.

**29 CFR CHAPTER XVII (PARTS 1900 TO 1910)**
**OCCUPATIONAL SAFETY AND HEALTH ADMINISTRATION, DEPARTMENT OF LABOR**

(Copies of the documents listed in this table are available through the Technical Data Center, U.S. Department of Labor, Washington, D.C., and through Regional Offices of the Occupational Safety and Health Administration. For a complete listing of these addresses, see the end of this table.)

*PART 1910*

| | 29 CFR |
|---|---|
| **American Conference of Governmental Industrial Hygienists** | |
| ACGIH Manual "Industrial Ventilation" (1970) | 1910.94 |
| Threshold Limit Values and Biological Exposure Indices for 1986–87 (1986). | 1910.120 |
| **American Society of Agricultural Engineers** | |
| ASAE Emblem for Identifying Slow Moving Vehicles, ASAE S276.2 (1968). | 1910.145 |
| **Agriculture Ammonia Institute—Rubber Manufacturers Association** | |
| AAI—RMA Specifications for Anhydrous Ammonia Hose | 1910.111 |
| **American National Standards Institute** | |
| ANSI A10.2–44 Safety Code for Building Construction | 1910.144 |
| ANSI A10.3–70 Safety Requirements for Explosive-Actuated Fastening Tools. | 1910.243 |
| ANSI A11.1–65 (R 70) Practice for Industrial Lighting | 1910.178; 1910.219; 1910.261; 1910.265 |
| ANSI A11.1–65 Practice for Industrial Lighting | 1910.262; 1910.265 |
| ANSI A12.1–67 Safety Requirements for Floor and Wall Openings, Railings, and Toe Boards. | 1910.66; 1910.68; 1910.261; 1910.264 |
| ANSI A13.1–56 Scheme for the Identification of Piping Systems | 1910.253; 1910.261; 1910.262; 1910.264 |
| ANSI A14.1–68 Safety Code for Portable Wood Ladders, Supplemented by ANSI A14.1a–77. | 1910.261 |
| ANSI A14.2–56 Safety Code for Portable Metal Ladders, Supplemented by ANSI A14.2a–77. | 1910.261 |
| ANSI A14.3–56 Safety Code for Fixed Ladders | 1910.68; 1910.179; 1910.261 |

**Figure 11.1** Material approved for incorporation by reference (revised as of June 29, 1990).

*PART 1910*—Continued
OCCUPATIONAL SAFETY AND HEALTH ADMINISTRATION, DEPARTMENT OF
LABOR—Continued

**29 CFR**

ANSI A17.1–65 Safety Code for Elevators, Dumbwaiters and Moving Walks, Including Supplements, A17.1a (1967); A17.1b (1968); A17.1c (1969); A17.1d (1970). — 1910.261

ANSI A17.2–60 Practice for the Inspection of Elevators, Including Supplements, A17.2a (1965), A17.2b (1967). — 1910.261

ANSI A90.1–69 Safety Standard for Manlifts..................................... — 1910.68

ANSI A92.2–69 Standard for Vehicle Mounted Elevating and Rotating Work Platforms. — 1910.67; 1910.268

ANSI A120.1–70 Safety Code for Powered Platforms for Exterior Building Maintenance. — 1910.66

ANSI B7.1–70 Safety Code for the Use, Care and Protection of Abrasive Wheels. — 1910.94; 1910.215; 1910.218

ANSI B15.1–53 (R 58) Safety Code for Mechanical Power Transmission Apparatus. — 1910.68; 1910.261

ANSI B20.1–57 Safety Code for Conveyors, Cableways, and Related Equipment. — 1910.218; 1910.261; 1910.265; 1910.266

ANSI B30.2–43 (R 52) Safety Code for Cranes, Derricks, and Hoists........ — 1910.261

ANSI B30.2.0–67 Safety Code for Overhead and Gantry Cranes.............. — 1910.179; 1910.261; 1910.266

ANSI B30.5–68 Safety Code for Crawler, Locomotive, and Truck Cranes. — 1910.180; 1910.261; 1910.266

ANSI B30.6–69 Safety Code for Derricks........................................ — 1910.181; 1910.268

ANSI B31.1–55 Code for Pressure Piping....................................... — 1910.261

ANSI B31.1a–63 Addenda to ANSI B31.1 (1955) ............................. — 1910.261

ANSI B31.1.0–67 and Addenda B31.1.0a (1969) Code for Pressure Piping — 1910.106; 1910.218; 1910.261

ANSI B31.2–68 Fuel Gas Piping ................................................ — 1910.103; 1910.104; 1910.106; 1910.252; 1910.261

ANSI B31.3–66 Petroleum Refinery Piping ..................................... — 1910.103; 1910.106

ANSI B31.5–66 Addenda B31.5a (1968) Refrigeration Piping.................. — 1910.103; 1910.111

ANSI B56.1–69 Safety Standard for Powered Industrial Trucks .............. — 1910.178; 1910.261

ANSI B57.1–65 Compressed Gas Cylinder Valve Outlet and Inlet Connections. — 1910.253

ANSI B71.1–68 Safety Specifications for Power Lawn Mowers ................ — 1910.243

ANSI C1–71 National Electrical Code........................................... — 1910.66; 1910.68; 1910.94; 1910.103; 1910.178

ANSI C33.2–56 Safety Standard for Transformer-Type Arc Welding Machines. — 1910.252

ANSI D8.1–67 Practices for Railroad Highway Grade Crossing Protection. — 1910.265

ANSI H23.1–70 Seamless Copper Water Tube Specification.................... — 1910.110

ANSI H38.7–69 Specification for Aluminum Alloy Seamless Pipe and Seamless Extruded Tube. — 1910.110

ANSI J6.1–50 (R 62) Standard Specifications for Rubber Insulating Line Hose. — 1910.137

ANSI J6.2–50 (R 62) Standard Specifications for Rubber Insulating Hood. — 1910.137

ANSI J6.4–70 Standard Specification for Rubber Insulating Blankets ...... — 1910.137

ANSI J6.4–71 Standard Specification for Rubber Insulating Blankets ...... — 1910.268

**Figure 11.1** Material approved for incorporation by reference. (*Continued*)

*PART 1910*—Continued
OCCUPATIONAL SAFETY AND HEALTH ADMINISTRATION, DEPARTMENT OF
LABOR—Continued

|  | **29 CFR** |
|---|---|
| ANSI J6.5–62 Standard Specification for Rubber Insulating Sleeves ........ | 1910.137 |
| ANSI J6.6–67 Standard Specification for Rubber Insulating Gloves ......... | 1910.137 |
| ANSI J6.6–71 Standard Specification for Rubber Insulating Gloves ......... | 1910.268 |
| ANSI J6.7–35 (R 62) Standard Specifications for Rubber Matting for Use Around Electric Apparatus. | 1910.137 |
| ANSI K13.1–67 Identification of Gas Mask Canisters .................................. | 1910.261 |
| ANSI K61.1–60 Safety Requirements for the Storage and Handling of Anhydrous Ammonia. | 1910.111 |
| ANSI K61.1–66 Safety Requirements for the Storage and Handling of Anhydrous Ammonia. | 1910.111 |
| ANSI O1.1–54 (R 61) Safety Code for Woodworking Machinery............... | 1910.261 |
| ANSI S1.4–71 (R 76) Specification for Sound Level Meters......................... | 1910.95 |
| ANSI S1.11–71 (R 76) Specification for Octave, Half-Octave and Third-Octave Band Filter Sets. | 1910.95 |
| ANSI S1.25–78 Specification for Personal Noise Dosimeters..................... | 1910.95 |
| ANSI S3.6–69 Specifications for Audiometers ............................................. | 1910.95 |
| ANSI Z4.1–68 Requirements for Sanitation in Places of Employment...... | 1910.261; 1910.264 |
| ANSI Z4.2–42 Standard Specifications for Drinking Fountains.................. | 1910.142 |
| ANSI Z9.1–51 Safety Code for Ventilation and Operation of Open Surface Tanks. | 1910.94; 1910.261 |
| ANSI Z9.2–60 Fundamentals Governing the Design and Operation of Local Exhaust Systems. | 1910.94; 1910.261; 1910.264 |
| ANSI Z12.12–68 Standard for the Prevention of Sulfur Fires and Explosions. | 1910.261; 1910.265 |
| ANSI Z12.20–62 (R 69) Code for the Prevention of Dust Explosions in Woodworking and Wood Flour Manufacturing Plants. | 1910.265 |
| ANSI Z21.30–64 Requirements for Gas Appliances and Gas Piping Installations. | 1910.264; 1910.265 |
| ANSI Z24.22–57 Method of Measurement of Real-Ear Attenuation of Ear Protectors at Threshold. | 1910.261 |
| ANSI Z33.1–61 Installation of Blower and Exhaust Systems for Dust, Stock, and Vapor Removal or Conveying. | 1910.261; 1910.265 |
| ANSI Z33.1–66 Installation of Blower and Exhaust Systems for Dust, Stock, and Vapor Removal or Conveying. | 1910.94 |
| ANSI Z35.1–68 Specifications for Accident Prevention Signs ................... | 1910.261 |
| ANSI Z41.1–67 Men's Safety Toe Footwear ................................................. | 1910.94; 1910.136; 1910.261; 1910.266 |
| ANSI Z48.1–54 Method for Marking Portable Compressed Gas Containers to Identify the Material Contained. | 1910.103; 1910.110; 1910.253 |
| ANSI Z48.1–54 (R 70) Method for Marking Portable Compressed Gas Containers To Identify the Material Contained. | 1910.111; 1910.134 |
| ANSI Z49.1–67 Safety in Welding and Cutting ............................................ | 1910.252 |
| ANSI Z53.1–67 Safety Color Code for Marking Physical Hazards and the Identification of Certain Equipment. | 1910.97; 1910.145; 1910.154 |
| ANSI Z54.1–63 Safety Standard for Non-Medical X-Ray and Sealed Gamma Ray Sources. | 1910.252 |
| ANSI Z87.1–68 Practice of Occupational and Educational Eye and Face Protection. | 1910.133; 1910.252; 1910.261 |
| ANSI Z88.2–69 Practices for Respiratory Protection ................................... | 1910.94; 1910.134; 1910.261; 1910.266 |

**Figure 11.1**   Material approved for incorporation by reference. (*Continued*)

*PART 1910*—Continued
OCCUPATIONAL SAFETY AND HEALTH ADMINISTRATION, DEPARTMENT OF
LABOR—Continued

|  | 29 CFR |
|---|---|
| ANSI Z89.1–69 Safety Requirements for Industrial Head Protection........ | 1910.135; 1910.261; 1910.266 |
| ANSI Z89.2–71 Safety Requirements for Industrial Protective Helmets for Electrical Workers, Class B. | 1910.268 |

**American Petroleum Institute**

| | |
|---|---|
| API 12A (Sept. 1951) Specification for Oil Storage Tanks With Riveted Shells, 7th Ed.. | 1910.106 |
| API 12B (May 1958) Specification for Bolted Production Tanks, 11th Ed., With Supplement No. 1, Mar. 1962. | 1910.106 |
| API 12D (Aug. 1957) Specification for Large Welded Production Tanks, 7th Ed.. | 1910.106 |
| API 12F (Mar. 1961) Specification for Small Welded Production Tanks, 5th Ed.. | 1910.106 |
| API 620, Fourth Ed. (1970) Including Appendix R, Recommended Rules for Design and Construction of Large Welded Low Pressure Storage Tanks. | 1910.103; 1910.106; 1910.111 |
| API 650 (1966) Welded Steel Tanks for Oil Storage, 3rd Ed....................... | 1910.106 |
| API 1104 (1968) Standard for Welding Pipelines and Related Facilities .. | 1910.252 |
| API 2000 (1968) Venting Atmospheric and Low Pressure Storage Tanks. | 1910.106 |
| API 2201 (1963) Welding or Hot Tapping on Equipment Containing Flammables. | 1910.252 |

**American Society of Mechanical Engineers**

| | |
|---|---|
| ASME Boiler and Pressure Vessel Code, 1949 Ed., Sec. VIII, Paragraph U–68 and U–69. | 1910.168 |
| ASME Boiler and Pressure Vessel Code, Sec. VIII, 1949, 1950, 1952, 1956, 1959, and 1962 Ed.. | 1910.110; 1910.111; 1910.168 |
| ASME Code for Pressure Vessels, 1968 Ed..................................................... | 1910.106; 1910.217 |
| ASME Boiler and Pressure Vessel Code, Sec. VIII, 1968 ........................... | 1910.103; 1910.104; 1910.106; 1910.107; 1910.110; 1910.111; 1910.169 |
| ASME Boiler and Pressure Vessel Code, Sec. VIII, Paragraph UG–84, 1968. | 1910.104 |
| ASME Boiler and Pressure Vessel Code, Sec. VIII, Unfired Pressure Vessels, Including Addenda (1969). | 1910.261; 1910.262; 1910.263 |
| Code for Unfired Pressure Vessels for Petroleum Liquids and Gases of the API and the ASME, 1951 Ed.. | 1910.110; 1910.168 |

**American Society for Testing and Materials**

| | |
|---|---|
| ASTM A 47–68 Malleable Iron Castings ......................................................... | 1910.111 |
| ASTM A 53–69 Welded and Seamless Steel Pipe ......................................... | 1910.110; 1910.111 |
| ASTM A 126–66 Gray Iron Casting for Valves, Flanges and Pipe Fitting | 1910.111 |
| ASTM A 391–65 (ANSI G61.1–1968) Alloy Steel Chain................................ | 1910.184 |
| ASTM A 395–68 Ductile Iron for Use at Elevated Temperatures.............. | 1910.111 |
| ASTM B 88–69 Seamless Copper Water Tube ............................................... | 1910.110 |
| ASTM B 88–66A Seamless Copper Water Tube............................................. | 1910.252 |
| ASTM B 117–64 Salt Spray (Fog) Test ................................................. | 1910.268 |
| ASTM B 210–68 Aluminum-Alloy Drawn Seamless Tubes ........................ | 1910.110 |
| ASTM D 5–65 Test for Penetration by Bituminous Materials.................... | 1910.106 |
| ASTM D 56–70 Test for Flash Point by Tag Closed Tester ....................... | 1910.106 |
| ASTM D 86–62 Test for Distillation of Petroleum Products ...................... | 1910.106 |
| ASTM D 88–56 Test for Saybolt Viscosity..................................................... | 1910.106 |

**Figure 11.1** Material approved for incorporation by reference. (*Continued*)

*PART 1910—*Continued
**OCCUPATIONAL SAFETY AND HEALTH ADMINISTRATION, DEPARTMENT OF LABOR—**Continued

|  | **29 CFR** |
|---|---|
| ASTM D 93–71 Test for Flash Point by Pensky Martens ............................ | 1910.106 |
| ASTM D 445–65 Test for Viscosity of Transparent and Opaque Liquids. | 1910.106 |
| ASTM D 1692–68 Test for Flammability of Plastic Sheeting and Cellular Plastics. | 1910.103 |
| ASTM D 2161–66 Conversion Tables For SUS............................................. | 1910.106 |

**American Welding Society**

| | |
|---|---|
| AWS A3.0 (1969) Terms and Definitions...................................................... | 1910.251 |
| AWS A6.1 (1966) Recommended Safe Practices for Gas Shielded Arc Welding. | 1910.254 |
| AWS B3.0–41 Standard Qualification Procedure ......................................... | 1910.67 |
| AWS D1.0–1966 Code for Welding in Building Construction..................... | 1910.27 |
| AWS D2.0–69 Specifications for Welding Highway and Railway Bridges. | 1910.67 |
| AWS D8.4–61 Recommended Practices for Automotive Welding Design | 1910.67 |
| AWS D10.9–69 Standard Qualification of Welding Procedures and Welders for Piping and Tubing. | 1910.67 |

**Commerce, Department of**

| | |
|---|---|
| Commercial Standard, CS 202–56 (1961) "Industrial Lifts and Hinged Loading Ramps". | 1910.30 |
| Pub., "Model Performance Criteria for Structural Fire Fighters' Helmets". | 1910.156 |

**Compressed Gas Association**

| | |
|---|---|
| CGA C–6 (1968) Standards for Visual Inspection of Compressed Gas Cylinders. | 1910.101; 1910.157 |
| CGA C–8 (1962) Standard for Requalification of ICC–3HT Cylinders...... | 1910.101; 1910.166 |
| CGA G–1 (1966) Acetylene............................................................................ | 1910.102 |
| CGA G–1.3 (1959) Acetylene Transmission for Chemical Synthesis......... | 1910.102 |
| CGA G–1.4 (1966) Standard for Acetylene Cylinder Charging Plants....... | 1910.102 |
| CGA G–7.1 (1966) Commodity Specification................................................ | 1910.134 |
| CGA G–8.1 (1964) Standard for the Installation of Nitrous Oxide Systems at Consumer Sites. | 1910.105 |
| CGA P–1 (1965) Safe Handling of Compressed Gases ............................... | 1910.101 |
| CGA P–3 (1963) Specifications, Properties, and Recommendations for Packaging, Transportation, Storage and Use of Ammonium Nitrate. | 1910.109 |
| CGA S–1.1 (1963) and 1965 Addenda. Safety Release Device Standards—Cylinders for Compressed Gases. | 1910.101; 1910.103; 1910.167 |
| CGA S–1.2 (1963) Safety Release Device Standards, Cargo and Portable Tanks for Compressed Gases. | 1910.101; 1910.103; 1910.167; 1910.168 |
| CGA S–1.3 (1959) Safety Release Device Standards—Compressed Gas Storage Containers. | 1910.103; 1910.104; 1910.111 |
| CGA 1957 Standard Hose Connection Standard......................................... | 1910.253 |
| CGA and RMA (Rubber Manufacturer's Association) Specification for Rubber Welding Hose (1958). | 1910.253 |
| CGA 1958 Regulator Connection Standard.................................................. | 1910.253 |

**Crane Manufacturer's Association of America, Inc.**

| | |
|---|---|
| CMAA Specification #61, Specifications for Electric Overhead Traveling Cranes. | 1910.179 |

**General Services Administration**

| | |
|---|---|
| GSA Pub. GG–B–0067b, Air Compressed for Breathing Purposes, or Interim Federal Specifications, Apr. 1965. | 1910.134 |

**Figure 11.1**  Material approved for incorporation by reference. (*Continued*)

PART 1910—Continued
OCCUPATIONAL SAFETY AND HEALTH ADMINISTRATION, DEPARTMENT OF
LABOR—Continued

| | 29 CFR |
|---|---|
| NFPA 203M–1970 Manual on Roof Coverings | 1910.109 |
| NFPA 251–1969 Standard Methods of Fire Tests of Building Construction and Materials. | 1910.106 |
| NFPA 302–1968 Fire Protection Standard for Motor-Craft (Pleasure and Commercial). | 1910.265 |
| NFPA 385–1966 Recommended Regulatory Standard for Tank Vehicles for Flammable and Combustible Liquids. | 1910.106 |
| NFPA 496–1967 Standard for Purged Enclosures for Electrical Equipment in Hazardous Locations. | 1910.103 |
| NFPA 505–1969 Standard for Type Designations, Areas of Use, Maintenence, and Operation of Powered Industrial Trucks. | 1910.110; 1910.189 |
| NFPA 566–1965 Standard for the Installation of Bulk Oxygen Systems at Consumer Sites. | 1910.252 |
| NFPA 656–1959 Code for the Prevention of Dust Ignition in Spice Grinding Plants. | 1910.263 |
| NFPA 1971-1975 Protective Clothing for Structural Fire Fighting | 1910.156 |

**National Food Plant Institute**

| | |
|---|---|
| Definition and Test Procedures for Ammonium Nitrate Fertilizer (Nov. 1964). | 1910.109 |

**National Institute for Occupational Safety and Health**

| | |
|---|---|
| Registry of Toxic Effects of Chemical Substances, 1978 | 1910.20 |
| Development of Criteria for Fire Fighters Gloves; Vol. II, Part II; Test Methods, 1976. | 1910.156 |
| NIOSH Recommendations for Occupational Safety and Health Standards (September 1987). | 1910.120 |

**Public Health Service**

| | |
|---|---|
| U.S. Pharmacopeia | 1910.134 |
| Publication No. 934 (1962), Food Service Sanitation Ordinance and Code, Part V of the Food Service Sanitation Manual. | 1910.142 |

**Society of Automotive Engineers**

| | |
|---|---|
| SAE 765 (1961) SAE Recommended Practice: Crane Loading Stability Test Code. | 1910.180 |

**The Fertilizer Institute**

| | |
|---|---|
| Standard M–1 (1953, 1955, 1957, 1960, 1961, 1963, 1965, 1966, 1967, 1968), Superseded by ANSI K61.1–1972. | 1910.111 |

**Underwriters Laboratories**

| | |
|---|---|
| UL 58–61 Steel Underground Tanks for Flammable and Combustible Liquids, 5th Ed.. | 1910.106 |
| UL 80–63 Steel Inside Tanks for Oil-Burner Fuel | 1910.106 |
| UL 142–68 Steel Above Ground Tanks for Flammable and Combustible Liquids. | 1910.106 |

*Addresses*
Technical Data Center: Frances Perkins Department of Labor Building, Room N2439, 200 Constitution Ave., N.W., Washington, D.C. 20210.
Boston Regional Office—Region I: Regional Administrator, U.S. Department of Labor—OSHA, 16–18 North St., 1 Dock Square Bldg., 4th Fl., Boston, MA 02109.
New York Regional Office—Region II: Regional Administrator, U.S. Department of Labor—OSHA, 1515 Broadway (1 Astor Plaza), Room 3445, New York, NY 10036.
Philadelphia Regional Office—Region III: Regional Administrator, U.S. Department of Labor—OSHA, Gateway Bldg., Suite 2100, 3535 Market St., Philadelphia, PA 19104.

**Figure 11.1** Material approved for incorporation by reference. (*Continued*)

*PART 1910*—Continued
OCCUPATIONAL SAFETY AND HEALTH ADMINISTRATION, DEPARTMENT OF
LABOR—Continued

**29 CFR**

**Health and Human Services, Department of**
Publication No. 76–120 (1975), List of Personal Hearing Protectors and  1910.95
Attenuation Data.

**Institute of Makers of Explosives**
IME Pamphlet No. 17, 1960, Safety in the Handling and Use of Explo-  1910.261
sives.

**National Electrical Manufacturer's Association**
NEMA EW–1 (1962) Requirements for Electric Arc Welding Apparatus.  1910.252

**National Fire Protection Association**
NFPA 30 (1969) Flammable and Combustible Liquids Code......................  1910.178
NFPA 32–1970 Standard for Dry Cleaning Plants.........................................  1910.106
NFPA 33–1969 Standard for Spray Finishing Using Flammable and  1910.94
Combustible Material.
NFPA 34–1966 Standard for Dip Tanks Containing Flammable or Com-  1910.94
bustible Liquids.
NFPA 35–1970 Standard for the Manufacture of Organic Coatings ..........  1910.106
NFPA 36–1967 Standard for Solvent Extraction Plants..............................  1910.106
NFPA 37–1970 Standard for the Installation and Use of Stationery  1910.106; 1910.110
Combustion Engines and Gas Turbines.
NFPA 51B–1962 Standard for Fire Protection in Use of Cutting and  1910.252
Welding Processes.
NFPA 54–1969 Standard for the Installation of Gas Appliances and  1910.110
Gas Piping.
NFPA 54A–69 Standard for the Installation of Gas Piping and Gas  1910.110
Equipment on Industrial Premises and Certain Other Premises.
NFPA 58–1969 Standard for the Storage and Handling of Liquefied  1910.168; 1910.178
Petroleum Gases (ANSI Z106.1–1970).
NFPA 59–1968 Standard for the Storage and Handling of Liquefied  1910.110
Petroleum Gases at Utility Gas Plants.
NFPA 62–1967 Standard for the Prevention of Dust Explosions in the  1910.263
Production, Packaging, and Handling of Pulverized Sugar and Cocoa.
NFPA 68–1954 Guide for Explosion Venting ................................................  1910.94
NFPA 70–1971 National Electrical Code .......................................................  1910.66; 1910.68;
                                                                                                                      1910.94; 1910.103;
                                                                                                                      1910.178
NFPA 78–1968 Lightning Protection Code ......................................................  1910.109
NFPA 80–1968 Standard for Fire Doors and Windows ...............................  1910.106
NFPA 80–1970 Standard for the installation of Fire Doors and Win-
dows ....................................................................................................................  1910.253
NFPA 86A–1969 Standard for Oven and Furnaces Design, Location and  1910.107; 1910.108
Equipment.
NFPA 91–1961 Standard for the Installation of Blower and Exhaust  1910.107
Systems for Dust, Stock, and Vapor Removal or Conveying (ANSI
Z33.1–61).
NFPA 91–1969 Standards for Blower and Exhaust Systems ......................  1910.108
NFPA 96–1970 Standard for the Installation of Equipment for the  1910.110
Removal of Smoke and Grease Laden Vapors from Commercial
Cooking Equipment.
NFPA 101–1070 Code for Life Safety From Fire in Buildings and  1910.261
Structures.

Figure 11.1   Material approved for incorporation by reference. (*Continued*)

# Appendix B  POTENTIALLY INTERACTIVE CODES & STANDARDS

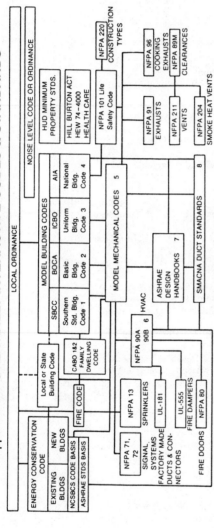

1. Southern Building Code Congress, 3617 8th Avenue, S., Birmingham, AL 35222
2. Building Officials & Code Administrators International, Inc., 17926 South Halsted, Homewood, IL 60430
3. International Conference of Building Officials, 5360 S. Workman Mill Road, Whittier, CA 90601
4. Formerly by American Insurance Association, 85 John Street, New York, NY 10038, now by NCSBCS.
5. Model Mechanical Code, Published by the Model Building Code Agency.
6. National Fire Protection Association, 470 Atlantic Avenue, Boston, MA 02210
7. American Society of Heating, Refrigerating and Air Conditioning Engineers, Inc., 345 E. 47th St., New York, NY 10017
8. Sheet Metal and Air Conditioning Contractors National Association, P.O. Box 70, Merrifield, VA 22116

Notice: Lines with direct connection to Item 8 denote incorporation by reference (except ICBO case). Other recognition may occur indirectly or directly.

Underwriters Laboratories: 207 East Ohio St., Chicago, IL 60611
333 Pfingsten Rd., Northbrook, IL 60062
1285 Walt Whitman Rd., Melville, NY 11746
1655 Scott Blvd., Santa Clara, CA 95050

### OTHER INFLUENTIAL AGENCIES

A. NCSBCS, National Conference of States on Building Codes and Standards, seeks to promote development, publication and use of standardized, uniform code practices. NCSBCS, 481 Carlisle Drive, Herndon, VA 22070.
B. CABO - SBCC, BOCA and ICBO cooperatively operate the Council of American Building Officials, which promotes uniformity and produces standard practice documents. CABO 2233 Wisconsin Ave., N.W., Washington, DC 20007.
C. For federal government construction other conditions prevail. Interagency standardization is promoted by the Federal Construction Council. General Services Administration, Veterans Administration, The Corps of Engineers, Naval Facilities Engineering Command and other government agencies adopt SMACNA standards by reference.

**Figure 11.2**  Potentially interactive codes and standards.

111,000 members, mostly engineers, and is very active in writing standards, with 120 main committees dealing with 600 standards.

Other very active standards-writing organizations of the 94 listed for building construction are

1. National Fire Protection Association (NFPA), which publishes more than 250 standards
2. Underwriters' Laboratories (UL), which publishes more than 550 standards
3. Factory Mutual (FM), which publishes more than 500 standards
4. Industrial Risk Insurers (IRI)
5. American Petroleum Institute (API)

Figure 11.1 provides a listing of enforced standards from OSHA. Figure 11.2 provides a typical diagram of how codes, regulations, and standards can form an interlocking image. Similar lists and diagrams could be made from building and fire codes and process safety and environmental regulations references. See the section on Interlocking Maze of Enforced Codes, Regulations, and Standards on page 8.

# Fire and Explosion Suppression

This chapter outlines the contents of a typical state fire code and discusses the design and installation requirements for fixed manual hose systems (standpipes), automatic sprinkler systems, other special automatic fire suppression systems, portable fire extinguishers, and explosion suppression systems. This chapter also provides sample plan-review checklists for some of these systems.

## Origin of Fire Codes

The first rules for the installation of automatic sprinklers were written by the Mutual Fire Insurance Corporation of Manchester, England, in 1885. In 1896, a set of rules was completed by a group of inspection bureau men in New York. That same year the National Fire Protection Association (NFPA) was established, and it issued the 1896 rules as its first standard for the installation of sprinkler systems (NFPA 13).

## Three Model Fire Codes

The three model building codes discussed in Chapter 8 each contain separate volumes for fire codes. Most states adopt one of these three model codes with some degree of amendment. In addition, both the building and fire codes enforce other standards in their appendices, and, as usual, all the enforced standards must be read and complied with in the design of an industrial facility. (See Chap. 11.)

## A Typical State Fire Code

The Ohio Fire Code, which is a typical state fire code, starts with this introduction:

The purpose and intent of state and local building/fire protection codes is to prescribe minimum requirements and controls to safeguard life, property or public welfare from the hazards of fire and explosion arising from the storage, handling or use of substances, materials or devices. All matters within the intent of this code and not covered by this shall comply with the accepted engineering practice standard listed in Rule 1301:7-7-34 of the Administration Code (Appendix A).

Then Rule 1301:7-7-34, Referenced Standards, states

The following is a listing of standards in the Ohio Fire Code, the effective date of the standard, the promulgating agency of the standard and the section(s) of the Ohio Fire Code that refer to the standard.

There are approximately 100 enforced standards listed over 2½ pages.

### Table of contents

Following is the table of contents from a typical state fire code:

Article 21. Cellulose Nitrate Motion Picture Film
Article 22. Cellulose Nitrate (Pyroxylin) Plastics
Article 23. Combustible Fibers
Article 24. Compressed Gases
Article 25. Cryogenic Liquids
Article 26. Explosives, Ammunition and Blasting Agents
Article 27. Fireworks
Article 28. Flammable and Combustible Liquids
Article 29. Hazardous Materials and Chemicals
Article 30. Liquefied Petroleum Gases and Maintenance
Article 31. Magnesium
Article 32. Matches
Article 33. Organic Coatings

Referenced Standards
Underground Storage Tank Regulations
Corrective Actions and the Cost Recovery Standards for Petroleum
  Underground Storage Tanks (see Chap. 21 for more information)

## Detail of fire codes

The fire code is extensive in important detail, and the sections that are applicable to your project must be read before the design process is begun. For example, Article 28, "Flammable and Combustible Liquids," states:

> This rule shall apply to the transportation, storage, handling and processing of flammable combustible liquids and to any underground storage tank system. The provisions of NFPA 30, NFPA 30A, NFPA 329, PEI RP 100-87, API 1604, API 1631 and ASTM G57-78 listed in Rule 1301: 7-7-34 of the Administrative Code shall apply where the provisions of this rule do not specifically cover conditions and operations.

Article 28 continues for nine pages and contains more important detail. Section F-2801, "Fire Safety Requirements," states that facilities engaging in the activities specified in Article 28 must be provided with fire protection and fire extinguishing equipment. It also states the requirements for bulk, processing, and industrial plants. Article 28 goes on to list detailed requirements for outside above-ground and underground flammable liquid tank farms and inside storage of flammable liquids, specifying such details as size of containers, quantities and maximum heights of storage, minimum ventilation, explosion relief, ignition sources, and where bonding and grounding are required. This article must be reviewed jointly with NFPA 30, which in paragraph 5-5.1.3 specifies six engineering evaluation criteria in deciding the type of fire control systems for industrial plants; bulk plants and terminals; processing plants; and refineries, chemical plants, and distilleries:

1. Analysis of fire and explosion hazards of the liquid operations.

2. Analysis of hazardous materials, hazardous chemicals, or hazardous reactions in the operations and the safeguards taken to control such materials.

3. Analysis of the facility design requirements described in NFPA 30.

4. Analysis of the liquid handling, transfer, and use requirements described in NFPA 30.

5. Analysis of local conditions, such as exposure to and from adjacent properties, flood potential, and earthquake potential.

6. Consideration of fire department of mutual aid response.

### Fire official's right of entry

Fire codes generally give the fire official "right of entry" by such statements as, "Whenever necessary for the purpose of enforcing the provisions of this code or whenever the fire official has reasonable cause to believe there exists in any structure or upon any premises any condition which makes such structure or premises unsafe, the fire official may enter...at all reasonable times to inspect...." Most fire codes also give the fire official the authority to revoke an occupancy permit or to stop unsafe operations.

### Alternate methods

Most codes allow alternate methods and materials. Generally, a code will contain a statement such as the following: "The fire official may accept alternate methods of satisfying the intent of this code if the material, method or work is at least the equivalent of that required by this [code] in quality." For example, Table 12.1 illustrates the code-approved alternatives in the selection of a fire suppression system for various facilities and areas within facilities. See also Figure. 12.1 for Grinnell Corporation's special fire hazard recommendations.

### Automatic Sprinkler Systems

### Building codes

Building codes generally specify where sprinkler systems are required. However, fire codes also specify sprinkler locations for specific areas, specify design details, and enforce a number of NFPA fire protection standards and the standards of other organizations.

TABLE 12.1 Guide for Suppression System Selection

| Hazard | Water sprinklers or spray 1004.0 to 1006.0 | Foam 1007.0 | Carbon dioxide or halogenated 1008.0 to 1009.0 | Dry chemical 1010.0 | Wet chemical 1011.0 |
|---|---|---|---|---|---|
| Class A fire potential | X | X | X | X | X |
| Class B fire potential | X | X | X | X | X |
| Class C fire potential | X | | X | | |
| Special Fire Hazard Areas[a] | | | | | |
| Aircraft hangars | X | X | X | X | |
| Alcohol storage | X | X | X | X | |
| Ammunition loading | X | | | | |
| Ammunition magazines | X | | | | |
| Asphalt impregnating | X | X | | | |
| Battery rooms | | | X | | |
| Carburetor overhaul shops | X | X | X | X | |
| Cleaning plant equipment | X | X | X | X | |
| Computer rooms | X | | X | | |
| Dowtherm | X | | | | |
| Drying ovens | X | | X | X | |
| Engine test cells | X | X | X | | |
| Escalator, stair wells | X | | | | |
| Explosives: manufacturing, storage | X | | | | |
| Flammable liquids storage | X | X | X | | |
| Flammable solids storage | X | | | | |
| Fuel oil storage | X | X | | | |
| Hangar decks | X | X | | | |
| High piled storage in excess of 15 ft in height | X | X | | | |
| HPM use facility: Fabrication areas (ordinary hazard group 3) | X | | | | |
| Service passages (ordinary hazard group 3) | X | | | | |
| Separate inside HPM storage rooms without dispensing (ordinary hazard group 3) | X | | | | |
| Separate inside HPM storage rooms with dispensing (extra hazard group 2) | X | | | | |
| Egress corridors (ordinary hazard group 3) | X | | | | |
| Hydraulic oil, lubricating oil | X | | X | | |
| Hydroturbine generators | X | | X | | |
| Jet engine test cells | X | X | X | | |
| Library stacks | X | | X | | |
| Lignite storage and handling | X | | | | |
| Liquefied petroleum gas storage | X | | | | |
| Oil quenching bath | X | X | X | X | |
| Paints: manufacturing, storage | X | X | X | X | |
| Paint spray booths | X | | X | X | |
| Petrochemical storage | X | X | X | | |
| Petroleum testing laboratories | X | X | X | | |
| Printing presses | X | | X | | |
| Rack and palletized storage in excess of 12 ft (3658 mm) in height | X | X | | | |
| Range hoods | X | | X | X | X |
| Reactor and fractionating towers | X | | | | |
| Record vaults | | | X | | |
| Rubber mixing and heat treating | X | | | | |

TABLE 12.1   Guide for Suppression System Selection (*Continued*)

| Hazard | Water sprinklers or spray 1004.0 to 1006.0 | Foam 1007.0 | Carbon dioxide or halogenated 1008.0 to 1009.0 | Dry chemical 1010.0 | Wet chemical 1011.0 |
|---|---|---|---|---|---|
| Service stations (inside buildings) | X | | X | | |
| Shipboard storage | X | | X | | |
| Solvent cleaning tanks | | X | X | X | |
| Solvent thinned coatings | | X | X | X | |
| Switchgear rooms | | | X | | |
| Transformers, circuit breakers (outdoors) | X | | | | |
| Transformers, circuit breakers (indoors) | X | | X | | |
| Turbine lubricating oil | X | X | X | X | |
| Vegetable oil, solvent extraction | X | X | | | |

ªWithin buildings or areas, so classified, as to require a suppression system.
SOURCE: Reprinted from BOCA, *National Building Code*, Vol. 1. Country Club Hills, Ill.: Building Officials and Code Administrators International, Inc., 1990. Reprinted by permission of BOCA.

**Existing buildings.**   Fire codes apply to both new and existing buildings. For existing buildings, the codes usually contain statements such as the following:

Buildings built under, and in full compliance with, the codes in force at the time of construction or alterations thereof, and that have been properly maintained and used for such use as originally permitted, shall be exempt from the requirements of this code pertaining to: (1) Fire protection of structural elements, except as provided for existing buildings under the building code; (2) exits required, except as provided for existing buildings under this code and the building code; and (3) isolation of hazardous materials, provided, however, that the fire official may require the installation of fire safety devices or systems....

### New buildings

Building codes specify where automatic fire extinguishing systems are required for new buildings based on their occupancy classifications. Fire codes also specify where automatic sprinklers are required. For example, the BOCA *National Fire Code*, Article 10, Sections 1002.2 through 1002.21, identifies the buildings and occupancy classifications that must have automatic suppression systems. Some of the industrial occupancies that require automatic fire suppression are listed in Table 12.2.

Table 501 of the BOCA code (see Table 8.3 of this book), which sets limits for area and height of new buildings, allows increases in some of these limitations as well as in maximum egress distances when a

| SPECIAL FIRE HAZARD | WATER SPRAY | FOAM | CARBON DIOXIDE | DRY CHEMICAL | HALON |
|---|---|---|---|---|---|
| Aircraft Hangars | • | • | | | |
| Alcohol Storage | • | • | • | | |
| Ammunition Loading | • | | | | |
| Ammunition Magazines | • | | | | |
| Asphalt Impregnating | • | | | | |
| Battery Rooms | | | • | | |
| Carburetor Overhaul Shops | • | • | • | • | |
| Cleaning Plant Equipment | • | • | • | • | |
| Computer Rooms | | | | | • |
| Dowtherm | • | | | | |
| Drying Ovens | • | | • | • | |
| Engine Test Cells | • | • | • | | |
| Escalators, Stair Wells | • | | | | |
| Explosives: Manufacturing, Storage | • | | | | |
| Flammable Liquids Storage | • | • | • | | |
| Flammable Solids Storage | • | | | | |
| Fuel Oil Storage | • | • | | | |
| Hangar Decks | • | • | | | |
| Hydraulic Oil, Lubricating Oil | • | | • | | |
| Hydro-Turbine Generators | • | | • | | • |
| Jet Engine Test Cells | • | • | • | | • |
| Lignite Storage and Handling | • | | | | |
| Liquefied Petroleum Gas Storage | • | | | | |
| Oil Quenching Bath | • | • | • | • | |
| Paints: Manufacturing, Storage | • | • | • | • | • |
| Paint Spray Booths | • | | • | • | |
| Petrochemical Storage | • | • | • | | • |
| Petroleum Testing Laboratories | • | • | • | | • |
| Printing Presses | | | • | | |
| Reactor and Fractionating Towers | • | | | | |
| Record Vaults | | | • | | • |
| Rubber Mixing and Heat Treating | • | | | | |
| Shipboard Storage | • | | • | | • |
| Solvent Cleaning Tanks | | • | • | • | |
| Solvent Thinned Coatings | | • | • | • | |
| Switchgear Rooms | | | • | | • |
| Transformers, Circuit Breakers (outdoors) | • | | | | |
| Transformers, Circuit Breakers (indoors) | • | | • | | |
| Turbine Lubricating Oil | • | • | • | • | |
| Vegetable Oil, Solvent Extraction | • | • | | | |

**Figure 12.1**   Quick selector chart. The most commonly used extinguishing agents are indicated by the bullets. (*From Grinnell's Special Hazard Fire Protection Catalogue, p. 34. Reprinted with permission of Grinnell Corporation, Exeter, NH.*)

building is equipped with an automatic sprinkler system (see notes at the bottom of Table 8.3).

**Use group H**   Section 1002.7, "Use Group H," of the BOCA *National Fire Code* states, as do most codes, "Because of the high hazard nature of buildings of Use Group H and a fire grading of 4 hours (Table 902),

TABLE 12.2    Where Automatic Fire Suppression Is Required

| Use group or area | Cross-reference |
|---|---|
| Use group H | See Chap. 8 |
| Use groups S and F when larger than limits listed | See Chap. 8 |
| Unlimited-area buildings | See Chap. 8 |
| Windowless buildings | See Chap. 8 |
| Basements | See Chap. 8 |
| Special rooms | See Chap. 12 |

all buildings or portions thereof constituting such a hazard are to be protected by an automatic suppression system."

**Use groups F and S**    Section 1002.9, "Use Groups S and F" (S = storage; F = factory), of the BOCA code requires automatic fire suppression systems in all buildings or structures or portions thereof in use groups S1 and F1

1. When they are more than 12,000 ft$^2$ (1116 m$^2$) in area, or

2. When they are more than 24,000 ft$^2$ (2232 m$^2$) in total area on all floors, or

3. When they are more than three stories high.

**Unlimited-area buildings**    Section 1002.13 of the BOCA code requires automatic fire suppression systems in unlimited-area buildings as required by Section 504.0, except special industrial uses, as indicated in Section 501.1.1.

**Windowless buildings**    Section 1002.15 of the BOCA code also requires windowless buildings or buildings with windows that are too small or too few in number to have automatic fire suppression systems because of the lack of firefighter access from a fire ladder. In addition, a 20-ft-wide paved fire truck access road is required on one or more sides of such buildings. Variances have been granted, however, when such buildings were made of metal panels that could easily be punctured by a firefighter's ax.

**Basements**    Section 1002.15 of the BOCA code requires automatic fire suppression systems in every story or basement of all buildings in which there is not provided at least 20 ft$^2$ (1.86 m$^2$) of openings entirely above the adjoining ground level in each 50 linear feet (15.24 m) or fraction thereof of exterior wall on at least one side of the building. Each opening must have a minimum dimension of not less than 22 in (559 mm), and such openings must be accessible to the fire department from the exterior and must be unobstructed to allow rescue operations from the exterior.

When openings in any story are provided on only one side and the opposite wall of such a story is more than 75 ft (22.86 m) from the openings, the story also must have an approved fire suppression system. If any portion of a basement is located more than 75 ft (22.86 m) from the openings required by this section, the basement also must have an approved automatic fire suppression system.

**Special rooms** The BOCA code also requires automatic fire suppression systems in the following locations, generally considered "special rooms":

1. Spray painting rooms or shops where painting, brushing, dipping, or mixing is regularly conducted using flammable materials (Section 1002.16)

2. Rooms or areas used for incineration, trash and laundry collection, or similar uses and at alternate floor levels and the tops of all chutes used in conjunction with these rooms or areas (Section 1002.17)

3. Furnace rooms, boiler rooms, and rooms for similar uses (Section 1002.18)

4. Unenclosed vertical openings as required by Section 606.3 (Section 1002.19)

5. Kitchen exhaust systems when such are required by the mechanical code (Section 1002.20)

6. Duct systems exhausting hazardous materials in accordance with the mechanical code (Section 1002.21)

7. Special-use areas of buildings or structures (Section 1002.22). Alternatively, in special-use rooms, an automatic fire detection system can be installed in lieu of a fire suppression system if the fire suppression system would be detrimental or dangerous to the specific use or occupancy.

Section 1003 covers suppression system selection; Section 1004 covers water sprinkler systems; Section 1005 covers limited-area sprinkler systems; Section 1006 covers water-spray fixed systems; Section 1007 covers foam systems; Section 1008 covers carbon dioxide systems; Section 1009 covers halogenated systems; and Section 1010 covers dry chemical systems.

## OSHA

Under the *Code of Federal Regulations* (*CFR*), Title 29, Part 1910, the Occupational Safety and Health Administration (OSHA) also sets out requirements for fire protection. The OSHA regulations that pertain to sprinkler systems are found under Subpart L, "Fire Protection." In addition, the specific areas that must have automatic fire suppression systems are found under the specific industries described throughout the regulations. Section 1910.55 covers applicable scope, application, and definitions for fire protection. This section applies to all employments except maritime, construction, and agriculture. Section 1910.164 covers fire detection systems. Section 1910.165 covers employee alarm systems.

Appendices A through C of Subpart L provide extensive nonmandatory details applicable to fire protection systems. Appendix B covers national consensus standards, and Appendix C lists fire protection references for further information. (See Chaps. 10 and 11 for more information on OSHA.)

### Other standards

Certain NFPA standards written for specific hazardous materials also have a fire protection section that must be complied with when it is enforced by the building or fire codes. (See Supplementary Sources for a list.)

### Success of automatic sprinkler systems

Recent NFPA statistics indicate that more than 145 industrial fires occur each day. Fire-loss analyses have shown that large plant fires result from a combination of factors, including

1. Lack of or inadequate automatic sprinklers

2. Hazardous processes and building contents

3. Building construction deficiencies

In the *Life Safety Code Handbook,* the NFPA states, "Automatic sprinkler protection in industrial occupancies has been a principal factor in ensuring safety to life through the control of 'fire spread.' Limiting the size of the fire by the operation of sprinklers provides sufficient time for the safe evacuation of people exposed to a fire." Today, sprinkler systems can be designed to automatically detect a fire, alarm local occupants, alarm remote occupants when desired, and either extinguish or keep a fire from spreading, all unattended. Obviously, sprinkler systems deserve careful consideration in the design of any industrial facility, especially those discussed throughout this section.

### Manual Fixed Systems (Standpipes)

#### Building codes

Requirements governing manual fixed fire protection systems, or standpipes, are covered in Section 1012 of the BOCA *National*

*Building Code.* The fire codes often list the same requirements. Section 1013 of the BOCA code covers standpipes for buildings during construction. Water-supply reliability is specified in Section 1015. Fire codes also require manual systems for all floors with human occupancy above the standard fire department ladder truck reach of 75 ft (22.86 m) above grade. Fire codes enforce NFPA 14.

## OSHA

OSHA regulations governing standpipes and hose systems are found in *CFR*, Subpart L, Section 1910.158.

## Other standards

Certain NFPA standards written for specific hazardous materials also have a fire protection section that must be complied with when it is enforced by the building or fire codes.

## Portable Extinguishers

### Building codes

Section 1021 of the BOCA *National Building Code* sets out requirements pertaining to portable fire extinguishers. Section 10 covers where portable fire extinguishers are required. Fire codes also specify specific areas where portable fire extinguishers are required and sometimes give the number, size, and type. Fire codes enforce NFPA 10, Portable Fire Extinguishers, which is a 51-page standard that covers selection of the extinguishing agent and the type, size, and location of these units. NFPA 10 also specifies the maximum travel distances to an extinguisher, and the appendix to NFPA 10 lists additional references. Many other NFPA standards give portable fire extinguisher requirements for special occupancies. For example, NFPA 30 specifies the number and size of portable fire extinguishers for flammable liquid container storage areas, processing areas, and outdoor areas.

### OSHA

Under the *Code of Federal Regulations (CFR)*, Title 29, OSHA also provides requirements for portable fire extinguishers. (See the section OSHA Fire Protection Requirements in this chapter and Chap. 10 for additional requirements.)

## Other standards

Certain NFPA standards written for specific hazardous materials also have a fire protection section that must be complied with when it is enforced by the building or fire codes.

## OSHA Fire Protection Requirements

The Occupational Safety and Health Administration (OSHA) fire protection regulations are covered under Title 29, Part 1910, of the *Code of Federal Regulations* (*CFR*). Installation of sprinklers is covered under Subpart L, "Fire Protection." Section 1910.155 covers scope, application, and definitions for fire protection. Section 1910.156 covers fire brigades. This section does not require an employer to organize a fire brigade, but if he or she does, then this section applies. Portable fire extinguishers are specified under Section 1910.157. Section 1910.158 covers standpipes and hose systems (manual). Automatic sprinkler systems are specified under Section 1910.159. Section 1910.160 covers fixed extinguishing systems in general. Section 1910.161 covers dry chemical fixed extinguishing systems. Section 1910.162 covers gaseous agent systems, and Section 1910.163 covers water-spray and foam systems. Appendix A, Fire Protection, provides supplemental detail information called *nonmandatory guidelines,* which assist employers in complying with these sections. Appendix B covers national consensus standards, and Appendix C lists fire protection references for further information.

## Design Considerations

### Automatic sprinkler systems

Fire codes specify the details of installation for sprinkler systems. In addition, NFPA 13, Installation of Sprinkler Systems, is enforced by almost all municipal codes. It contains 112 pages detailing minimum requirements.

Chapter 1 of NFPA 13 provides general information, including classifications of sprinkler systems and the information required on working plans, approvals, and acceptance tests. It also mandates that all equipment, devices, and materials be approved or listed by a recognized testing laboratory for fire protection services. The only exceptions allowed are certain special devices that have never been submitted for test by any manufacturer.

Chapter 2 of NFPA 13 sets out minimum water-supply requirements and rules governing connection to municipal water supplies and the use of tanks, pumps, and so on. Sprinkler head water flow rates are also specified based on the amount of combustible materials protected by the sprinklers. However, other standards also must be reviewed. In some instances, specific sprinkler head flow rates are mandated by other enforced NFPA standards. For example, NFPA 850 specifies sprinkler water flow densities for coal conveyors. Others specify sprinkler water flow densities for dust collectors.

Chapter 3 of NFPA 13 covers system components, listing the approved pipe material standards in the form of ANSI numbers. Chapters 4 and 9 cover sprinkler head details. Paragraph 4-1.3, "High-Piled Storage," indicates that when materials are stored above 12 ft (3.66 m), either NFPA 231, General Storage, or NFPA 231C, Rack Storage of Materials, applies because of the increased difficulty in extinguishing fires in high-piled or rack-stored combustible materials.

Chapter 5 covers types of systems, such as wet, dry, deluge, and so on. Chapter 6 covers outside sprinklers for building protection from adjacent property fires. Chapter 7 covers hydraulical design for economical pipe sizing. Chapter 8 covers pipe sizing by table for more flexibility in protecting changing building contents. This is considered more expensive, however, than hydraulically calculated pipe sizing systems. Chapter 10 covers referenced publications.

Municipal water mains are the cheapest source of water supply when they have adequate pressure and flow and only a single source of water is required. See Chapter 14 of this book for code requirements in terms of backflow prevention to protect the municipal water supply from contamination. Fire water pumps and fire water tanks, when required, are covered by NFPA 20 and 22, respectively.

**Tests and reports.**    After a sprinkler system is installed, most codes require a pressure and flow test to be conducted with the fire inspector present. NFPA has published a form, NFPA 13A, Inspection, Testing and Maintenance of Sprinkler Systems, to facilitate this process.

**Other literature**    In addition to NFPA 13, the NFPA also publishes the *Automatic Sprinkler Systems Handbook,* which includes the complete texts of NFPA 13 and 13A plus explanatory comments that are often helpful in resolving complicated situations that arise. Underwriters such as Factory Mutual and Industrial Risk Insurers also have extensive standards for the design of these systems. If your facility is insured by one of these underwriters, you are required to submit detailed installation drawings for their review and approval before you begin construction.

### Fixed manual systems (standpipes)

Standpipes are a system of piping that supplies either fixed 1½-in, 100-ft-long (30.48 m) hoses with valves for occupant use (Class II system) or 2½-in valves without hoses for firefighter use (Class I system). A combination of the two is a Class III system. Fire codes specify the details of installation and enforce NFPA 14, Installation of Standpipes and Hose Systems. The codes generally require standpipes in multistory buildings with or without sprinklers, in storage buildings, and in certain other spaces. NFPA 14 consists of over 20 pages and includes the following chapters: Chapter 1, General Information; Chapter 2, Size and Arrangement of Standpipes; Chapter 3, The Number and Location of Standpipes; Chapter 4, Hose Connections; Chapter 5, Water Supplies; and Chapter 6, Combined Systems. The rest specifies materials and tests.

Another helpful source is a handbook entitled, *Industrial Fire Protection,* published by Fire Protection Publications of Oklahoma State University and validated by the International Fire Service Training Association. This handbook describes the various standpipe systems and presents information on the inspection and testing of all systems.

### Special extinguishing systems

Alternate methods and materials are allowed by most fire codes through such statements as, "The fire official may accept alternate methods of satisfying the intent of this code if the material, method or work is at least the equivalent of that required by this [code] in quality." Fire codes often will specify the type and agent for manual and automatic fire extinguishing systems (for example, see Table 12.1). As mentioned earlier, underwriters also frequently have standards that apply to special systems, and these also must be reviewed for design details.

Other enforced NFPA standards that govern the installation of special fire extinguishing systems are listed in Table 12.3.

### Explosion Suppression Systems

Generally, the building or fire codes, OSHA, or other enforced standard such as NFPA 654 require explosion containment for vessels, explosion venting to outdoors for buildings and/or vessels, vessel inerting, or explosion suppression whenever explosive materials such as vapors and dusts exist (including dust collectors). The codes also re-

TABLE 12.3    Other NFPA Fire Extinguishing System Standards

| | |
|---|---|
| NFPA 11 | Low Expansion Foam and Combined Agent Systems |
| NFPA 11A | Medium and High Expansion Foam Systems |
| NFPA 12 | Carbon Dioxide Extinguishing Systems |
| NFPA 12A | Halon 1301* Fire Extinguishing Systems |
| NFPA 12B | Halon 1211* Fire Extinguishing Systems |
| NFPA 13A | Inspection, Testing and Maintenance of Sprinkler Systems |
| NFPA 14A | Inspection, Testing and Maintenance of Standpipe and Hose Systems |
| NFPA 15 | Water Spray Fixed Systems for Fire Protection |
| NFPA 16 | Deluge Foam-Water Sprinkler Systems |
| NFPA 16A | Installation of Closed-Head Foam-Water Sprinkler Systems |
| NFPA 17 | Dry Chemical Extinguishing Systems |
| NFPA 17A | Wet Chemical Extinguishing Systems |
| NFPA 18 | Wetting Agents |
| NFPA 20 | Installation of Centrifugal Fire Pumps |
| NFPA 22 | Water Tanks for Private Fire Protection |
| NFPA 24 | Installation of Private Fire Service Mains |
| NFPA 26 | Supervision of Valves Controlling Water Supplies |
| NFPA 69 | Explosion Prevention Systems |
| NFPA 231 | General Storage |
| NFPA 231C | Rack Storage of Materials |

Note: Also see Tables 5.2, 15.1, and 15.2.
*Halon 1211, 1301, and 2402. The EPA is presently authorized to allow production of limited quantities of these fire suppression materials, since no safe substitute has yet been developed. No exception can be granted to permit production after 1999. See Chapter 17 for more information.

quire explosion isolation in equipment in the form of chokes, rotary valves, or instant-acting dampers or valves (these units are closed with a small explosive cartridge).

Explosion suppression systems, when required for flammable gases, vapors, or suspended flammable dusts, are installed in accordance with NFPA 69, Chapter 4. These systems can be used to protect certain kinds of processing equipment, storage tanks, materials handling equipment, and laboratory and pilot plant equipment. NFPA 654, Chemical, Dye, Pharmaceutical and Plastic Industry, provides valuable information on what to consider and sets out test data to determine if these systems can be effective.

## Drawing Reviews and Specifications Checklists

Before a contractor can begin construction of a fire suppression system, the building authorities and underwriters frequently require the submission of completely detailed construction drawings for review and approval. The installing contractor cannot deviate from the approved drawings without fire marshall approval. The data that must be included in these drawings are itemized in the referenced fire codes.

Tables 12.4 through 12.7 are checklists that can serve as guides to ensure that your design documents for fire protection are complete prior to installer bidding.

**TABLE 12.4  Automatic Sprinkler Systems Specifications Checklist**

*Item 1:* Check both building and fire code requirements for where sprinklers are required and other items (most codes include a table giving approved suppression systems and agents).

*Item 2:* Check NFPA 13 and 24 for detail requirements.

*Item 3:* Check water supply demand against water supply available (municipal water systems must be flow tested by the fire department and a report issued giving maximum flow and pressure).

*Item 4:* Check type of sprinkler system (closed or open/deluge heads, dry when required due to lack of building heat, and if allowed, preaction systems, on/off head recycling systems, etc.).

*Item 5:* Check classification of water flow density (low-, ordinary-, or extra-hazard water density flow) with adequate pipe sizes.

*Item 6:* Check sprinkler head type (pendant, upright, open, quick-acting, etc.).

*Item 7:* Check riser pipe locations (for inspection and maintenance access and interference checks).

*Item 8:* Check materials, equipment, and devices (almost all items must be approved for fire service by a recognized testing laboratory or it will be rejected by the local fire inspector and an occupancy permit may not be issued).

*Item 9:* Check all required accessories (automatic and manual rise valves, alarm devices, testing connections, etc.).

*Item 10:* Check outside post indicator valves and location of fire department connections.

*Item 11:* Check coordination of electrical and fire alarm services (flow indicators and manual valve position indicators).

**TABLE 12.5  Standpipe/Manual Fire Hose Systems Specifications Checklist**

*Item 1:* Check building and fire code requirements.

*Item 2:* Check NFPA 14 and 24 for detail requirements.

*Item 3:* Class I, II, or III service (1½-in hoses for building occupant use or 2½-in valves for fire department use).

*Item 4:* Check water supply demand with water supply available (pressure at each valve must be a minimum of 65 lb/in² to provide the minimum throw and a maximum of 100 lb/in² to prevent excessive unmanageable hose nozzle force).

*Item 5:* Check location, length, and spacing of fire hoses (just outside stairway enclosures for 1½-in hoses and inside stairway enclosure for 2½-in hoses).

*Item 6:* Check pipe sizes per NFPA 14.

*Item 7:* Check materials, equipment, and devices (see item 8 in Table 12.4).

*Item 8:* See item 10 Table 12.4.

*Item 9:* Coordinate flow switches and valve position indicators with fire alarm service.

**TABLE 12.6   $CO_2$/Halon\* Systems Specifications Checklist**

*Item 1:*   Check building and fire code requirements.
*Item 2:*   Check applicable NFPA standard (12, 12A, or 12B).
*Item 3:*   Check type, location, and size of extinguishing agent container.
*Item 4:*   Check type and location of detectors.
*Item 5:*   Check type and location of nozzles.
*Item 6:*   Check materials, equipment, and devices.
*Item 7:*   Check location of control panel, abort switches, and alarm lights and horns.
*Item 8:*   Coordinate electrical service.

\*At this writing, Halon has no substitute as a fire extinguishing agent and therefore is not banned (see Chap. 17 for more information). Limitations to its release when testing systems is undergoing review. Most releases of Halon in fire extinguishing is due to testing, and room air pressure tests are sometimes substituted. Rooms often leak, preventing the Halon from reaching the necessary concentrations to extinguish a fire. Check with your fire marshall before specifying Halon.

**TABLE 12.7   Dry Chemical Systems Specifications Checklist**

*Item 1:*   Check building and fire code requirements.
*Item 2:*   Check NFPA 17 for details.
*Item 3:*   Check type of extinguishing agent.
*Item 4:*   Check size and locations of agent supply containers.
*Item 5:*   Check type and locations of detectors.
*Item 6:*   Check type and locations of nozzles.
*Item 7:*   Check materials, equipment, and devices.
*Item 8:*   Check location of control panel, abort switches, and alarm lights and horns.
*Item 9:*   Coordinate electrical service.

# 13

# Ventilation, Smoke Control, Energy Conservation, and Chlorofluorocarbons (CFCs)

This chapter discusses local and general mechanical ventilation codes, smoke control codes, energy conservation codes, and code-required chlorofluorocarbon (CFC) replacement for industrial facilities.

## Ventilation

The various codes specify plant ventilation in order to ensure that any hazardous vapors and/or dusts that accumulate in a plant's atmosphere are removed or diluted. Frequently, ventilation is required by the codes even if there is just a potential for the release of hazardous dusts or vapors. Both local and general building ventilation is sometimes specified in the same facility.

General building ventilation is required in the storage of flammable liquids to prevent the accumulation of vapors from leaking containers or accidental spills. The ventilation must be low level when the vapors are heavier than air. Local ventilation is required whenever operations normally generate vapors and/or dusts at material transfer points, for example, or at other operations. Such operations must be enclosed by hoods as much as possible, and a sufficient air velocity entering the hood openings must be induced to prevent flammable, explosive, or toxic vapors and/or dusts from escaping into the building and accumulating to a level where they will ignite, burn, explode, or exceed the maximum allowable concentrations specified by OSHA. The air that is exhausted from the building must be replaced by an equal volume of air from the outside to prevent the room with the exhaust hood from developing a negative atmospheric pressure, because a negative pressure would reduce the air velocity at the hood and thus permit the accumulation of hazardous vapors and/or dusts (see Chap. 5).

After these systems are installed, they must be balanced to be sure that the fans are moving the minimum amount of air prescribed by code. This is done to ensure safety. See the *Engineer's Project Design Checklist and Design Guide Manual* and the Exhaust Fan Test Sheet published by the Associated Air Balance Council.

### BOCA *National Building Code*

The BOCA *National Building Code,* Article 7, "Interior Environmental Requirements," specifies mechanical ventilation to exhaust contaminants in the breathing air of industrial facilities and enforces the BOCA *National Mechanical Code.* The fire codes also specify mechanical ventilation for operations that generate hazardous conditions. For example, the Ohio Fire Code, Article 33, Organic Coatings, states, "Enclosed buildings in which class 1 liquids are processed or handled shall be ventilated."

Article 25 of the BOCA *National Building Code* sets out requirements for the construction, inspection, and maintenance of all mechanical equipment in both new and existing buildings with respect to structural strength, fire safety, and operation. This article also enforces the BOCA *National Mechanical Code.* The article's specifications cover air distribution systems and duct work, as well as exhaust and ventilation systems. Also see NFPA 30 for ventilation rates in buildings with flammable liquids. Section 617.3 of the BOCA National Building Code permits mechanical ventilation to be substituted for explosion-relief vents when the ventilation is designed in strict accordance with the provisions of the BOCA *National Mechanical Code.*

The BOCA *National Mechanical Code* sets out requirements for building ventilation in general and for exhausts systems that remove hazardous vapors and/or dusts. Article 1 covers administration and enforcement. Article 2 lists definitions. Article 3 delineates air distribution. Article 4 covers all mechanical equipment, including when special rooms are required for mechanical equipment and when fire suppression is required. Article 5 covers kitchen exhaust equipment, including when automatic fire suppression is required in exhaust hoods and ducts. Article 10 specifies combustion air requirements. Article 16 covers ventilation air. Article 17 addresses air quality. Article 18 deals with solar heating and cooling systems. And Article 19 covers energy conservation.

The articles dealing with requirements for pressure vessels and piping (not listed above) are examined in Chapter 14. The BOCA *National Mechanical Code* also lists referenced standards in Appendix A.

Section M-309 in Article 3 contains provisions for hazardous exhaust systems. This section mandates the removal of flammable vapors, spray paint residues, corrosive fumes, and dusts. It also requires that such systems be independent from each other and states other conditions. Section M-311 of the same article gives the criteria for fire dampers.

## A typical state mechanical code

A typical state mechanical code establishes the minimum general ventilation rate in cubic feet per minute per occupant for specific factory and industrial operations and directs that system be designed in accordance with other sections of the code. Generally, the locations of air intakes are specified, requirements for hazardous exhaust systems are mandated, and the details of duct construction and specifications for air filters are stated. The typical state mechanical code specifies that exhaust systems for hazardous materials be independent of each other and indicates when smoke detectors, explosion venting, and automatic fire suppression systems are required. NFPA 90A, 91, and 96, which cover general ventilation and local exhaust system details, are enforced in the state fire code. (See the section The Interlocking Maze of Enforced Codes, Regulations, and Standards in Chap. 1 for information on this circumstance and Figure 11.1 for an example.)

## OSHA requirements

In various subparts, the Occupational Safety and Health Act (OSHA) requires ventilation and local exhaust systems for different hazardous operations. Subpart Z, "Toxic and Hazardous Substances," of the OSHA safety and health standards (29 *CFR* 1910) specifies maximum allowable concentration values for hundreds of hazardous substances in the workplace and defines the permissible extent of employee exposure. See Chapter 10 for more information on maximum allowable concentrations of toxic and hazardous substances in the workplace.

## Air pollution limitations

The 1990 Clean Air Act amendments list 189 hazardous air pollutants that are controlled by law (see Chap. 17). Under regulations included in the Clean Air Act amendments of 1990, a chemical safety and hazard committee will issue a report to the Environmental Protection Agency (EPA) and OSHA recommending regulations for risk management plans (RMPs) and hazard assessments (HAs). The regulations will cover each facility that produces, processes, handles, or stores any of the extremely hazardous substances (EHSs) listed in the 1990

amendments. Sixteen such substances were listed initially, and more
are to be added by November 15, 1992, which will bring the list to
about 100 substances (see Chap. 17). The EPA will set threshold limits for the handling and storage of these materials. Chapter 17 also
should be consulted for the requirements to reduce emissions of the
189 hazardous air pollutants (HAPs) from industrial sources. See
Chapters 4 and 10 for information from the new OSHA process safety
management standards (PSMs) issue (February 24, 1992) that covers
130 toxic and reactive chemicals and all flammable liquids and gases
in quantities over 10,000 lb, except heating fuels.

### Other enforced standards

Table 13.1 lists other enforced ventilation standards by the NFPA,
American Conference of Governmental Industrial Hygienists
(ACGIH), American Society of Heating, Air Conditioning, and Refrigerating Engineers (ASHRAE), EPA, and ANSI. Legislation is also
pending to authorize the EPA to analyze the adequacy of existing ventilation standards. The proposed legislation specifically mentions

**TABLE 13.1   Other Enforced Ventilation Standards***

| | |
|---|---|
| NFPA 90A | Installation of Air Conditioning and Ventilating Systems (see Figure 13.1 for fire damper locations) |
| NFPA 91 | Installation of Blower and Exhaust Systems for Dust, Stock and Vapor Removal or Conveying |
| NFPA 96 | Installation of Equipment for the Removal of Smoke and Grease-Laden Vapors from Commercial Cooking Equipment |
| ACGIH | *Industrial Ventilation: A Manual of Recommended Practices*, 20th ed. (1989). Specifies quality of air used for ventilation of industrial operations (p. 61.1.1) and specifies that carbon dioxide concentrations shall not exceed 1000 ppm (p. 6.1.3). |
| ASHRAE-62, 1989 | Acceptable Indoor Air Ventilation |
| ASHRAE | Ventilation for Control of the Work Environment |
| EPA AP-40 | *Air Pollution Engineering Manual*, 2d ed.† |
| ANSI 29.5 | New Standard for Laboratory Ventilation |
| ANSI 29.2 1979 | Design and Operation of Local Exhaust Systems |

*Note that these standards are sometimes not enforced in some states. The state codes must
be checked to determine this.

†EPA AP-40 provides extensive detail on the design of all types of exhaust systems and
control equipment. It contains almost 1000 pages of diagrams and includes 10 pages of references.

Chapter headings are (1) Introduction, (2) Air Contaminants, (3) Design of Local Exhaust
Systems, (4) Air Pollution Control Equipment for Particulate Matter, (5) Control Equipment
for Gases and Vapors, (6) Metallurgical Equipment, (7) Mechanical Equipment, (8) Incineration, (9) Combustion Equipment, (10) Petroleum Equipment, (11) Chemical Processing Equipment, and (12) Organic Solvent Emitting Equipment.

The locations of dust and vapor collectors are specified in a number of codes, enforced standards, and OSHA regulations. For control equipment required to separate air contaminants
in the airstream before discharge into the atmosphere, see Chapter 17 of this source. Also see
Chapter 12.

ASHRAE Standard 62, which would require the EPA to determine the adequacy of indoor air standards and assess the cost of compliance. The ASHRAE standard requires adequate and effective ventilation. ASHRAE 62 does allow a reduction of outdoor air below the 20 ft$^3$ per person, to conform to the energy code requirements when improved filtration is provided.

## Smoke Control

Smoke is a major threat to life safety in fire situations: It migrates to egresses, stairways, and elevator shafts and can overcome persons attempting to exit a building during a fire.

Section 1019.0 of the BOCA *National Building Code* and Section M-312.0 of the BOCA *National Mechanical Code* specify smoke-control systems. Although such systems are generally required for high-rise buildings, covered mall buildings, atriums, and elevator lobbies, they also can be required for large industrial buildings in the form of smoke and heat vents to assist in firefighting and the safe exit of building occupants.

The codes allow a number of smoke-control methods:

1. Smoke barriers
2. Smokeproof stair towers for high-rise buildings
3. Mechanical smoke-control systems
4. Automatic or manual smoke and heat vents, generally installed in the roofs of industrial buildings (at present, there is some controversy on the need for these; check the local building code for requirements)
5. Smoke detectors (to automatically trip systems or give fire alarms)
6. Smoke dampers

### Design

Smoke partition and damper locations are specified in NFPA 90A, Installation of Air Conditioning and Ventilating Systems. See Figure 13.1 for an example. Table 13.2 lists some of the standards governing the design of smoke-control systems.

## Energy Conservation

Article 31 of the BOCA *National Building Code* and Article 19 of the BOCA *National Mechanical Code* cover energy. ASHRAE 90A-1980,

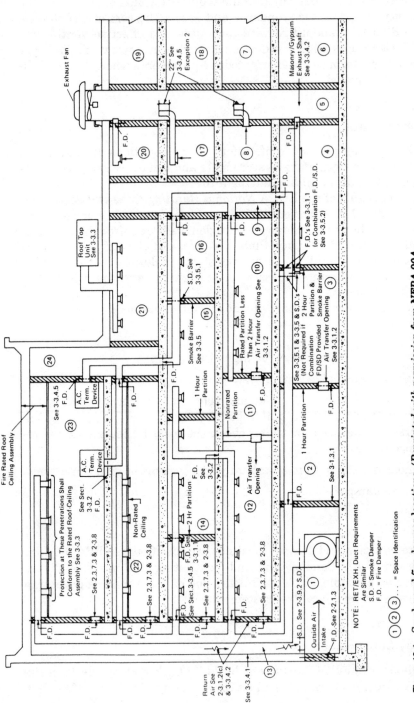

**Figure 13.1** Smoke and fire damper locations. (*Reprinted with permission from NFPA 90A-1989 Installation of Air Conditioning and Ventilating Systems © 1989, National Fire Protection Association. Quincy, MA. This reprinted material is not the complete and official position of the National Fire Protection Association on the referenced subject, which is represented only by the standard in its entirety.*)

TABLE 13.2   Smoke-Control Design Standards

| | |
|---|---|
| NFPA 92A | Smoke Control Systems |
| NFPA 92B | Smoke Management Systems in Malls, Atria and Large Areas |
| NFPA 204M | Smoke and Heat Venting |
| ASHRAE | Design of Smoke Control Systems for Buildings |
| ASHRAE | Smoke Control Technology |

Energy Conservation in New Building Design (IES co-sponsored), including Addendum 90A-a-1987, is generally the recognized standard enforced by most state codes. In addition, the National Conference of States on Building Codes and Standards, Inc., publishes *Energy Directory* (1989 edition), which is a combined source of technical and administrative energy criteria in building codes and regulations in the United States.

## Chlorofluorocarbon (CFC) Ozone Depletion

The Montreal Protocol of 1987, which was developed as a result of a meeting of nations in Vienna in 1985, set guidelines for cutting back on the use of chlorofluorocarbons (CFCs). Another meeting in London in June of 1990 accelerated the scale-down and expanded the number of compounds to be regulated. See Chapter 17 for new requirements under the Clean Air Act amendments of 1990. Eight chemicals are subject to reduction: Freon-11, Freon-12, Freon-13, Freon-14, and Freon-15 and Halon-1211, Halon-1301, and Halon-2402. Also refer to ASHRAE 3-1990, Guidelines for Reducing Emissions of Fully Halogenated Chlorofluorocarbon (CFC or Freon) Refrigerants in Refrigeration and Air Conditioning Equipment and Applications, and the new ASHRAE book, *Alternative Refrigerants,* which contains nine papers on alternatives to CFCs and HCFCs that were presented at ASHRAE's 1991 annual meeting.

Research and development on the depletion of the ozone layer is an active concern. New requirements and regulations will be issued.

# Boilers and Pressure Vessels, Piping, and Plumbing

This chapter discusses the codes governing pressure vessels, pressure piping, natural gas piping, and plumbing.

## Boilers and Pressure Vessels

### ASME codes

Records indicate that in the 40-year period between 1870 and 1910 there were at least 10,000 boiler-related explosions, or nearly one explosion every day. As a consequence, some states started writing their own boiler specifications. Since these specifications were not identical, manufacturers had a difficult time making boilers that could be sold nationally. To remedy this situation, in 1911 the American Society of Mechanical Engineers (ASME) assumed responsibility and formed a boiler-code committee. The ASME is a nonprofit national technical organization, and one of its activities is to develop codes and standards. In 1984 it had more than 120 main committees responsible for regularly reviewing and revising nearly 600 standards. The ASME is one of 200 voluntary members of the American National Standards Institute (ANSI) (see Chap. 11).

### Content

The ASME *Boiler and Pressure Vessel Code* establishes rules of safety governing the design, fabrication, and inspection of boilers and pressure vessels. The code also provides allowances for the deterioration of boilers and pressure vessels in service. The code consists of 11 sections, as listed in Table 14.1.

TABLE 14.1    ASME *Boiler and Pressure Vessel Code* Sections

I. Power Boilers
II. Materials Specifications
III. Rules for the Construction of Nuclear Power Plant Components
IV. Heating Boilers
V. Nondestructive Examination
VI. Recommended Rules for Care and Operation of Heating Boilers
VII. Recommended Guidelines for Care of Power Boilers
VIII. Pressure Vessels
IX. Welding and Brazing Qualifications
X. Fiberglass-Reinforced Plastic Pressure Vessels
XI. Rules for Inservice Inspection of Nuclear Power Plant Components

TABLE 14.2    The Six General Boiler Categories of
the ASME Code

1. PWT: Requirements for water tube boilers
2. PFT: Requirements for fire tube boilers
3. PFH: Requirements for feed water heaters
4. PMB: Requirements for miniature boilers
5. PEB: Requirements for electric boilers
6. PVG: Requirements for organic fluid vaporizers

TABLE 14.3    Boiler Safety Devices

1. Safety valves
2. Pressure gauges
3. Relief valves
4. Safety relief valves
5. Rupture disks
6. Low water–fuel cutoff

Section I of the code is organized into six general boiler categories, as shown in Table 14.2.

Boiler safety devices are also specified by the code and are listed in Table 14.3.

### State boiler codes

The ASME *Boiler and Pressure Vessel Code* has been adopted into law by 48 states, numerous municipalities, Canada, and several other countries. The states also publish rules governing the inspection, repair, and modification of existing boilers.

The BOCA *National Building Code* specifies fire wall and egress requirements for boiler equipment rooms in Article 6, "Special Use and

Occupancy Requirements." Article 25 of the BOCA *National Building Code* also must be read for requirements governing all the mechanical equipment in a building in communities where this code is enforced. This code covers building specifications for facilities containing boilers, furnaces, collectors, dryers, conveyor systems, and oxygen systems and requires ventilation and explosion-relief vents. It also enforces the BOCA *National Mechanical Code*. In addition, some of these equipment rooms are required to have automatic sprinklers (see Chap. 12).

## BOCA *National Mechanical Code*

The BOCA *National Mechanical Code* also specifies installation requirements for mechanical equipment. Article 6, "Boilers and Water Heaters," discusses the following:

1. General features

2. Water heaters

3. Boiler connections

4. Safety and pressure relief valves

5. Steam boiler equalizing pipes

6. Steam boiler low-water cutoffs

7. Steam blowoff valves

8. Hot water boiler expansion tanks

9. Gauges

Article 10 specifies combustion air requirements. Article 11 covers clearance reductions. Article 12 sets out requirements for chimneys and vents. Article 13 discusses mechanical refrigeration. Article 14 specifies solid-fuel–burning appliances. Article 15 covers incinerators. And Article 20 delineates boiler and pressure vessel maintenance and inspection. Articles not listed above that discuss ventilation, air handling systems, and exhaust systems are examined in Chapter 13 of this book. The BOCA *National Mechanical Code* also lists referenced standards in Appendix A.

Piping is covered in the BOCA *National Mechanical Code* in the following articles:

Article 7: Hydronic Piping

Article 8: Gas Piping Systems

Article 9: Flammable and Combustible Liquid Storage and Piping Systems

Article 13: Mechanical Refrigeration (including piping)

NFPA 54, National Fuel Gas Code, also sets out requirements for the safe design and installation of vented gas appliances in industrial applications.


## Piping

Pressure piping of flammable or combustible liquids or gases can pose a serious threat when such piping is exposed to fires. Failure of pipes, valves, and fittings during a fire can convert a small fire into a major conflagration. Minimum standards for flammable and combustible piping are specified in Chapter 3 of NFPA 30, Flammable and Combustible Liquids Code. Minimum standards for natural gas piping, including pressure limits, are specified in NFPA 54, National Fuel Gas Code. Piping for other hazardous materials is specified in other enforced standards, and all these piping standards are enforced by most building and fire codes.

For example, one state piping code reads: "Incorporated in the rules under each specific system type, reference is made to the published national codes or standards which are to be followed. The board of building standards adopts existing published standards by year of issue...as well as amendments and addenda published by the same authority." The piping code often consists primarily of a list of approved recognized standards, as shown in Table 14.4. Table 14.5 lists other enforced piping standards. See Table 5.2 for other enforced standards pertaining to boilers and furnaces.


**TABLE 14.4   Enforced Piping Standards**

| Authority | Designation | Edition | Title |
|---|---|---|---|
| ANSI/ASME | B31.1 | 1986 | Power Piping |
| ANSI | B31.2 | 1968 | Fuel Gas Piping |
| ANSI/ASME | B31.3 | 1987 | Chemical Plant and Petroleum Refinery Piping |
| ANSI/ASME | 31.4c | 1986 | Liquid Petroleum Transportation Piping Systems |
| ANSI | B31.5 | 1987 | Refrigeration Piping |
| ANSI/NFPA | 58 | 1986 | Liquefied Petroleum Gases |
| ANSI/NFPA | 59 | 1984 | LP Gases at Utility Gas Plants |
| NFPA (ANSI) | 54 (Z223.1) | 1984 | National Fuel Gas Code |
| NFPA | 51 | 1987 | Oxygen Fuel Gas Systems for Welding and Cutting |
| ASME | Section IX | 1986 | Welding and Brazing Qualifications |

TABLE 14.5   Other Enforced Piping Standards

| | |
|---|---|
| ANSI/ASME B31.8: | Gas Transmission and Distribution Piping System |
| ANSI/ASME B31.9: | Building Services Piping |
| ANSI/ASME B31G: | Determining the Remaining Strength of Corroded Pipelines |
| ANSI/ASME B31.11: | Slurry Transportation Systems |

## Plumbing

In 1928, the American Standards Association (ASA) organized its Sectional Committee on Minimum Requirements for Plumbing Equipment. ASA A40, the first nationally recognized plumbing code, was published in 1942 and expanded in 1944. In 1933, the National Association of Master Plumbers published a Standard Plumbing Code, and they revised it in 1942. After 1933, other plumbing codes were published by the model code-writing agencies, and these were followed by state and local adopted issues. In addition the *National Plumbing Code Handbook,* by Vincent T. Manas, P.E., provides some very informative technical explanations of various parts of these plumbing codes.

### BOCA *National Plumbing Code*

Article 28 of the BOCA *National Building Code* sets out general and scope requirements for building plumbing systems. It also discusses plan-review submittals and permit procedures. Also included in this article are general requirements for sanitary drains, storm drains, water supply, and private sewage disposal. The code mandates compliance with these stated general requirements and the BOCA *National Plumbing Code.*

The BOCA *National Plumbing Code,* which is used by many communities in the Northeast, is set up as follows: Article 1 covers administration and enforcement. Article 2 list definitions. Article 3 sets out general regulations. Article 4 lists materials. Article 5 specifies joints and connections. Article 6 covers sanitary drainage systems. Article 7 addresses indirect waste piping and special waste. Article 8 covers storm drainage systems.* Article 9 specifies vents and venting systems. Article 10 discusses traps, interceptors, separators, and backwater valves. Article 11 addresses drainage pipe cleanouts. Article 12 covers plumbing fixtures. Article 13 specifies hangers and supports.

---

*Many codes require overflow protection for building roof drains that can become plugged from solids that collect on the roof. Plugged roof drains can result in a buildup of water during a heavy rain that can threaten the collapse of the supporting structure. Scuppers or overflow roof drains are specified in the building codes and sometimes are not mentioned in the companion plumbing code.

Article 14 discusses health care plumbing. Article 15 covers water supply and distribution. Article 16 specifies individual water supplies. Article 17 delineates inspections, tests, and maintenance. And Article 18 covers engineered plumbing systems. The BOCA *National Plumbing Code* also lists reference standards in Appendix A.

### Municipal water service

Tapping into municipal water mains can only be done by city crews in some localities and only by authorized contractors in others. The codes frequently specify the exact materials, valves, and meters that can be used. Municipalities often also adopt standards for meter pit layouts, including arrangements of meters, valves, backflow preventers, and so on. The water authorities often require the submission of drawings that give the exact dimensions and location of all piping and valves with respect to property lines, and these drawings must be followed exactly.

### Process waste and vent systems

Process areas with many floor drains are sometimes allowed by code to use combination waste and vent systems. Such combination systems can result in savings by eliminating the individual vent required by each floor drain trap. However, special design features are required, such as oversizing and so on, as specified in the local plumbing code. Figure 14.1 presents an example of a combination waste and vent system with explanatory text.

The plumbing codes require the installation of interceptors or separators for flammable liquid wastes, grease, and chemical wastes. They also specify minimum pH levels for discharges into municipal sewers (see Chap. 18). One important precaution required for hazardous area plumbing is to prevent the water seals in drains in flammable liquid rooms from transmitting flammable vapors through the drain piping to other rooms with ignition sources.

### Plastic pipe

Before deciding to use plastic pipe, particularly in a code-required fire resistive building, the building, piping, and plumbing codes must be reviewed. Almost all codes publish an overall list of approved materials that is referenced throughout the text of the code. Such lists give material specification numbers, usually in the form of ANSI/ASTM numbers, for materials that can be used. Then the chapter covering the specific installation must be reviewed for approval. For example, the plumbing code allows the use of certain materials for above ground and inside buildings for drains and different materials for

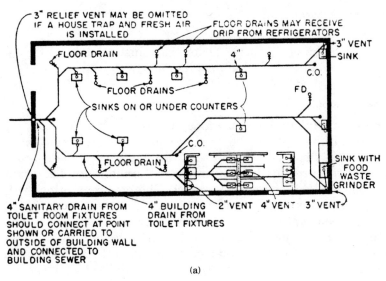

(a)

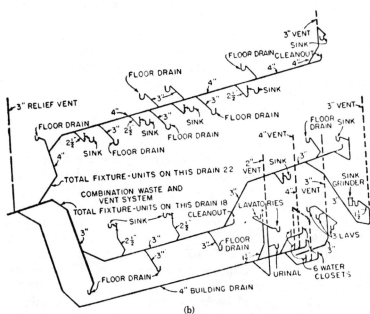

(b)

**Figure 14.1** Combination waste and vent system. (*a*) A system of waste piping which also serves as horizontal wet venting of one or more sinks or floor drains. The dual function is accomplished by installing a common waste and vent pipe of sufficient size to provide free movement of air above the flow line of the drain. This system is relatively new, having been developed during the past few years. The Code permits a combination waste-and-vent system as a means of avoiding complicated design. The designer, however, must plan the sizing and runouts of piping necessary to maintain a balance within the system and prevent trap siphonage. It should be noted that this combination waste-and-vent system is for floor drains and sinks only. It is not for water closets or urinals or other fixtures having high fixture-unit ratings. Toilet-room fixtures are roughed in the conventional manner. Their discharge is carried separately to the building sewer or may be connected to the building drain on the sewer side of the combination waste and unit. (*b*)A plumbing isometric of (*a*).

drains under buildings. Another factor that must be checked for approval is location and method of installation.

## Potable water supply

The Environmental Protection Agency (EPA), on May 7, 1991, set 15 parts per billion (ppb) as the maximum allowable lead content in drinking water. Lead is a poison that can cause permanent brain damage and often results in gastrointestinal complaints. Lead cannot be seen, smelled, or tasted in water. The new regulations will require municipal water systems to monitor drinking water. Until about 1926, lead pipes were commonly installed to supply water. After 1926, copper pipes were used, but they were still soldered with a 50-50 mixture of lead and tin. It was not until 1989 that the EPA banned lead-based solders. However, in buildings with the old lead pipes or with copper pipes with lead-based solder, the lead can be kept out of the water by a calcium carbonate coating that forms on the inside of the pipes after 5 years when the system is treated with lime. The new standards will require lime treatment. Alternatively, zinc orthophosphate treatment also prevents the dissolution of lead into water.

## Backflow prevention

Backflow prevention for an industrial facility is necessary and complex. Many processes that are potential sources of contamination access the community water supply. All municipalities now require that their potable water supply in the public street main be protected from contamination from connection(s) to industrial facilities. Therefore, they usually require a backflow preventer in the valve pit at the property line. However, such preventers protect only the city water supply main. Frequently, the industrial facility will have drinking water and washing and shower fixtures that also must be protected from contaminating processes that require water supply connections. Table 14.6 lists the different degrees of backflow protection required and the types of devices or fixtures used to address those hazards for some typical applications found in industry.

Another possibility allowed by codes is to separate domestic and process water supply systems at the valve pit or municipal water main and incorporate suitable protections. This obviously requires an economic review when the water supply system is complex.

## Emergency eyewashes and showers

State plumbing codes and OSHA generally require emergency eyewashes and safety showers whenever a person is exposed to injurious

TABLE 14.6    Guide to the Assessment of Hazard and Application of Devices

| Description of cross-connection | Assessment of hazard | Recommended device at fixture | Recommended additional device for area of premise isolation |
|---|---|---|---|
| Aspirator (medical) | Severe | DCAP, AVB, or PVB | RPBD |
| Bed pan washers | Severe | DCAP, AVB, or PVB | RPBD |
| Autoclaves | Severe | DCAP, AVB, or PVB | RPBD |
| Specimen tanks | Severe | DCAP, AVB, or PVB | RPBD |
| Sterilizers | Severe | DCAP, AVB, or PVB | RPBD |
| Cuspidors | Severe | DCAP, AVB, or PVB | RPBD |
| Lab bench equipment | Severe | DCAP, AVB, or PVB | RPBD |
| Autopsy and mortuary equip. | Severe | AVB or PVB | RPBD |
| Sewage pumps | Severe | RPBD | |
| Sewage ejectors | Severe | RPBD | |
| Firefighting system (toxic-foamite) | Severe | RPBD | |
| Connection to sewer pipe | Severe | AG | |
| Connection to plating tanks | Severe | RPBD | RPBD |
| Irrigation system or chemical injectors or pumps | Severe | RPBD | |
| Connection to saltwater cooling system | Severe | RPBD | |
| Tank vats or other vessels containing toxic substances | Severe | RPBD | |
| Connection to industrial fluid systems | Severe | RPBD | |
| Dye vats or machines | Severe | RPBD | |
| Cooling towers with chemical additives | Severe | RPBD | |
| Trap primer | Severe | AG | |
| Steam generators | Moderate | DCV | |
| Heating equipment | Moderate | DCV | |
| Irrigation systems | Moderate | DCV, AVB, or PVB | |
| Swimming pools | Moderate | DCV or AG | |
| Vending machines | Moderate | DCV or PVB | |
| Ornamental fountains | Moderate | DCV or AVB or PVB | |
| Degreasing equipment | Moderate | DCV | |
| Lab bench equipment | Minor | AVB, PVB, or CVP | |
| Hose bibbs | Minor | AVB | |
| Trap primers | Minor | AG | |
| Flexible shower heads | minor | AVB | |
| Steam tables | Minor | AVB | |
| Washing equipment | Minor | AVB | |
| Shampoo basins | Minor | AVB | |
| Kitchen equipment | Minor | AVB | |
| Aspirators | Minor | AVB | |
| Domestic heating boiler | Minor | CVP | |

*Note:* Where a higher hazard exists (due to toxicity or health hazard), additional area protection with RPBD is required.

SOURCE: American Society of Plumbing Engineers, "Cross Connection Control," *ASPE Data Book: Special Plumbing Systems Design,* 1982. Reprinted by permission.

materials. ANSI Z58.1, Emergency Eyewash and Shower Equipment, specifies the minimum performance requirements for such equipment. This standard also specifies distance and maximum time to reach such devices and requires the use of highly visible signs. It gives recommendations in the appendix on water temperature, minimum water pressure, water capacity, alarm devices, and so on. The wording of the state code needs to be reviewed, since sometimes state codes enforce not only the main content but also all the appendices.

## Plant drains

Table 14.7 contains a sample plumbing code checklist for plant drains.

TABLE 14.7  Sample Plumbing Code Checklist for Plant Drains

*Step 1:* Check materials specifications, including pipe, joints, and fittings (must use latest ANSI numbers). Check process locations for corrosion-resistance requirements, and specify extraheavy materials where required.

*Step 2:* Check that pipe direction is least expensive routing.

*Step 3:* Underground pipe should avoid excessive depths.

*Step 4:* Review trench loads.

*Step 5:* Consider future additions or process updating in routing and sizing.

*Step 6:* Allow for waste process flows when these flows are permitted to discharge directly into sanitary drains or provide separate process drain system with required treatment (see Chap. 18).

*Step 7:* Check sizes of drains and vents required by code.

*Step 8:* Check capacities of any trench drains.

*Step 9:* Check drains and inverts for minimum pitch required or minimum velocities.

*Step 10:* Check for minimum cover under floor slabs allowing for underground vent connections, trap arms, and bell and spigot hubs and review trench loads from heavy equipment.

*Step 11:* Coordinate with civil drawings for locations and inverts of municipal sewers.

*Step 12:* Check cleanout requirements, spacing, and accessibility, and allow for floor and wall finishes where applicable.

*Step 13:* Check for all interferences, including columns, piers or footings, beams, and other services. Check for undercutting of footings.

*Step 14:* Provide minimum separation from other pipe services for access and for excavating underground sewers. Separate domestic water from sewers in common trenches.

*Step 15:* Avoid connections to horizontal pipes within 10 ft downstream of risers.

*Step 16:* Remove dead ends from alterations to existing sewers.

*Step 17:* Provide backwater valves where required.

*Step 18:* Check for maximum unvented distance from traps.

*Step 19:* Avoid routing underground sewers below heavy and vibrating equipment.

*Step 20:* Provide protection sleeves when passing through underground walls that settle and where others are required.

*Step 21:* Check for maximum waste temperatures and pressures and prohibited direct connections to floor drains.

*Step 22:* Check traps for freezing locations and for priming code requirements.

*Step 23:* Provide antisplash arrangements in food plants or other required areas. Check for potential contamination of any direct connections to sewer.

*Step 24:* Provide grease and solid interceptors where required.

# National Electrical Code and Electrical Classifications for Hazardous Areas

This chapter discusses the origin and scope of the *National Electrical Code,* the *Lightning Protection Code,* and the *Static Electricity Code,* and examines electrical classifications for hazardous (classified) locations.

### National Electrical Code

In 1881, the National Association of Fire Engineers passed a proposal that later resulted in the development of the *National Electrical Code (NEC).* In 1895, the National Board of Fire Underwriters (NBFU), now the American Insurance Association (AIA), published the first nationally recommended electric code. In 1911, the National Fire Protection Association (NFPA) assumed control of the *National Electrical Code.* Today the code is published as ANSI/NFPA Standard 70.

The *National Electrical Code* is now the most widely recognized set of electrical standards in the world. It is offered for use as a law and regulation in the interest of life safety and property protection.

The *National Electrical Code* has nine chapters. Chapters 1 through 4 are general rules. Chapters 5 through 7 apply to special occupancies, special equipment, or other special conditions and supplement the general rules. Chapter 8 specifies communication systems and is independent of the other chapters unless specifically referenced. Chapter 9 consists of tables and examples of use. There is also a 24-page index.

Equipment and conductors required or permitted by this code are acceptable only where tested by a qualified testing laboratory, such as

Underwriter's Laboratories, approved by Factory Mutual or by the authority having jurisdiction for a specific environment or application.

## State and Local Electrical Codes

State and local electrical codes generally enforce NFPA 70 for all buildings and structures and often follow with a list of exceptions, such as elevators, dumbwaiters, and escalators and installations in spaces under control of the electric utilities and communication utilities for purposes of generation, transmission, distribution, metering, and communication.

Elevators, dumbwaiters, and escalators are covered by Article 26 of the BOCA *National Building Code.* The article is extensive and detailed, containing provisions specific to these conveyances, such as special permits, inspections, tests, accident reporting, and others. This article enforces ASME A17.1, Elevator Code; ASME A17.3, Safety Code for Existing Elevators and Escalators; ASME A17.4, Emergency Evacuation of Passengers from Elevators; ANSI A117.1, Buildings and Facilities—Providing Accessibility and Usability for Physically Handicapped People; ASME A90.1, Safety Standard for Manlifts; ANSI A10.4, Safety Requirements for Personnel Hoists; and ANSI A10.5, Safety Requirements for Material Hoists. This article also specifies the fire wall ratings for shaft enclosures, venting of smoke, and elevator recall for emergency operation in the event of a fire. In addition, it forbids the installation of pipes in elevator shafts for safety reasons.

A typical state or local electrical code generally includes the following:

1. General information

2. Plans and specifications

3. Inspections and tests

4. Temporary use

5. Permits and certificates of inspection

6. Existing installations

7. Emergency electrical systems

8. Standby power systems

9. General lighting levels by either natural or artificial means

10. Exit signs and lights

11. Means-of-egress lighting

Installation of lighting fixtures is usually referred to in Article 410 of NEC 70.

## Hazardous (Classified) Locations

Chapter 5, "Special Occupancies," and Article 500, "Hazardous (Classified) Locations," of Chapter 5 of the *National Electrical Code* specifies classified electrical service for all areas with hazardous materials that would be ignited easily with normal electrical service because of arcs, sparking, or high temperatures. Articles 500 through 504 cover the requirements for electrical equipment and wiring for all voltages in locations where fire or explosion hazards may exist due to flammable liquids, combustible dusts, or ignitable fibers or flyings. These articles provide considerable detail (see Table 15.1). The *NEC Handbook* also provides much supporting commentary.

Article 504, "Intrinsically Safe Systems, Installation," defines such systems as any assembly of interconnected intrinsically safe apparatuses, associated apparatuses, and interconnecting cables in which those parts of the system which may be used in hazardous (classified) locations are intrinsically safe circuits. It requires that such systems be installed in accordance with the requirements of Article 504 of the *National Electrical Code*. In terms of locations for such systems, the article states, "Intrinsically safe apparatuses shall be permitted to be installed in any hazardous (classified) location for which they have been approved." For construction and performance requirements for intrinsically safe equipment, see ANSI/UL 913, Standard for Intrinsically Safe Apparatuses and Associated Apparatuses for Use in Class I, II, and III, Division 1, Hazardous (Classified) Locations. Article 510 of the *National Electrical Code* states that Articles 511 through 517 cover occupancies or parts of occupancies that are or may be hazardous because of atmospheric concentrations of flammable liquids, gases, or vapors or because of deposits or accumulations of materials that may be readily ignitable.

**TABLE 15.1**  *National Electrical Code* **Article 500, "Hazardous (Classified) Locations"**

| Article | Title |
|---|---|
| 500-1 | Scope |
| 500-2 | Location and General Requirements |
| 500-3 | Special Precautions |
| 500-4 | Special Occupancies |
| 500-5 | Class I Locations; Division 1 and Division 2, Defined |
| 500-6 | Class II Locations; Division 1 and Division 2, Defined |
| 500-7 | Class III Locations; Division 1 and Division 2, Defined |
| 501 | Class I Locations, General Rules |
| 502 | Class II Locations, General Rules |
| 503 | Class III Locations, General Rules |
| 504 | Intrinsically Safe Systems, Installation |
| 510 | Hazardous (Classified) Locations—Specific Hazardous Occupancies |

## Other standards specifying hazardous electrical areas

In addition to NFPA 70, Table 15.2 lists some additional state and local codes, enforced industry standards, and federal regulations that specify requirement or show diagrams for minimum distances for the installation of hazardous electrical (classified) locations.

The list in Table 15.2 may not be complete, and readers are advised to check the local codes, regulations, and enforced standards. Some underwriter standards also specify hazardous (classified) locations. In addition, the American Petroleum Institute (API) also issues some standards that may be enforced, which specify hazardous (classified) locations.

**TABLE 15.2     Enforced Standards Specifying Classified (Hazardous) Locations**

| Standard | Title |
|---|---|
| NFPA 30 | Flammable and Combustible Code |
| NFPA 31 | Installation of Oil Burning Equipment |
| NFPA 33 | Spray Applications Using Flammable and Combustible Materials |
| NFPA 34 | Dipping and Coating Processes Using Flammable or Combustible Liquids |
| NFPA 35 | Manufacture of Organic Coatings |
| NFPA 36 | Solvent Extraction Plants |
| NFPA 37 | Installation and Use of Stationary Combustion Engines and Gas Turbines |
| NFPA 40E | Storage of Pyroxylin Plastic |
| NFPA 43A | Storage of Liquid and Solid Oxidizing Materials |
| NFPA 43B | Storage of Organic Peroxide Formulations |
| NFPA 43C | Storage of Gaseous Oxidizing Materials |
| NFPA 45 | Fire Protection for Laboratories Using Chemicals |
| NFPA 50 | Bulk Oxygen Systems at Consumer Sites |
| NFPA 50A | Gaseous Hydrogen Systems at Consumer Sites |
| NFPA 50B | Liquefied Hydrogen Systems at Consumer Sites |
| NFPA 51 | Design and Installation of Oxygen–Fuel Gas Systems for Welding, Cutting and Allied Processes |
| NFPA 51A | Acetylene Cylinder Charging Plants |
| NFPA 51B | Cutting and Welding Processes |
| NFPA 52 | Compressed Natural Gas (CNG) Vehicular Fuel Systems |
| NFPA 53M | Fire Hazards in Oxygen-Enriched Atmospheres |
| NFPA 58 | Storage and Handling of Liquefied Petroleum Gases |
| NFPA 59A | Production, Storage and Handling of Liquefied Natural Gas (LNG) |
| NFPA 70B | Electrical Equipment Maintenance |
| NFPA 70E | Electrical Safety Requirements for Employee Workplaces |
| NFPA 79 | Electrical Standards for Industrial Machinery |
| NFPA 325M | Fire Hazard Properties of Flammable Liquids, Gases and Volatile Solids |
| NFPA 493 | Intrinsically Safe Apparatuses and Associated Apparatuses for Use in Class I, II, and III, Division 1, Hazardous Locations |
| NFPA 496 | Purged and Pressurized Enclosures for Electrical Equipment |
| NFPA 497A | Electrical Installations, Classification of Class I Hazardous Locations |
| NFPA 497M | Electrical Equipment in Hazardous (Classified) Locations, Gases, Vapors, Dusts |
| NFPA 505 | Powered Industrial Trucks, Including Type Designations, Areas of Use, Maintenance and Operations |
| OSHA | 29 *CFR* 1910, Subpart S |

NOTE: Also see Tables 5.2, 6.1, 12.3, and 15.1.

## Transformer locations

Transformers are generally located as follows:

1. Outdoors with minimum spacing
2. Indoors with the required fire protection, ventilation, and security
3. On roofs with structural reinforcement and fire protection

However, the local electric utility must be consulted for approval of this choice. Article 450 of the *National Electric Code* must be reviewed for the type and installation.

Askarel insulating fluids have been used for many years in indoor transformer installations without special fire protection. However, production of askarel fluids, which contain polychlorinated biphenyls (PCBs), has been discontinued in the United States for environmental reasons.

## Lightning Protection

Lightning protection is specified by NFPA 78, Lightning Protection Code. This standard also sets out requirements for lightning protection for facilities that use hazardous materials. Chapter 1 of this standard discusses scope, purpose, and listed and labeled devices. Under scope, it states, "this code covers lightning protection requirements for ordinary structures, miscellaneous structures, special occupancies, heavy duty stacks, and structures containing flammable vapors, flammable gases, or liquids which can give off flammable vapors. Chapter 2 lists terms and definitions. Chapter 3 delineates the protection of ordinary structures. Chapter 4 discusses the protection requirements for miscellaneous structures and special occupancies. Under this heading is included grain, coal, and coke handling and processing structures; metal towers and tanks; concrete tanks and silos; and other such structures. Chapter 5 specifies protection for heavy duty stacks. And Chapter 6 covers protection for structures containing flammable vapors, flammable gases, or liquids that can give off flammable vapors. Appendices A through N contain more informative data. Appendix I is a "Risk Assessment Guide," and Appendix M lists "principles of lightning protection that are of special interest."

## Static Bonding

NFPA 77, Recommended Practice on Static Electricity, specifies static bonding and is enforced by state fire codes and other enforced standards, such as NFPA 70 and NFPA 30, Flammable and Combustible Liquids Code.

The contents of NFPA 77 include the following:

Chapter 1: General Purpose and Scope

Chapter 2: The Hazards of Static Electricity

Chapter 3: Control of Ignition Hazards

Chapter 4: Flammable and Combustible Liquids

Chapter 5: Dusts and Fibers

Chapter 6: Gases

Chapter 7: Industrial and Commercial Processes

Chapter 8: Detection and Measurement of Static Accumulation

## OSHA

The Occupational Safety and Health Act (OSHA) sets out electrical system requirements in Subpart S and throughout other parts of 29 *CFR* 1910 (see Chap. 10). NFPA 70E, "Electrical Safety Requirements for Employee Workplaces," was written to assist OSHA in preparing electrical safety standards.

# Chapter 4

# Fire Alarm Systems

This chapter discusses the host of codes, regulations, and enforced standards that specify requirements for the design and installation of complete automatic fire detection and alarm systems in industrial facilities.

## Development

The rapid technical developments in fire detection and alarm systems over the last two decades have contributed to a multitude of codes, regulations, and enforced standards that apply to such systems. Today's modern fire alarm systems are so complex that they can employ field-programmable computers, multiplexing, remote annunciation, remote control of fire suppression and smoke exhaust systems, and automatic self-supervision, and they can even send a trouble alarm if the sensing system fails. Systems also can be programmed to automatically alarm all plant areas or specific areas in the event of a fire signal and to automatically notify the municipal fire department or a local security firm. They also can include warnings for special toxic hazards such as the escape of ammonia in an unoccupied equipment room. Modern alarm systems also incorporate intrusion or burglar alarms and other security measures and can monitor the entrance and exit of employees.

## State and Local Building Codes

State and local building codes generally specify where manual and automatic fire protective signaling systems or fire alarms systems are required. State codes also specify such items as manual pull stations, emergency power supplies, electrical or mechanical supervision, alarms, the zoning of floors, maximum areas of zones, and the testing of these systems.

## State and Local Fire Codes

State and local fire codes also specify where manual and/or automatic signaling systems are required and provide testing data. A section on fire safety requirements generally indicates which areas should be provided with fire protection and fire extinguishing equipment that requires some degree of alarm. Automatic and manual extinguishing systems require some type of signaling method to warn occupants and summon the fire department.

NFPA 30 specifies an engineering evaluation to include six criteria (see Chap. 12) in deciding the type of fire control systems for industrial plants, bulk plants and terminals, processing plants, and refineries, chemical plants, and distilleries. It continues, "An approved means for prompt notification of fire or emergency to those within the plant and to the available public or mutual aid fire department shall be provided." Areas, including buildings, where a potential exists for a flammable liquid spill also require monitoring as appropriate. Some methods may include

1. Personnel observation or patrol
2. Process monitoring equipment that would indicate that a spill or leak has occurred
3. Gas detectors to continuously monitor areas that are unattended

As usual, the method used requires the approval of the local authority.

## State and Local Mechanical Codes

State and local mechanical codes generally enforce NFPA 90A, which specifies smoke detectors in air-handling units that move more than 2000 ft$^3$/min of air. Then NFPA 90A, in turn, states that when an approved detection system is installed in a building, the air-handling unit detectors must be connected thereto in accordance with NFPA standards 71, 72A, 72B, 72C, or 72D, whichever is appropriate.

When elevator recall is required for fire department operation by the state or local elevator code, ASME A17.1, Elevators and Escalators, ASME A17.4, Emergency Evacuation of Passengers from Elevators, or ANSI A117.1, Buildings and Facilities—Providing Accessibility and Usability for Physically Handicapped People, it also must be connected to the fire detection with the elevator lobby smoke detectors.

## State and Local Electrical Codes and NFPA 70

NFPA 70, the *National Electrical Code,* specifies the installation of fire alarm systems in Article 760, "Fire Protective Signaling Systems." the article references NFPA 71, 72A, 72B, 72C, 72D, 72E, and 72F. Article 760-4, "Locations and Other Articles," requires the compliance of circuits and equipment with

(a) Spread of Fire or Products of Combustion, Section 300-21.

(b) Ducts, Plenums and Other Air-Handling Spaces, Section 300-22, where installed in ducts or plenums or other spaces used for environmental air with an exception allowed.

(c) Hazardous (Classified) Locations, Articles 500 through 516 and Article 517, Part D, where installed in hazardous (classified) locations.

(d) Corrosive, Damp or Wet Locations, Sections 110-11, 300-6, and 310-9, where installed in corrosive damp or wet locations.

(e) Building Control Circuits, Article 725, where building control circuits (e.g., elevator capture fan shut down) are associated with the fire protective signaling system.

The code also states that fire alarm systems must include fire alarms, guard tours, sprinkler waterflow, and sprinkler supervisory systems. Article 501-14 of NFPA 70 specifies the requirements for signaling, alarms, remote control, and communication systems for hazardous (classified) locations (see Chap. 15).

## OSHA

The Occupational Safety and Health Act (OSHA) specifies fire detection and fire alarm systems in Subpart L and throughout 29 *CFR* 1910 (see Chap. 10). The areas that are required by OSHA to have fire alarm systems are found under the specific industries described throughout the regulations. Section 1910.155 covers applicable scope, application, and definitions for fire protection. This section applies to all employments except maritime, construction, and agriculture.

Section 1910.164 covers fire detection systems. Section 1910.165 details employee alarm systems. Appendices A through C of Subpart L provide extensive nonmandatory details related to fire protection systems. Appendix B lists national consensus standards, and Appendix C provides fire protection references for further information.

### List of Fire Alarm Standards

A list of some of the enforced standards that specify requirements for automatic fire alarm systems in industrial facilities is given in Table 16.1. See also Figures 16.1 to 16.3.

**TABLE 16.1    List of Enforced Fire Alarm Standards**

| Standard | Title |
|---|---|
| NFPA 70 | *National Electrical Code* |
| NFPA 71 | Installation, Maintenance and Use of Signaling Systems for Central Station Service |
| NFPA 72A* | Installation, Maintenance and Use of Local Protective Signaling Systems for Guard's Tour, Fire Alarm and Supervisory Service |
| NFPA 72B* | Installation, Maintenance and Use of Auxiliary Protective Signaling Systems for Fire Alarm Service |
| NFPA 72C* | Installation, Maintenance and Use of Remote Station Protective Signaling Systems |
| NFPA 72D* | Installation, Maintenance and Use of Proprietary Protective Signaling Systems |
| NFPA 72E | Automatic Fire Detectors |
| NFPA 72G | Installation, Maintenance and Use of Notification Appliances for Protective Signaling Systems |
| NFPA 72H | Testing Procedures for Local, Auxiliary, Remote Station and Propriety Protective Signaling Systems |
| NFPA 11 | Low Expansion Foam and Combined Agent Systems |
| NFPA 11A | Medium and High Expansion Systems |
| NFPA 12 | Carbon Dioxide Extinguishing Systems |
| NFPA 12A | Halon 1301 Fire Extinguishing Systems |
| NFPA 13 | Installation of Sprinkler Systems |
| NFPA 14 | Installation of Standpipe and Hose Systems |
| NFPA 15 | Water Spray Fixed Systems |
| NFPA 16 | Installation of Deluge Foam-Water Sprinkler Systems and Foam-Water Spray Systems |
| NFPA 16A | Installation of Closed-Head Foam-Water Sprinkler Systems |
| NFPA 17 | Dry Chemical Extinguishing Systems |
| NFPA 17A | Wet Chemical Extinguishing Systems |
| NFPA 20 | Installation of Centrifugal Fire Pumps |
| NFPA 22 | Water Tanks for Private Fire Protection |
| NFPA 24 | Installation of Private Service Mains and Their Appurtenances |
| NFPA 26 | Supervision of Valves Controlling Water Supplies |
| NFPA 90A | Installation of Air Conditioning and Ventilating Systems |
| NFPA 92B | Smoke Management Systems in Malls, Atria and Large Areas |
| NFPA 101 | Safety to Life from Fire in Buildings and Structures |

NOTE: Also see Tables 15.1 and 15.2.

*Check the new NFPA 72. In 1990, NFPA combined standards 72A, 72B, 72C, and 72D into 72; however, it will take many municipalities many years to update their codes to enforce this latest revision due to normal lag time. Meanwhile, the old NFPA issues are legally enforceable.

**MANUAL**

**Pull Station**

**AUTOMATIC**

**Smoke Detector**

**Heat Detector**

**Flame Detector**

**Water Flow**

## Life Safety® 101® (1988 EDITION)

7-6.2.3 A manual fire alarm station shall be provided in the natural path of escape near each required exit from an area, unless modified by another section of this code.

7-6.2.4 Additional fire alarm stations shall be so located that, from any part of the building, not more than 200 feet (60m) horizontal distance on the same floor shall be traversed in order to reach a manual fire alarm station.

7-6.2.6 Where a sprinkler system provides automatic detection and alarm system initiation, it shall be provided with an approved alarm initiation device that will operate when the flow of water is equal to or greater than that from a single automatic sprinkler.

## BOCA® Smoke Detection (1988 EDITION)

602.6 Automatic fire detection: A smoke detector suitable for the intended use shall be installed in each of the following rooms: mechanical equipment; electrical, transformer, telephone equipment; elevator machine; or similar room. The actuation of any detector shall sound an alarm at a constantly attended location and shall place into operation all equipment necessary to prevent the recirculation of smoke.

602.6.1 Duct locations: A smoke detector shall be installed in each connection to a vertical duct or riser serving two or more stories from return air ducts or plenums of heating, ventilating and air conditioning systems. In buildings of Use Group R, an approved smoke detector shall be installed as required by this section or such smoke detectors shall be installed in each return air riser carrying not more than 5,000 cubic feet per minute (cfm) (2.36 m³/s) and serving not more than ten air inlet openings.

## S.B.C. High-Rise Section (1988 EDITION)

506.2.1 At least one approved smoke detector suitable for the intended use shall be installed in:
1. Every mechanical equipment, electrical, transformer, telephone equipment, elevator machine or similar room.
2. In every elevator lobby.
3. In the main return and exhaust air plenum of each air conditioning system serving more than one story and located in a serviceable area downstream of the last duct inlet.
4. Each connection to a vertical duct or riser serving two or more stories from return air ducts or plenums of heating, ventilating and air conditioning systems, except that in Group R occupancies, an approved smoke detector may be used in each return air riser carrying not more than 5,000 cfm and serving not more than 10 air inlet openings.

506.2.2 The actuation of any detector required by this section shall operate the voice alarm system and shall place into operation all equipment necessary to prevent the recirculation of smoke.

## NFPA 72E (1987 PRINTING)

4-4.2 Spot-type smoke detectors shall be located on the ceiling not less than 4 inches (100 mm) from a sidewall to the near edge, or if on a sidewall, between 4 and 12 inches (100 and 300 mm) down from the ceiling to the top of the detector.

4-4.3 Beam-type smoke detectors shall be normally located with their projected beams parallel to the ceiling, and in accordance with the manufacturers instructions.

4-4.3.1 The beam length shall not exceed the maximum permitted by the equipment listing.

5-5.1 Since flame detectors are essentially line-of-sight devices, special care shall be taken in applying them to assure that their ability to respond to the required area of fire in the zone, which is to be protected will not be unduly compromised by the presence of intervening structural members or other opaque objects or materials.

## Uniform Building Code (1988 EDITION)

Special Provisions for Group B, Division 2 Office Buildings and Group R, Division 1 Occupancies*

1807(d) Smoke Detection Systems. At least one approved smoke detector suitable for the intended use shall be installed:
1. In every mechanical equipment, electrical, transformer, telephone equipment, elevator machine or similar room.
2. In the main return and exhaust air plenum of each air-conditioning system and located in a serviceable area downstream of the last duct inlet.
3. At each connection to a vertical duct or riser serving two or more stories from a return-air duct or plenum of an air-conditioning system. In group R, Division 1 Occupancies, an approved smoke detector may be used in each return-air riser carrying not more than 5,000 cfm and serving not more than 10 air inlet openings.

The actuation of any detector required by this section shall operate the voice alarm system and shall place into operation all equipment necessary to prevent the recirculation of smoke.

**SPACING FOR RECTANGLES OF ODD DIMENSIONS**
(Fig. A-3-5.1C; NFPA 72E)

Example A: If a heat detector is rated for 900 sq. ft. of coverage (30' x 30'), the maximum distance between detectors in a 10' wide corridor would be 41'.

Rectangle A = 10' x 41' = 410 sq. ft.
B = 15' x 39' = 585 sq. ft.
C = 20' x 37' = 740 sq. ft.
D = 25' x 34' = 850 sq. ft.

**Edition Dates**
1988 NFPA Life Safety Code 101
1987 NFPA 72A, B
1987 NFPA 72C, E
1988 NFPA 72H
1986 NFPA 72D
1988 Standard Building Code
1990 BOCA National Building Code
1988 Uniform Building Code

## Fire Detector Selection

| TYPICAL APPLICATION GUIDELINES | TYPE OF DETECTOR | | | | OPTICAL LINEAR BEAM |
| --- | --- | --- | --- | --- | --- |
| | PHOTO-ELECTRONIC SMOKE | IONIZATION SMOKE | HEAT | I.R. FLAME | |
| OFFICES | ••• | ••• | • | • | •• |
| HOTEL ROOMS | ••• | •• | | | |
| KITCHENS | | | ••• | | |
| EDP FACILITIES | ••• | •• | | | ••• |
| ATRIUMS | •• | •• | | | ••• |
| DEPT. STORES | ••• | ••• | | • | •• |
| FACTORIES, WAREHOUSES | •• | •• | | • | ••• |
| PETROCHEMICAL PLANTS | • | • | | ••• | ••• |
| CHURCHES, MUSEUMS | •• | •• | | | ••• |
| PARKING GARAGES | • | | •• | • | •• |
| HIGH RACK STORAGE | •• | •• | | | ••• |
| AIRCRAFT HANGARS | •• | | | ••• | ••• |

**LEGEND:** • FAIR  •• GOOD  ••• EXCELLENT
Note: Selection may vary depending upon configuration of protected area

**Figure 16.1** Alarm initiation. (*From The New Reference for Life Safety Wall Chart, The Gamewell Company, 10 Forge Park, Franklin, Mass. 02038*)

## Life Safety 101 (1988 EDITION)

7-6.3.8 Recorded or live voice evacuation or relocation instructions to occupants shall be permitted.

7-6.3.9 Audible and visible fire alarm indicating appliances shall be used only for fire alarm system or other emergency purposes.

*Exception No. 1: Voice communication systems may be used for other purposes, subject to the approval of the authority having jurisdiction, if the fire alarm system takes precedence over all other signals.*

*Exception No. 2: Where otherwise permitted by another section of this Code.*

## BOCA® High-Rise Section (1990 EDITION)

602.9 **Central control station:** A central control station for fire department operations shall be provided in a location approved by the fire department. The central control station shall contain: the voice alarm system panels; the fire department communications panel; the fire detection and alarm system annunciator panels; an annunciator which visually indicates the floor location of elevators and whether they are operational; status indicators and controls for air-handling systems; controls for unlocking all stairway doors simultaneously; sprinkler valve and water-flow detector display panels; emergency and standby power; status indicators and a telephone for fire department use with controlled access to the public telephone system.

## S.B.C. High-Rise Section (1988 EDITION)

506.4 **Central Control Station**
A central control station for fire department operations shall be provided in location approved by the fire department. It shall contain:
1. The voice alarm and public address system panels.
2. The fire department communications panel.
3. Fire detection and alarm system annunciator panels.
4. Status indicators showing location of elevators in the hoistways and switches to selectively turn on or off power to elevators.
5. Status indicators and controls for air handling systems.
6. Controls for unlocking all stairway doors simultaneously.
7. Sprinkler valve, waterflow detector and fire pump display panels.
8. Emergency power, light and emergency system controls and status indicators.
9. A telephone for fire department use with controlled access to the public telephone system.

506.7.3 **Emergency Power Loads**
The transition time from the instant of failure of the normal power source to the generating source shall not exceed 10 seconds. The following loads are classified as emergency power loads:
1. Voice alarm systems.
2. Voice communication system.
3. Fire alarm systems.
4. Fire detection systems.
5. Elevator car lighting.
6. Escape route lighting and exit sign illumination.

## NFPA 72A (1987 PRINTING)

2-7.3.2 **Silencing Switch.** A switch for silencing the audible trouble signal sounding appliance shall be permitted if it transfers the trouble indication to a lamp or other acceptable visible indicator on or adjacent to the switch. The visual indication shall persist until the trouble has been corrected. The audible trouble signal shall sound if the switch or valve is in its "silence" position and no trouble exists.

2-7.3.2.1 Where an audible supervisory signal is used to indicate a trouble condition, as permitted in 2-8.5(b), a trouble silencing switch shall not be permitted to prevent subsequent sounding of supervisory signals.

## NFPA 72

Power Supply Sources.
Reference the following sections from NFPA 72 for primary and secondary power supply requirements.
72A 2-6 (1987) 72B 2-9 (1986)
72C 2-6 (1986) 72D 2-6 (1986)

## NFPA 72D (1986 PRINTING)

**Proprietary Protective Signaling Systems**
4-2.2 Provision shall be made to designate the building in which a signal originates. The floor, section, or other subdivision of the building shall be designated at the central supervising station or at the building protected, except that the authority having jurisdiction may waive this detailed designation where the area, height, or special conditions of occupancy make it unessential. The indication of location shall utilize indicating appliances acceptable to the authority having jurisdiction.

**Distinctive Signals**
4-4.1 Audible signal appliances of a fire alarm system shall produce signals which are distinctive from other similar appliances used for other purposes in the same area. The distinction among signals shall be as follows:
(a) Fire alarm signals shall be distinctive in sound from other signals, and this sound shall be used for no other purpose.
(b) Supervisory signals shall be distinctive in sound from other signals, and this sound shall not be used for any other purpose.
(c) Fire alarm, supervisory, and trouble signals shall take precedence over all other signals.

4-4.2 **Coded Alarm Signal.** A coded alarm signal shall consist of not less than three complete rounds of the number transmitted and each round shall consist of not less than three impulses.

**System Operation**
4-5.1 The central supervising station shall have, in addition to a recording device, two different means, one of which shall be audible, for alerting the operator when each signal is received indicating a change of state of any connected initiating device circuit. The audible signal shall persist until manually acknowledged. This shall include the receipt of alarm signals, supervisory signals and trouble signals including signals indicating restoration to normal.

4-5.2 All signals received by the central supervising station that show a change in status shall be automatically and permanently recorded, including time and date of occurrence.

## NFPA 72G (1989 EDITION)

AMBIENT SOUND LEVEL
Chapter 3 Notification Characteristcs
Audible Characteristics.

3-1.1 **Performance.** Sound measurements should be made in a free field condition.

3-1.1.1 Audible signals intended for operation in the public mode should have a sound level of not less than 75dBA at 10 ft (3m) or more than 130 dBA at the minimum hearing distance from the audible appliance.

3-1.1.2 Audible signals intended for operation in the private mode should have a sound level of not less than 45dBA at 10 ft (3m) or more than 130 dBA at the minimum hearing distance from the audible appliance.

3-1.1.3 The sound level of an installed signal should be adequate to perform its intended function and should meet the requirements of the authority having jurisdiction or other applicable standards.

3-1.1.4 The average ambient sound level for the various occupancies as listed below may be used for design guidance as follows:

Locations
| | |
|---|---|
| Business Occupancies | 45 dBA |
| Educational Occupancies | 45 dBA |
| Industrial Occupancies | 80 dBA |
| Institutional Occupancies | 50 dBA |
| Mercantile Occupancies | 40 dBA |

**Figure 16.2** Central controls. (*From The New Reference for Life Safety Wall Chart, The Gamewell Company, 10 Forge Park, Franklin, Mass. 02038*)

Piers and Water Surrounded Structures . . . . . . . . . . . . 40 dBA
Places of Assembly . . . . . . . . . . . . . . . . . . . . . . . . . . . 40 dBA
Residential Occupancies . . . . . . . . . . . . . . . . . . . . . 35 dBA
Storage Occupancies . . . . . . . . . . . . . . . . . . . . . . . . . 30 dBA
Thoroughfares, High Density Urban . . . . . . . . . . . . . 70 dBA
Thoroughfares, Medium Density Urban . . . . . . . . . . . 55 dBA
Thoroughfares, Rural and Suburban . . . . . . . . . . . . . 40 dBA
Tower Occupancies . . . . . . . . . . . . . . . . . . . . . . . . . 35 dBA
Underground Structures and Windowless Buildings . . . 40 dBA
Vehicles and Vessels . . . . . . . . . . . . . . . . . . . . . . . . 50 dBA

## NFPA 72H (1988 PRINTING)

**Periodic Equipment and Circuit Testing Procedures**

**3-1 Periodic Testing:** Periodic tests should be performed in accordance with the schedules in Chapter 4 or more frequently when required by the authority having jurisdiction. When less than a 100 percent test is being performed, a record should be maintained of individual initiating devices and indicating appliances tested each time, so that different devices and appliances are tested in subsequent tests.

INS 2

## Uniform Building Code
### (1988 EDITION)

**Special Provisions for Group B, Division 2 Office Buildings and Group R, Division 1 Occupancies***

**Sec. 1807(e) Alarm and Communication Systems.** The alarm and communication systems shall be designed and installed so that damage to any terminal unit or speaker will not render more than one zone of the system inoperative.
The voice alarm and public address system may be a combined system. When approved the fire department communications system may be combined with the voice alarm system and the public address system.

Three communication systems which may be combined as set forth above shall be provided as follows:
1. **Voice alarm system.** The operation of any smoke detector, sprinkler, water flow device or manual fire alarm station shall automatically sound an alert signal to the desired areas followed by voice instructions giving appropriate information and direction to the occupants.
The central control station shall contain controls for the voice alarm system so that a selective or general voice alarm may be manually initiated.
The system shall be supervised to cause the activation of an audible trouble signal in the central control station upon interruption or failure of the audiopath including amplifiers, speaker wiring, switches and electrical contacts and shall detect opens, shorts and grounds which might impair the function of the system.
The alarm shall be designed to be heard clearly by all occupants within the building or designated portions thereof as is required for the public address system.

2. **Public address system.** A public address communication system designed to be clearly heard by all occupants of the building shall operate from the central control station. It shall be established on a selective or general basis to the following terminal areas:

A. Elevators.
B. Elevator lobbies.
C. Corridors.
D. Exit stairways.
E. Rooms and tenant spaces exceeding 1000 square feet in

area.
F. Dwelling units in apartment houses.
G. Hotel guest rooms or suites.

3. **Fire department communication system.** A two-way fire department communication system shall be provided for fire department use. It shall operate between the central control station and every elevator, elevator lobby and entry to every enclosed exit stairway.

**Sec. 1807 (f) Central Control Station.** A central control station for fire department operations shall be provided. The location of the central control station shall be approved by the fire department. The central control station room shall have a minimum of 96 square feet with a minimum dimension of 8 feet. It shall contain the following as a minimum:
1. The voice alarm and public address system panels.
2. The fire department communications panel.
3. Fire detection and alarm system annunciator panels.
4. Annunciator visually indicating the location of the elevators and whether they are operational.
5. Status indicators and controls for air-handling systems.
6. Controls for unlocking all stairway doors simultaneously.
7. Sprinkler valve and water-flow detector display panels.
8. Emergency and standby power status indicators.
9. A telephone for fire department use with controlled access to the public telephone system.
10. Fire pump status indicators.
11. Schematic building plans indicating the typical floor plan and detailing the building core, exit facilities, fire protection systems, fire-fighting equipment and fire department access.
12. Work table.

All control panels in the central control station shall be permanently identified as to function.

FlexAlert  Flex 300

## *Uniform Building Code
### (1988 Edition)

**Group B Occupancies Defined**

**Sec. 701.** Group B Occupancies shall be:
Division 1. Gasoline service stations, garages where no repair work is done except exchange of parts and maintenance requiring no open flame, welding or use of Class I, II or III-A liquids.
Division 2. Drinking and dining establishments having an occupant load of less than 50 wholesale and retail stores, office buildings, printing plants, municipal police and fire stations, factories and workshops using materials not highly flammable or combustible, storage and sales rooms for combustible goods, paint stores without bulk handling. (See Section 402 for definition of assembly buildings.)
Buildings or portions of buildings having rooms used for educational purposes beyond the 12th grade with less than 50 occupants in any room
Division 3. Aircraft hangars where no repair work is done except exchange of parts and maintenance requiring no open flame, welding or the use of Class I or II liquids
Open parking garages
Heliports
Division 4. Ice plants, power plants, pumping plants, cold storage and creameries. Factories and workshops using noncombustible and nonexplosive materials. Storage and sales rooms containing only noncombustible and nonexplosive materials that are not packaged or crated in or supported by combustible material.

Group R Occupancies Defined.

**Sec. 1201.** Group R occupancies shall be:
Division 1. Hotels and apartment houses Convents and monasteries (each accommodating more than 10 persons)
Division 2. Not used
Division 3. Dwellings and lodging houses

**Figure 16.2** Central controls. *(Continued)*

## Municipal & Central Control Connections

**Auxiliary Connection to Municipal Fire Department**

**Direct Connection to Municipal or Central Station**

### Life Safety 101 (1988 EDITION)

7-6.4 Emergency Forces Notification. Where required by another section of this *Code*, emergency forces notification shall be provided to alert the local fire brigade or municipal fire department of fire or other emergency.

Where fire department notification is required by another section of this *Code*, the fire alarm system shall be arranged to transmit the alarm automatically via any of the following means:
(a) An auxiliary alarm system in accordance with NFPA 72B, *Standard for the Installation, Maintenance, and Use of Auxiliary Protective Signaling Systems for Fire Alarm Service*, or
(b) A central station connection in accordance with NFPA 71, *Standard for the Installation, Maintenance, and Use of Signaling Systems for Central Station Service*, or
(c) A proprietary system in accordance with NFPA 72D, *Standard for the Installation, Maintenance, and Use of Proprietary Protective Signaling Systems*, or
(d) A remote station connection in accordance with NFPA 72C, *Standard for the Installation, Maintenance, and Use of Remote Station Protective Signaling Systems*.

### NFPA 72B (1983 PRINTING)

2-5.4 Transmission of alarms to the municipal communications center shall not be delayed in cases where provision has been made for delaying evacuation alarm signals.

2-5.11 Auxiliary alarm systems shall be so arranged that one municipal transmitter or master box does not serve more than 100,000 square feet (9,290 sq. meters) total fire area.

## Audible & Visual Alarm Indicating Circuits

**Combination Strobe-Horn**   **Visual**

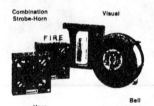

**Horn**   **Bell**

### Life Safety 101 (1988 EDITION)

7-6.3.3. Where a standard evacuation signal is required by another section of this *Code*, the evacuation signal shall be the standard fire alarm evacuation signal described in NFPA 72A, *Standard for Installation, Maintenance, and Use of Local Protective Signaling Systems for Guard's Tour, Fire Alarm, and Supervisory Service.*

7-6.3.4 Notification signals for occupants to evacuate shall be by audible signals and, where deemed necessary by the authority having jurisdiction, shall also be by visible signals.

7.6.3.7 Audible alarm indicating appliances shall produce signals that are distinctive from audible signals used for other purposes in the same building.

### NFPA 72A (1987 PRINTING)

2-8.4* Distribution of Evacuation Signals. Fire alarm systems provided for evacuation of occupants shall have one or more audible signaling appliances approved for the purpose on each floor of the building, so located that their operation will be heard clearly, regardless of the maximum noise level obtained from machinery or other equipment under normal conditions of occupancy. Each section of a floor divided by a fire wall may be considered as a separate floor for the purpose of this protection.

A-2-8.4 To ensure that audible evacuation signals are clearly heard, it is recommended that their sound level be at least 15 dBA above the equivalent sound level or 5 dBA above the maximum sound level having a duration of at least 60 seconds (whichever is greater) measured 5 ft (1.5 m) above the floor in the occupiable area. The equivalent sound level is the mean square A-weighted sound pressure measured over a 24-hour period. Refer to NFPA 72G, *Guide for the Installation, Maintenance, and Use of Notification Appliances for Protective Signaling Systems.*

A-2-8.5(a) When a distinctive fire alarm signal is to be used to notify the building occupants of the need to evacuate (leave the building), the use of a national standard fire alarm evacuation signal is recommended to facilitate quick and positive recognition of the signal.

The recommended fire alarm evacuation signal is a uniform Code 3 temporal pattern, using any appropriate sound, keyed 1/2 to 1 second "ON," 1/2 second "OFF," 1/2 to 1 second "ON," 1/2 second "OFF," 1/2 to 1 second "ON," and 2 1/2 seconds "OFF," with timing tolerances of ± 25 percent, repeated for not less than 3 minutes.

*Exception. The minimum repetition time may be manually interrupted.*

The recommended standard fire alarm evacuation signal is intended for use only as an an evacuation signal. Its use should be restricted to situations where it is desired to have all occupants hearing the signal evacuate the building immediately. It should not be used when, with the approval of the authority having jurisdiction, the planned action during a fire emergency is not evacuation, but relocation of the occupants from the affected area to a safe area within the building, or their protection in place (e.g., high rise buildings, health care facilities, penal institutions, etc.)

**Figure 16.3**   Alarm action/response. (*From The New Reference for Life Safety Wall Chart, The Gamewell Company, 10 Forge Park, Franklin, Mass. 02038*)

## Life Safety 101 (1988 EDITION)

7-6.3.9 Audible and visible fire alarm indicating appliances shall be used only for fire alarm or other emergency purposes.

*Exception No. 1: Voice communication systems may be used for other purposes, subject to the approval of the authority having jurisdiction, if the fire alarm system takes precedence over all other signals.*

*Exception No. 2: Where otherwise permitted by another section of this Code.*

7-6.3.10 Alarm notification signals shall take precedence over all other signals.

## S.B.C. High-Rise Section (1988 EDITION)

**506.3 Alarm and Communication Systems**

506.3.1 A voice alarm system, public address system and fire department communication system shall be provided.

**506.3.2 Voice Alarm System.**

506.3.2.1 The operation of any smoke detector required by this section, sprinkler, waterflow device or manual fire alarm system, shall automatically activate a voice alarm system. The voice alarm system shall provide a predetermined message on a selective basis to the area where the alarm originated.

506.3.2.2 The voice alarm shall provide information and give direction to the occupants.

506.3.2.3 The central control system shall contain controls for the voice alarm system so that a selective or general voice alarm may be manually initiated.

506.3.2.4 The system shall be continuously electrically supervised against component failure of the audiopath including amplifiers, speaker wiring, switches and electrical contacts and shall detect opens and shorts which might impair the function of the system.

506.3.2.5 Activation of the system shall automatically sound an alert signal to the desired areas followed by voice instructions giving appropriate information.

506.3.2.6 The alarm shall be designed to be heard clearly by all occupants within the building or designated portions thereof as is required for the public address system.

**506.3.3 Public Address System**

A public address commmunication system designed to be clearly heard by all occupants of the building shall operate from the central control station. It shall be established on a selective or general basis to the following terminal areas:

    1. Elevators.
    2. Elevator lobbies.
    3. Corridors.
    4. Exit stairways.
    5. Rooms and tenant spaces exceeding 1000 sq ft in area.
    6. Dwelling units in apartment houses.
    7. Hotel guest rooms or suites.

Speakers

## BOCA® Fire Protective Signaling Systems (1990 EDITION)

1016.7.3 **Activation**: The alarm-indicating appliances shall be automatically activated by all of the following where provided:

    1. Smoke detectors, other than single-station smoke detectors, as required by Section 1018.0;
    2. Sprinkler water-flow devices;
    3. Manual fire alarm boxes; and
    4. Other approved types of automatic fire detection devices or suppression systems.

*Exception: Smoke detectors in buildings of Use Group 1-3 are permitted to actuate an audible alarm-indicating appliance at a constantly attended location and are not required to activate a general alarm.*

1016.8 **Voice/alarm signaling system**: When activated in accordance with Section 1016.7.3, the voice/alarm signaling system shall automatically sound an alert signal to all occupants within the building on a general or selective basis to the following terminal areas: elevators, elevator lobbies, corridors, exit stairways, rooms and tenant spaces exceeding 1,000 square feet (93 m²) in area; dwelling units in Use Group R-2,; and guestrooms or suites in Use Group R-1. The fire command station shall contain controls to transmit manually an evacuation signal and voice instructions on a selective and all-call basis to the terminal areas indicated herein. The voice/alarm system shall be installed in accordance with the provisions of this code and NFPA 72F listed in Appendix A.

## BOCA® Hi-Rise Section (1990 EDITION)

602.7 **Voice alarm signaling systems**: A voice alarm signaling system shall be provided in accordance with Section 1016.8 and activated in accordance with Section 1016.7.3.

Emergency Telephone System

## BOCA® High-Rise Section (1990 EDITION)

602.8 **Fire department communication system**: A two-way fire department communication system shall be provided for fire department use. The communication system shall operate between the central control station and every elevator, elevator lobby and enclosed exit stairway. Acceptable types of fire department communications shall include:

    1. Telephone or fire department radio in lieu of a dedicated system, where approved by the fire department.

    2. Intercom or two-way public address system complying with NFPA 72F listed in Appendix A.

602.13.1 **Stairway communication system**: A telephone or other two-way communication system connected to an approved constantly attended station shall be provided at not less than every fifth floor in each required stairway where the doors to the stairway are locked.

**Figure 16.3** Alarm action/response. (*Continued*)

## S.B.C. High-Rise Section (1988 EDITION)

506.3.4 Fire Department Communication System: A two way fire department communication system shall be provided for fire department use. It shall operate between the central control station and every elevator, elevator lobby, entry to every enclosed exit stairway and in corridors.

## U.B.C. 1807(e)3 (1988 EDITION)

3. Fire department communication system. A two way fire department communication system shall be provided for fire department use. It shall operate between the central control station and every elevator, elevator lobby and entry to every enclosed exit stairway.

System Integration Controls

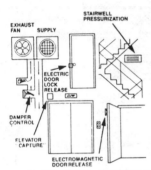

STAIRWELL PRESSURIZATION

EXHAUST FAN    SUPPLY

ELECTRIC DOOR LOCK RELEASE

DAMPER CONTROL

ELEVATOR "CAPTURE"

ELECTROMAGNETIC DOOR RELEASE

## Life Safety 101 (1988 EDITION)

7-6.5.2 Where required by another section of this Code, the following functions shall be actuated by the protective signaling and control system:
(a) Release of hold-open devices for doors or other opening protectives
(b) Stairwell or elevator shaft pressurization
(c) Smoke management or smoke control systems
(d) Emergency lighting control
(e) Unlocking of doors

7-6.5.3 The functions specified in 7-6.5.2 are permitted to be actuated by any protective signaling and control system where otherwise not required by this Code. Additionally, the protective signaling and control system may recall elevators, as required by 7-4.4, if the activation of the system for this purpose comes only from elevator lobby or associated machine room detectors, or if otherwise permitted by the authority having jurisdiction.

## S.B.C. (1988 EDITION)

1114.1.7 All doors in smoke barriers, horizontal exits, stairway enclosure and other doors opening between room and fire-rated exit access corridors shall be self closing and so maintained or shall be provided with approved door holding devices of the fail safe type which will release the door causing it to close when activated by approved listed smoke detectors. When doors are automatic closing by smoke detection, there shall be not more than a 10-second delay before the door starts to close after the smoke detector is actuated.

## S.B.C. High-Rise Section (1988 EDITION)

506.6.3 Each elevator lobby shall be provided with an approved smoke detector located on the lobby ceiling. When the detector is activated, elevator doors shall not open and all cars serving that lobby are to return to the main floor and be under manual control only. If the main floor detector or a transfer floor detector is activated, all cars serving the main floor or transfer floor shall return to a location approved by the fire department and Building Official and be under manual control only. The smoke detector is to operate before the optical density reaches 0.03 per foot. The detector may serve to close the lobby doors.

## BOCA® High-Rise Section (1990 EDITION)

602.10 Smoke control: A smoke control system conforming to Section 1019.2 shall be installed.

602.6 Automatic fire detection: A smoke detector suitable for the intended use shall be installed in each of the following rooms: mechanical equipment; electrical: transformer, telephone equipment; elevator machine; or similar room. The actuation of any detector shall sound an alarm at a constantly attended location and shall place into operation all equipment necessary to prevent the recirculation of smoke.

602.6.1 Duct locations: Smoke detectors in mechanical systems shall comply with the mechanical code listed in Appendix A. A smoke detector shall be installed in each connection to a vertical duct or riser serving two or more stories from return air ducts or plenums of heating, ventilating and air conditioning systems. In buildings of Use Group R, an approved smoke detector shall be installed as required by this section or such smoke detectors shall be installed in each return air riser carrying not more than 5,000 cubic feet per minute (cfm) (2.36 m³/s) and serving not more than ten air inlet openings.

1019.2.2 Mechanical system: Where an automatic sprinkler system in accordance with Section 1004.2.1 is installed throughout, and the mechanical air-handling equipment is designed to accomplish smoke containment, the return and exhaust air shall be moved directly to the outside without recirculation to other fire areas of the building under fire conditions. Containment of smoke shall be considered as confining smoke to the fire area involved without migration to other fire areas. Exhaust capacity in cubic feet per minute shall be a minimum of the volume of the fire area divided by 10. Supply air by mechanical means to the fire area is not required.

**Figure 16.3**    Alarm action/response. (*Continued*)

# Environmental Air Regulations

This chapter outlines the Clean Air Act and its amendments, including the latest 1990 amendments, with regard to industry. It is important to note, however, that some states enforce the Clean Air Act under state implementation plans (SIPs) and thus have different attainment requirements; therefore, compliance requirements can vary from one state to another. As a consequence, this information must be confirmed with the state or local agency where your facility is located. A list identifying the abbreviations used in the Clean Air Act is included at the end of the chapter.

## The Clean Air Act and 1990 Amendments

The Clean Air Act was passed in 1970, extended and substantially amended in 1977, and extensively amended with sweeping legislation in 1990. The 1990 amendments are 20 times the size of the original Clean Air Act and are over 700 pages long. They will require a decade to implement. They are found in 40 *CFR* Parts 1 to 800. The 1990 amendments are concerned primarily with toxic air pollution, urban air quality, acid deposition, and protection of the stratospheric ozone layer. The amendments impose new standards on industry and present detailed approaches, and for the first time, they also include regulations for small industries such as dry cleaners, print shops, and so on. Table 17.1 presents an outline of the Clean Air Act amendments. The amendments consist of Titles I through XI. Titles I, III, IV, V, VI, and VII contain regulations governing the design of industrial pollution control.

## Title I: National Ambient Air Quality Standards (NAAQS)

Before the 1990 amendments, Title I required the EPA to set health-based standards for ambient air and required the states to prepare

TABLE 17.1    1990 Clean Air Act Amendment Outline

| | |
|---|---|
| Title I | National Ambient Air Quality Standards (NAAQS), New or Revised Attainment and Nonattainment Areas |
| Title II | Motor Vehicles |
| Title III | Hazardous Air Pollutants (list of 189 hazardous air pollutants from stationary sources) |
| Title IV | Acid Rain |
| Title V | Permits (expanded form) |
| Title VI | Stratospheric Ozone |
| Title VII | Enforcement |
| Titles VIII–X | Miscellaneous |
| Title XI | Job-Loss Benefits |

and enforce state implementations plans (SIPs). The amended law has added requirements for volatile organic compounds (VOCs). The previous regulations required VOCs to be controlled as described in the EPA's guidance document entitled, *Control Technique Guidelines* (CTGs). Now the regulations mandate revision of the CTGs and development of new guidelines for state control of 11 new stationary sources.

Two kinds of air pollution standards are specified:

1. National ambient air quality standards (NAAQS)

2. Point-source emission limitations and standards

The national ambient air quality standards (NAAQS) determine the concentrations of pollutants allowed in the region. Point-source emissions are covered in a list of air pollutants published by the EPA (see Title III below).

### NAAQS attainment or nonattainment areas and state implementation plans (SIPs)

In the 1990 amendments to the Clean Air Act, Title I focuses on bringing all areas of the country into compliance with national ambient air quality standards (NAAQS). After new or revised national ambient air quality standards have been issued, Title I requires each state to designate all areas in the state as *attainment, nonattainment,* or *unclassifiable* so that the EPA can, in turn, classify all areas in the country; this is to be done with 2 years, with a possible 1-year extension. Attainment or nonattainment classifications are assigned separately for ozone or volatile organic compounds (VOCs) emitted by a variety of industrial sources, carbon monoxide (CO), suspended solid or liquid particles under 10 $\mu$m in diameter (PM-10), $SO_2$, $NO_x$, and lead. State implementation plans (SIPs) must include enforceable emission limits. Stationary sources also must monitor emissions, and the states must report these data to the EPA for NAAQS compliance.

**Attainment areas.**   All construction of new sources of pollution and virtually all modifications to existing sources in attainment areas require permit applications before construction is begun (see Title V below). A prevention of significant deterioration (PSD) permit also is required in an attainment area for a major new source or a modified major existing source, except sources covered specifically by national emission standards for hazardous air pollutants (NESHAPs). If a source emits less than significant amounts of any pollutant, the *prevention of significant deterioration* PSD permit must detail tested emission levels to verify this, except in nonattainment areas or if the pollutant is one of the hazardous air pollutants (HAPs) listed under Title III.

A PSD review involves six steps:

1. Best available control technology (BACT) must be applied. BACT is determined on a case-by-case basis and must start with the most stringent control technology available. Less stringent control cannot be used unless the source demonstrates that the most stringent controls cannot be achieved because of specific energy or economic impacts. In no case may emissions exceed established PSD increments.

2. Existing air quality in the source's area must be reviewed, and this may limit the PSD increment. One year of monitoring is required before permits are granted and operation is allowed.

3. The source must be reviewed to ensure that it does not violate NAAQS.

4. The air-quality impacts must be reviewed.

5. The impacts on soil and vegetation that have commercial or recreational value must be reviewed.

6. The impact of increased pollution on visibility must be reviewed, and this may cause some locations to be restricted.

**Nonattainment areas.**   New major source limitations for carbon monoxide (CO), ozone, and fine particulate matter of less than 10 $\mu$m diameter (PM-10) have been established for nonattainment areas. Stationary sources of CO are considered major when they emit 50 tons per year or more. A source emitting PM-10 pollutants can be classified as major if it has the potential to emit 70 tons or more per year.

**Volatile organic compounds (VOCs).**   Title I in addition covers emissions of volatile organic compounds (VOCs) (ozone-generating) from industry. These commonly found pollutants are emitted by industrial processes, which are the most common type of nonattainment area. VOCs are hydrocarbons (generally petroleum products) that react with $NO_x$ and other chemicals in the presence of sunlight to produce ozone. VOCs include most paint solvents, degreasers, lubricants, and liquid fuels. Emission quantities for any of the VOCs must be checked with the local EPA office to determine if they constitute major sources. Depending on the ozone nonattainment subclassification area (see Table 17.2), the amendments require existing sources to reduce emissions and new sources or modifications to obtain emission offsets applying the lowest achievable emission rate (LAER) and best available control technology (BACT). Some of the 189 hazardous air pollutants (HAPs) listed under Title III are also VOCs. Therefore, facilities must carefully review the requirements under both Title I and Title III, for determinations of compliance and estimates of cost.

**TABLE 17.2    Ozone Nonattainment Area Classifications**

1. Marginal
2. Moderate
3. Serious
4. Severe
5. Extreme for ozone

Nonattainment areas for ozone have the subclassifications shown in Table 17.2. Nonattainment areas for PM-10 pollutants and CO have the subclassifications of moderate or serious.

**Nonattainment plan provisions for ozone, CO, and PM-10s**  PM-10s, ozone, and CO require a comprehensive operating permit for new and modified sources in nonattainment areas. Levels of these substances must undergo new source reviews (NSRs) before construction, and NSRs must comply with the steps listed in Table 17.3. Existing stationary sources that are not modified are only required to apply reasonably available control technology (RACT) controls.

**Attainment schedule for all nonattainment areas.**  Title I requires that nonattainment areas reach attainment as promptly as possible or

**TABLE 17.3    New Source Review Steps**

*Step 1:* Application of the lowest achievable emission rate (LAER).
*Step 2:* Emission offsets greater than the potential increase.
*Step 3:* Compliance with NAAQS.
*Step 4:* Other sources operated by facility in compliance.
*Step 5:* Impact on visibility within guidelines.

within 5 years, with a possible extension up to 10 years. Title I sets out lengthy specifications for achieving attainment for all areas for all pollutants. For example, it requires ozone nonattainment areas or CO nonattainment areas to be expanded to include the entire consolidated metropolitan statistical area (CMSA) instead of county limits for major cities. It separately classifies attainment-nonattainment areas for particulate matter (PM-10s) and may require the state to designate areas as nonattainment for lead.

**PM-10s**  PM-10 nonattainment areas are initially classified as moderate but can be reclassified as serious if they do not reach the attainment date of December 31, 1994, or for some areas a date no later than 6 years after designation. Other extensions also may be applied. However, areas classified as serious have to apply control measures within 4 years.

**Point-source emission limitations**  Air pollution control laws and regulations have generally specified the amounts of pollutants that may be discharged from a source, but not the particular technology or method the source had to use to reduce or eliminate the discharge. However, maximum achievable control technology (MACT) standards published in November of 1991 by the EPA change this. Legal regulation of emissions considers the economic costs and best available technology. It is absolutely necessary to review air pollution control requirements with the local EPA office during the design process for an industrial facility. The requirements for the degree of control vary with the region, the toxic material, and potential emissions. The least costly option is reasonable available control technology (RACT); the next is best available control technology (BACT); the second most costly option is maximum achievable control technology (MACT) for major sources or generally achievable control technology (GACT) for area sources; and the most costly option is lowest achievable emission rate (LAER). Methods of control are well documented. Agreement with the local air pollution agency must be obtained to ensure that an operating permit to discharge is received. This is best done during the design stage to avoid needless costs and delays later.

**Major sources**  A *major source* is defined as a pollution source that emits 100 tons per year of an attainment pollutant, 250 tons per year of any pollutant, or any single source that emits more than 10 tons per year of any of the 189 hazardous air pollutants (HAPs) listed under Title III or more than 25 tons per year of any combination of HAPs. If a source is in a nonattainment area, its emissions must be checked by the local enforcing agency.

## Title III: Hazardous Air Pollutants (HAPs)
## and Accidental Releases from Industry

The Clean Air Act authorizes the EPA to set source performance standards and national emission standards for 189 hazardous air pollutants (HAPs). The 1990 amendments impose new standards for industry sources of 41 pollutants; these must be in place by 1995; standards for 148 other pollutants must be in place by 2003.

### Hazardous air pollutants (HAPs)

Part 61 of the 1991 issue of the *Code Federal Regulations* (EPA, 40 *CFR*, Subchapter C, "Air Programs") is entitled "National Emissions Standards for Hazardous Air Pollutants." Section 61.01 provides a list of hazardous air pollutants (HAPs) and specifies the applicability of Part 61. Section 61.02 sets out definitions of terms. Section 61.03 lists units and abbreviations. Section 61.04 provides the address. Section 61.05 delineates prohibited activities. Section 61.06 covers determinations for new construction or modifications. Section 61.07 covers applications for approval of new construction or modifications. Section 61.08 covers approval of new construction or modifications. Section 61.09 specifies notification of startup. Section 61.10 covers source reporting and requests for waivers of compliance. Section 61.11 specifies waivers of compliance. Section 61.12 sets out compliance and maintenance requirements. Section 61.13 covers emission tests and waivers of emission tests. Section 61.14 specifies monitoring requirements. Section 61.15 covers modifications. Section 61.16 discusses availability of information. Section 61.17 delineates state authority. Section 61.18 covers incorporation by reference. And section 61.19 addresses circumvention.

### Major emission reductions for
### industrial HAPs

Section 301 of Title III amends Section 112 of the Clean Air Act on national emission standards for hazardous air pollutants (NESHAP). It requires major emission reductions of hazardous air pollutants (HAPs) and imposes new maximum achievable control technology (MACT) standards for both new and existing emission sources of HAPs. It contains four major requirements for industry:

1. It lists the 189 HAPs (see Table 17.4) and 16 extremely hazardous substances (EHSs) (see Table 17.9) that apply to industry. The list of EHSs will be expanded to about 100 by the EPA in the near future.

**TABLE 17.4    Hazardous Air Pollutants (HAPs)**

| CAS number | Chemical name |
|---|---|
| 75070 | Acetaldehyde |
| 60355 | Acetamide |
| 75058 | Acetonitrile |
| 98862 | Acetophenone |
| 53963 | 2-Acetylaminofluorene |
| 107028 | Acrolein |
| 79061 | Acrylamide |
| 79107 | Acrylic acid |
| 107131 | Acrylonitrile |
| 107051 | Allyl chloride |
| 92671 | 4-Aminobiphenyl |
| 62533 | Aniline |
| 90040 | o-Anisidine |
| 1332214 | Asbestos |
| 71432 | Benzene (including benzene from gasoline) |
| 92875 | Benzidine |
| 98077 | Benzotrichloride |
| 100447 | Benzyl chloride |
| 92524 | Biphenyl |
| 117817 | Bis(2-ethylhexyl)phthalate (DEHP) |
| 542881 | Bis(chloromethyl)ether |
| 75252 | Bromoform |
| 106990 | 1,3-Butadiene |
| 156627 | Calcium cyanamide |
| 105602 | Caprolactam |
| 133062 | Captan |
| 63252 | Carbaryl |
| 75150 | Carbon disulfide |
| 56235 | Carbon tetrachloride |
| 463581 | Carbonyl sulfide |
| 120809 | Catechol |
| 133904 | Chloramben |
| 57749 | Chlordane |
| 7782505 | Chlorine |
| 79118 | Chloroacetic acid |
| 532274 | 2-Chloroacetophenone |
| 108907 | Chlorobenzene |
| 510156 | Chlorobenzilate |
| 67663 | Chloroform |
| 107302 | Chloromethyl methyl ether |
| 126998 | Chloroprene |
| 1319773 | Cresols/cresylic acid (isomers and mixture) |
| 95487 | o-Cresol |
| 108394 | m-Cresol |
| 106445 | p-Cresol |
| 98828 | Cumene |
| 94757 | 2,4-D, salts and esters |
| 3547044 | DDE |
| 334883 | Diazomethane |
| 132649 | Dibenzofurans |
| 96128 | 1,2-Dibromo-3-chloropropane |
| 84742 | Dibutylphthalate |

TABLE 17.4    Hazardous Air Pollutants (HAPs) (*Continued*)

| CAS number | Chemical name |
|---|---|
| 106467 | 1,4-Dichlorobenzene(*p*) |
| 91941 | 3,3-Dichlorobenzidene |
| 111444 | Dichloroethyl ether [bis(2-chloroethyl)ether] |
| 542756 | 1,3-Dichloropropene |
| 62737 | Dichlorvos |
| 111422 | Diethanolamine |
| 121697 | *N,N*-Diethyl aniline (*N,N*-dimethylaniline) |
| 64675 | Diethyl sulfate |
| 119904 | 3,3-Dimethoxybenzidine |
| 60117 | Dimethyl aminoazobenzene |
| 119937 | 3,3'-Dimethyl benzidine |
| 79447 | Dimethyl carbamoyl chloride |
| 68122 | Dimethyl formamide |
| 57147 | 1,1-Dimethyl hydrazine |
| 131113 | Dimethyl phthalate |
| 77781 | Dimethyl sulfate |
| 534521 | 4,6-Dinitro-*o*-cresol, and salts |
| 51285 | 2,4-Dinitrophenol |
| 121142 | 2,4-Dinitrotoluene |
| 123911 | 1,4-Dioxane (1,4-Diethyleneoxide) |
| 122667 | 1,2-Diphenylhydrazine |
| 106898 | Epichlorohydrin (1-chloro-2,3-epoxypropane) |
| 106887 | 1,2-Epoxybutane |
| 140885 | Ethyl acrylate |
| 100414 | Ethyl benzene |
| 51796 | Ethyl carbamate (urethane) |
| 75003 | Ethyl chloride (chloroethane) |
| 106934 | Ethylene dibromide (dibromoethane) |
| 107062 | Ethylene dichloride (1,2-dichloroethane) |
| 107211 | Ethylene glycol |
| 151564 | Ethylene imine (aziridine) |
| 75218 | Ethylene oxide |
| 96457 | Ethylene thiourea |
| 75343 | Ethylidene dichloride (1,1-dichloroethane) |
| 50000 | Formaldehyde |
| 76448 | Heptachlor |
| 118741 | Hexachlorobenzene |
| 87683 | Hexachlorobutadiene |
| 77474 | Hexachlorocyclopentadiene |
| 67721 | Hexachloroethane |
| 822060 | Hexamethylene-1,6-diisocyanate |
| 680319 | Hexamethylphosphoramide |
| 110543 | Hexane |
| 302012 | Hydrazine |
| 7647010 | Hydrochloric acid |
| 7664393 | Hydrogen fluoride (hydrofluoric acid) |
| 123319 | Hydroquinone |
| 78591 | Isophorone |
| 58899 | Lindane (all isomers) |
| 108316 | Maleic anhydride |
| 67561 | Methanol |
| 72435 | Methoxychlor |

TABLE 17.4   Hazardous Air Pollutants (HAPs) *(Continued)*

| CAS number | Chemical name |
|---|---|
| 74839 | Methyl bromide (bromomethane) |
| 74873 | Methyl chloride (chloromethane) |
| 71556 | Methyl chloroform (1,1,1-trichloroethane) |
| 78933 | Methyl ethyl ketone (2-butanone) |
| 60344 | Methyl hydrazine |
| 74884 | Methyl iodide (iodomethane) |
| 108101 | Methyl isobutyl ketone (hexone) |
| 624839 | Methyl isocyanate |
| 80626 | Methyl methacrylate |
| 1634044 | Methyl tert butyl ether |
| 101144 | 4,4-Methylene bis(2-chloroaniline) |
| 75092 | Methylene chloride (dichloromethane) |
| 101688 | Methylene diphenyl diisocyanate (MDI) |
| 101779 | 4,4'-Methylenedianiline |
| 91203 | Naphthalene |
| 98953 | Nitrobenzene |
| 92933 | 4-Nitrobiphenyl |
| 100027 | 4-Nitrophenol |
| 79469 | 2-Nitropropane |
| 684935 | *N*-Nitroso-*N*-methylurea |
| 62759 | *N*-Nitrosodimethylamine |
| 59892 | *N*-Nitrosomorpholine |
| 56382 | Parathion |
| 82688 | Pentachloronitrobenzene (quintobenzene) |
| 87865 | Pentachlorophenol |
| 108952 | Phenol |
| 106503 | *p*-Phenylenediamine |
| 75445 | Phosgene |
| 7803512 | Phosphine |
| 7723140 | Phosphorus |
| 85449 | Phthalic anhydride |
| 1336363 | Polychlorinated biphenyls (aroclors) |
| 1120714 | 1,3-Propane sulfone |
| 57578 | beta-Propiolactone |
| 123386 | Propionaldehyde |
| 114261 | Propoxur (baygon) |
| 78875 | Propylene dichloride (1,2-dichloropropane) |
| 75569 | Propylene oxide |
| 75558 | 1,2-Propylenimine (2-Methyl aziridine) |
| 91225 | Quinoline |
| 106514 | Quinone |
| 100425 | Styrene |
| 96093 | Styrene oxide |
| 1746016 | 2,3,7,8-Tetrachlorodibenzo-*p*-dioxin |
| 79345 | 1,1,2,2-Tetrachloroethane |
| 127184 | Tetrachloroethylene (perchloroethylene) |
| 7550450 | Titanium tetrachloride |
| 108883 | Toluene |
| 95807 | 2,4-Toluene diamine |
| 584849 | 2,4-Toluene diisocyanate |
| 95534 | *o*-Toluidine |
| 8001352 | Toxaphene (chlorinated camphene) |

TABLE 17.4  Hazardous Air Pollutants (HAPs) *(Continued)*

| CAS number | Chemical name |
|---|---|
| 120821 | 1,2,4-Trichlorobenzene |
| 79005 | 1,1,2-Trichloroethane |
| 79016 | Trichloroethylene |
| 95954 | 2,4,5-Trichlorophenol |
| 88062 | 2,4,6-Trichlorophenol |
| 121448 | Triethylamine |
| 1582098 | Trifluralin |
| 540841 | 2,2,4-Trimethylpentane |
| 108054 | Vinyl acetate |
| 593602 | Vinyl bromide |
| 75014 | Vinyl chloride |
| 75354 | Vinylidene chloride (1,1-dichloroethylene) |
| 1330207 | Xylenes (isomers and mixture) |
| 95476 | o-Xylenes |
| 108383 | m-Xylenes |
| 106423 | p-Xylenes |
| 0 | Antimony compounds |
| 0 | Arsenic compounds (inorganic including arsine) |
| 0 | Beryllium compounds |
| 0 | Cadmium compounds |
| 0 | Chromium compounds |
| 0 | Cobalt compounds |
| 0 | Coke oven emissions |
| 0 | Cyanide compounds[a] |
| 0 | Glycol ethers[b] |
| 0 | Lead compounds |
| 0 | Manganese compounds |
| 0 | Mercury compounds |
| 0 | *Fine mineral fibers[c]* |
| 0 | Nickel compounds |
| 0 | Polycylic organic matter[d] |
| 0 | Radionuclides (including radon)[e] |
| 0 | Selenium compounds |

NOTE: For all listings that contain the word *compounds* and for glycol ethers, the following applies: Unless otherwise specified, these listings are defined as including any unique chemical substance that contains the named chemical (i.e., antimony, arsenic, etc.) as part of that chemical's infrastructure. CAS = Chemical Abstract Service

[a] "X'CN, where X = H' or any other group where a formal dissociation may occur. For example, KCN or Ca(CN)2.

[b] Includes mono- and di- ethers of ethylene glycol, diethylene glycol, and triethylene glycol R = $(OCH2CH2)_n$ = OR', where $n$ = 1, 2, or 3; R = alkyl or aryl groups; R' = R, H, or groups which, when removed, yield glycol ethers with the structure: R = $(OCH2CH)_n$ = OH. Polymers are excluded from the glycol category.

[c] Includes mineral fiber emissions from facilities manufacturing or processing glass, rock, or slag fibers (or other mineral derived fibers) of average diameter 1 μm or less.

[d] Includes organic compounds with more than one benzene ring and that have a boiling point greater than or equal to 100°C.

[e] A type of atom that spontaneously undergoes radioactive decay.

2. It requires rigorous maximum achievable control technology (MACT) over a specified period of time for the list in item 1.

3. It requires further emissions reductions after MACT standards are installed if studies reveal that a risk to health and the environment remain.

4. It requires planning and procedures to prevent accidental releases of EHSs.

### Action required by industry

Table 17.5 provides a summary of design items that must be addressed in the planning phase for an industrial facility. Figure 17.1 presents a compliance flowchart.

**TABLE 17.5   Summary of Items for Industrial Pollution Design**

| No. | Action | Date* |
|-----|--------|-------|
| 1 | Determine the permitting agency: federal, state, or local. | — |
| 2 | Identify HAPs. | — |
| 3 | Estimate new source emission discharges and storage quantities of all regulated substances per EPA methods. | — |
| 4 | Determine if emissions will constitute a major or an area source. | — |
| 5 | Determine MACT standards for each category of the HAPs (189 substances listed in Table 17.4). | Published in Nov. 1991 |
| 6 | If not a major source, review GACT standard for compliance. | — |
| 7 | Review benefits and risks of early HAP (90 percent) emission reductions† if source is subject to MACT prior to 1994. | — |
| 8 | Review possibility of grouping emission sources to achieve compliance. | SIPs by 1992 |
| 9 | Review opportunities for banking emission reductions, obtaining credits, or trading with other emission sources. | SIPs by 1992 |
| 10 | List EHSs and threshold quantities (16 more substances to be added). | Complete by 1992 |
| 11 | Review potential for eliminating EHSs. | — |
| 12 | Develop risk management plan and coordinate with OSHA and SARA. | — |
| 13 | Perform a hazardous assessment for all EHSs. (See Chapter 10.) | 1993 |

*These scheduled dates may change as the EPA develops standards.
†Six-year MACT compliance extension is allowed for early reduction.

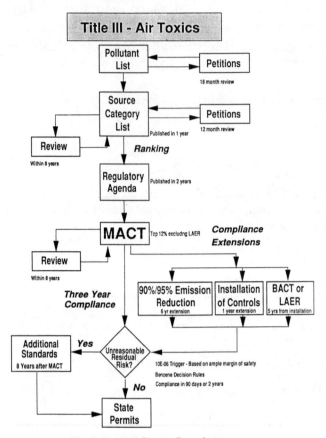

**Figure 17.1** Air toxics compliance flow chart.

### Definitions of industrial sources

Emissions are classified into sources categories (see Table 17.6), which are defined in Title III as follows:

1. A *major source* is any stationary source that emits, with or without emission reduction control equipment, more than 10 tons per year of any of the 189 HAPs or more than 25 tons per year of any combination of HAPs. This includes all the emission sources within a contiguous area. A major source is exempt from a PSD review. Over the next 10 years, EPA will promulgate MACT standards for each major source category. Existing operations have up to a three-year exemption from compliance with MACT standards; however, new operations do not.

2. An *area source* is any stationary source of HAPs that is not a major source. The area source regulation has been delayed for 5 years in order for EPA to study this category.

TABLE 17.6   Title III Industrial Emission
Sources

---

Major sources
Area sources
Stationary sources
New sources
Modified sources
Existing sources
Electric utility steam-generating units

---

3. A *stationary source* is a facility or installation that emits or will emit a HAP.

4. *Modified source* is any physical change or change in method of operation of a major source that increases the actual emissions or that adds emission of a new pollutant.

5. An *existing source* is any stationary source other than a new source.

6. An *electric utility steam-generating unit* supplies more than a third of its potential electric output and more than 25 MW to any utility power distributing system.

### Source categories and MACT standards

**Major sources.**   The EPA must publish a list of all categories and subcategories of major sources of HAPs within 12 months after the 1990 amendments were enacted. By November of 1995, the EPA will post categories for major sources of the pollutants listed in Table 17.7.

**Area sources.**   The EPA must publish a goal for regulation of 90 percent of the 30 most hazardous HAPs of area sources within 5 years of passage of the 1990 amendments. The EPA may require area-source categories to meet the less stringent generally available control technology (GACT). Cancer-causing emissions from area sources must be

TABLE 17.7   Pollutant Categories to Be Listed
in 1995

---

Alkylated lead compounds
Polycyclic organic matter
Hexachlorobenzene
Mercury
Polychlorinated biphenyls
2,3,7,8-Tetrachlorodibenzofurans (TCDFs)
2,3,7,8-Tetrachlorodibenzo-*p*-dioxin (TCDD)

reduced by 75 percent. The EPA will research and measure ambient HAP concentrations by November 15, 1993 and submit a strategy for controlling urban area sources by November 15, 1995.

**Specific pollutants.**  The EPA must publish a list of categories and subcategories of sources for the seven pollutants listed in Table 17.7.

**All pollutants.**  The EPA will publish a set of first-round technology-based emission standards for every category and subcategory on its list of sources, taking into consideration the cost of achieving them and the non-air-quality health and environmental impacts and energy requirements of new and existing sources. This first round of MACT standards (technology-based emission standards) will be issued for each listed source category. They will apply to new and existing sources, and they will be based on the best demonstrated control technology or practices within the regulated industry. Cost and any non-air-quality health and environmental impacts and energy requirements will be considered. Substitution of materials, process changes, technological pollution controls, and special operator training all can be used to reach the required emission reduction. MACT standards will be issued as shown in Table 17.8.

Industries that voluntarily reduce emissions according to certain conditions can get a 6-year extension for compliance with MACT standards. New sources are required to satisfy the most stringent emission limit achieved by an existing source in the same category or subcategory. Emission rates for new sources can be estimated through factors developed by EPA, or the synthetic and organic chemical manufacturers' industry and others. Emission rates can also be estimated by mass balance across a piece of equipment but this method is considered inaccurate. Existing source emission reductions can be less stringent than standards for new sources in the same category or subcategory if they are (1) as low as the average emission limitation of the best-performing 12 percent of sources in a similar category or subcategory or (2) as low as the average emission limitation of the five best-

**TABLE 17.8    Intended Schedule Dates for MACT Standard Issues**

| MACT standard | Date |
| --- | --- |
| Forty categories | 11/15/92 |
| Coke ovens | 12/31/92 |
| Twenty-five percent of categories | 11/15/94 |
| An additional 25 percent of categories | 11/15/97 |
| Seven specified pollutants | 1/15/2000 |
| All categories | 11/15/2000 |

performing sources in a category or subcategory with fewer than 30 sources.

An industrial facility may reduce the emissions from one source below the requirements of the EPA standard and earn credits for other sources that are above the EPA standards. Residual risk procedures will be applied after 10 years and all MACT standards are in place. These risk assessments will test the effectiveness of MACT controls. If the health risk exceeds the rate of one cancer per million in the most exposed urban population, further reductions will be required. Should the EPA determine that no technology or economically practical measurement technique is available for a certain HAP, it may allow alternative methods, such as equipment design or operation practices.

No emission standard set under this section can take precedence over any stricter standard set in other applicable sections of the Clean Air Act or by a state.

A compliance plan is needed for every regulated facility. An air emissions inventory should be conducted either independently or as part of an overall environmental audit. After an inventory, regulations should be reviewed to determine

1. Applicability of Title I
2. Categorization of Title III
3. Criteria of applicability
4. Timing of new regulations

### Prevention of accidental releases of EHSs

The Clean Air Act amendments direct the EPA to take a larger role in industrial process safety matters. As a result, the EPA has collected chemical release data from industry and has issued reports assessing the present status of accidental release-prevention activities. The EPA has identified common elements in hazardous chemical accidents and is assisting state and local emergency planning officials. The amendments also establish a new Chemical Safety and Hazard Investigation Board. It is an independent safety board modeled after the National Transportation Safety Board. The 1990 Clean Air Act amendments require that a report be issued to the EPA administrator by the Chemical Safety and Hazard Investigation Board on November 15, 1992 recommending regulations for risk management plans (RMPs) and hazard assessments (HAs). The regulations will cover each facility that produces, processes, handles, or stores any of the extremely hazardous substances (EHSs) listed in the 1990 amendments. Sixteen substances were listed initially, as shown in Table 17.9, and more will be added by November 15, 1992, bringing the list up to about 100 substances.

TABLE 17.9   Initial Extremely Hazardous
Substances

---

1. Ammonia
2. Anhydrous ammonia
3. Anhydrous hydrogen chloride
4. Anhydrous sulfur dioxide
5. Bromine
6. Chlorine
7. Ethylene oxide
8. Hydrogen cyanide
9. Hydrogen fluoride
10. Hydrogen sulfide
11. Methyl chloride
12. Methyl isocyanate
13. Phosgene
14. Sulfur trioxide
15. Toluene diisocyanate
16. Vinyl chloride

---

Recommended procedures will be consistent with standards established by ANSI, ASTM, and ASME. The EPA must publish the regulations by November 15, 1993, and compliance is required within 3 years. Hazardous assessments (HAs) must cover specific methodologies, techniques, parameters, and assumptions for simulating vapor and liquid/vapor releases. They must identify potential equipment and process failures and assess the magnitude of releases and their impacts on the health of people and environment. Section 301 of Title III adds a new subsection to Section 112 of the Clean Air Act that directs OSHA to publish regulations for a chemical process safety standard to protect employees from the hazards of accidental releases of highly hazardous chemicals (HHCs) using hazard assessments. A list of highly hazardous chemicals was published by the EPA on November 15, 1991.

OSHA issued its final standard, process safety management rule (PSM), on February 24, 1992, covering process safety management of highly hazardous substances. This standard, effective May 26, 1992, covers 130 toxic and reactive chemicals and all flammable liquids and gases, except heating fuel, in quantities over 10,000 lb. See Chaps. 4 and 10. Twenty-five percent of the initial process hazard analysis must be completed by May 1994.

## Title IV: Acid Rain or $SO_2$ and $NO_x$ Emissions

Title IV requires reductions in $SO_2$ and $NO_x$ emissions. It is concerned mainly with utilities. However, it also includes industrial sources that do not produce electricity and defines them as a nonutility unit or process sources. $SO_2$ emissions must be inventoried by the EPA every 5 years. The inventory also will include qualifying small power production facilities and qualifying cogeneration facilities ordinarily not subject to provisions under Title IV. This title also requires the EPA to issue new and revised standards in the future if industrial emissions of $SO_2$ should exceed 5.6 million tons.

### Title V: Permits

Operating permits are required for all existing, modified, or new sources. Permits are required for all facilities emitting the pollutants listed in Table 17.10. *New* operating permits are required for all major sources of the 189 hazardous air pollutants listed in Title III. Existing sources that are presently operating under old permits should contact their state EPA. Under the 1990 amendments, the new permit provisions are extensive. The amendments require comprehensive operating permits for stationary sources and most industrial operations. Permits are aimed at attaining and maintaining national ambient air quality standards. By 1993, state and local agencies must implement permit procedures with the EPA. Each state must develop a permitting and emission fee program subject to federal approval. The states must issue permits for major sources. Permits are then sent to the EPA for a 45-day period for review, modification, or rejection.

All of a facility's emissions are covered by one permit document that identifies the extent of compliance. All major sources are required to have a maximum 5-year fixed-term permit detailing compliance information. Title V specifies procedures for permitting several source categories, including HAPs, under Title III. Eighteen months after a mandated MACT date has passed, the owner-operator must submit an application for a permit. An existing source will have up to 3 years to achieve this classification. Almost all new sources and modifications to existing sources require evaluation before construction. A source

**TABLE 17.10  Pollutants Requiring Permits**

Sulfur dioxide $(SO_2)$
Carbon monoxide (CO)
Nitrogen oxides $(NO_x)$
Ozone (VOCs)
Lead
PM-10s
The 189 HAPs plus the initial sixteen EHSs

that emits less than significant amounts of any pollutant needs to submit enough application details to verify emission levels; however, in nonattainment areas, application requires more detail.

Many questions remain unanswered at this time regarding permit rule development, permit application procedures, interface with current permits, and assessment of permits. Some of these issues may not be resolved for years.

## Title VI: Stratospheric Ozone

The Montreal Protocol of 1987, which was developed as a result of a meeting of nations in Vienna in 1985, set guidelines to cut back on the use of chlorofluorocarbons (CFCs). Another meeting in London in June 1990 accelerated the scaledown and expanded the number of compounds to be regulated. Some of the important regulations expected as a result are a total ban on CFCs by the year 2000 and excise taxes on the sale of CFCs early in the 1990s. See Tables 17.11 and 17.12 for lists of ozone-depleting substances.

### Control of CFCs

Title VI defines substances that are known to or could reasonably be anticipated to cause or contribute to ozone depletion and classifies them into class I or class II. Title VI assigns each substance an ozone-depletion factor, as shown in the tables.

Class I includes CFCs. These substances will be scaled down in production and availability. Production and use of CFCs and carbon tetrachloride will be phased out by 2000. Methyl chloroform will be phased out no later than 2005.

Class II includes chlorofluorocarbons with the addition of hydrogen (HCFCs). These substances are to be phased out by 2030. Exceptions for CFCs, halons, and carbon tetrachloride will be granted to the production limits for medical devices, aviation safety, fire suppression,

**TABLE 17.11   Class I Ozone-Depleting Substances and Factors**

| No. | Substance | Ozone-depleting factor |
|---|---|---|
| 1 | CFCs 11, 12, 13, 111, 112 | 1.00 |
| 2 | CFC 113 | 0.80 |
| 3 | CFC 114 | 1.00 |
| 4 | CFC 115 | 0.60 |
| 5 | CFCs 211, 212, 213, 214, 215, 216, 217 | 1.00 |
| 6 | Halon 1211 | 3.00 |
| 7 | Halon 1301 | 10.00 |
| 8 | Carbon tetrachloride | 1.10 |
| 9 | Methyl chloroform | 0.10 |

TABLE 17.12    Class II Ozone-Depleting Substances and Factors

| No. | Substance | Factor |
|-----|-----------|--------|
| 1 | HCFC 22 | 0.05 |
| 2 | HCFCs 123 and 124 | 0.02 |
| 3 | HCFC 141(b) | 0.10 |
| 4 | HCFC 142(b) | 0.06 |

export to developing nations, and national security. The EPA will issue regulations limiting the use and emissions of all ozone-depleting chemicals. Methyl chloroform, which is used for metal cleaning and chemical processing, has a low ozone-depleting potential but a high volume of use. Under Title VI, CFC production is set not to exceed 1989 levels and will be reduced in increments starting in 1993. Title VI establishes five classes of ground-level ozone nonattainment areas. Accidental release planning under Title III does not apply to substances covered under Title VI. Current research and development may affect much of the present view stated above.

## Title VII: Enforcement

Title VII enforces the Clean Air Act with civil and criminal penalties. These penalties have been strengthened by the 1990 amendments. The new civil and criminal penalties clauses punish those who knowingly or negligently release unpermitted emissions.

The amendments include a civil penalty involving field-citation fines of up to $5000 per day. Civil penalties of up to $25,000 per day can be levied for violations of state implementation plans (SIPs) or provisions of attainment and maintenance of national air quality standards, control of hazardous air pollutants, permits or acid deposition control, or attempts to construct or modify a major stationary source in any nonattainment area without complying with the prevention of significant deterioration of air quality.

Criminal penalties of up to $250,000 for individuals and $500,000 for organizations or imprisonment for up to 5 years or both can be levied for first convictions. Penalties double for second convictions.

## Definitions

*Air toxics:*  Any air pollutant not included in the national ambient air quality standards (NAAQS), excluding ozone, carbon monoxide, PM-10s, sulfur dioxide, and nitrogen dioxide, that can be considered to cause the development of cancer, reproductive dysfunctions, neurologic disorders, heritable gene mutations, or other serious or irreversible chronic or acute health effects in humans.

*Attainment area:*    An area that complies with NAAQS. An area may be attainment for one pollutant and nonattainment area for another pollutant.

*BACT (best available control technology):*    Defined by the EPA as the best methods to control small or dispersed sources.

*CFC (chlorofluorocarbons):*    A group of inert, nontoxic, and easily liquefied chemicals used in refrigeration, air conditioning, packaging, insulation, or as solvents or aerosol propellants.

*CTGs (control techniques guidelines):*    Guidance documents to be issued by the EPA that define reasonably available control technology (RACT) to be applied to existing facilities that emit certain threshold quantities of air pollutants. They will specify both the economic and technologic feasibility of available control methods.

*EHS (extremely hazardous substances):*    The EPA has published an original list of 16 substances and expects to add another 80 or more generally achievable control technologies (GACTs) for the application of risk management procedures (RMP) and hazard assessments (HAs).

*HAPs (hazardous air pollutants):*    The 189 substances listed by the EPA under Title III of the Clean Air Act.

*HCFCs (chlorofluorocarbons with the addition of hydrogen):*    These are considered significantly less damaging to the ozone layer than CFCs.

*LAER (lowest achievable emission rate):*    Applies to pollutants under Title I. Cost and energy consideration cannot be applied.

*MACT (maximum achievable control technology):*    The degree of reductions in emissions achievable for new and existing sources, taking into consideration the cost of achieving them and the non-air-quality health and environment impacts and energy requirements.

*NAAQS (national ambient air quality standards):*    Established by the Clean Air Act to protect human health and the environment.

*PM-10s:*    Suspended solid or liquid particles under 10 $\mu$m in diameter.

*PSM:*    Process safety management (see Chaps. 4 and 10).

*RACT (reasonably available control technology):*    The emission limitations on existing sources in nonattainment areas defined by the EPA.

*VOCs (volatile organic compounds):*    A group of chemicals that react with nitrogen oxides in the presence of heat and sunlight.

# Environmental Water Regulations

### Robert D. Smith

This chapter outlines the environmental water regulations that apply to industry. It provides a list for engineers to review for compliance with the Clean Water Act when they are dealing with an industrial wastewater problem.

## Clean Water Act

The Clean Water Act (CWA) was passed in 1972, amended in 1977, and amended again in 1987. It is a successor to the Federal Water Pollution Control Act legislation that was passed in the 1950s and the 1960s (*CFR*, Title 40). The 1977 amendments to the Clean Water Act severely limit the industrial discharge of pollutants. Industries must control toxic pollutant discharges from plant-site runoff, spillage or leaks, sludge or waste disposal, and effluent from industrial manufacturing or processing operations. The CWA controls discharges from point sources into waters of the United States, regulating five types of discharges:

1. Direct discharges

2. Indirect discharges

3. Sources that spill oil or hazardous substances

4. Discharges of dredged or fill material

5. Sewage from vessels

## Effluent guidelines and standards

The Clean Water Act amendments of 1987 empowered the Environmental Protection Agency (EPA) to establish effluent guidelines and standards for wastewater discharges to public waterways. These guidelines and standards are listed in the *Code of Federal Regulations* (*CFR*) under Title 40, "Protection of All the Environment," which covers 15 volumes.

Part 400 of *CFR* 40 lists point-source categories according to type of industry (see Table 18.1). Point-source discharges are regulated by state environmental protection agencies, who have approved programs to achieve national pollutant discharge elimination standards (NPDES). NPDES permits are required for each point discharge. The permit specifies the amount of pollutant allowed based on the production rate. The permit also sets time limits for accomplishing specific objectives of compliance if the point-source discharge is not in compliance at the time of permit granting. Additionally, changes to discharges because of new processes or modifications of existing processes must be reported to the control agency. For a list of state agencies concerned with pollution guidelines and regulations, see the *1991 Conservation Directory,* published by the National Wildlife Federation.

Wastewater usually needs some treatment before discharge, and treatment costs may become burdensome. However, noncompliance can result in fines. Therefore, treatment costs can be a significant factor in the selection of a site for a new industrial facility. Feasibility studies should be performed to determine the most effective means of disposal.

### Sampling program

The pollutant content in any wastewater leaving a plant or percolating into the ground must be determined. This content is determined in accordance with *CFR* 40, Part 401.13, "Test Procedures for Measurement," and Part 136, "Guidelines Establishing Test Procedures for the Analysis of Pollutants." Averages and maximum concentrations must be noted.

A sampling program is established that should coordinate with the production schedule of the facility. Composite samples of the wastewater should be taken proportional to the flow. One method is to take "grab" samples of the waste stream at uniform intervals, portions corresponding to the flow rate measured simultaneously as the sample is taken and placed in a jar. See *CFR* 40, Part 403, Appendix E, "Sampling Procedures."

Analyses should include all potential pollutants, including those listed in the pertinent *CFR* 40, Part 400, series industry category. Since 129 pollutants are listed in the EPA regulations, a review of the production processes is needed to eliminate unlikely substances. Determine the amount of each pollutant from the concentration and flow rate. Then calculate the amount per production rate, that is, kilograms of pollutant per 1000 kg of production (pounds per 1000 lb of production). Compare the calculated amounts, and identify which require reduction or removal.

**TABLE 18.1  Water Pollution Effluent Guidelines and Standards for Point-Source Categories**

| Category | 40 *CFR* |
|---|---|
| Aluminum forming | 467 |
| Asbestos manufacturing | 427 |
| Battery manufacturing | 461 |
| Builders' paper and board mills | 431 |
| Carbon black manufacturing | 458 |
| Cement processing | 411 |
| Coal mining, BPT, BAT, BCT limitations and new source performance standards | 434 |
| Coil coating facilities | 465 |
| Copper forming | 468 |
| Dairy products processing | 405 |
| Electrical and electronic components | 469 |
| Electroplating | 413 |
| Explosives manufacturing | 457 |
| Feedlots | 412 |
| Ferroalloy manufacturing | 424 |
| Fertilizer manufacturing | 418 |
| Fruits and vegetables, canned and preserved | 407 |
| General provisions | 401 |
| Glass manufacturing | 426 |
| Grain mills | 406 |
| Gum and wood chemical industry | 454 |
| Hospitals | 460 |
| Ink formulating | 447 |
| Inorganic chemicals manufacturing | 415 |
| Iron and steel manufacturing | 420 |
| Leather tanning and finishing | 425 |
| Meat products | 432 |
| Metal finishing | 433 |
| Metal molding and casting | 464 |
| Mineral mining and processing | 436 |
| Nonferrous metals forming and metal powders | 471 |
| Nonferrous metals manufacturing | 421 |
| Oil and gas extraction | 435 |
| Ore mining and processing | 440 |
| Organic chemicals, plastics, and synthetic fibers manufacturing | 414 |
| Paint formulating | 446 |
| Pesticides chemicals manufacturing | 455 |
| Petroleum refining | 419 |
| Pharmaceutical manufacturing | 439 |
| Phosphate manufacturing | 422 |
| Photographic processing | 459 |
| Plastics molding and forming | 463 |
| Porcelain enameling | 466 |
| Pretreatment regulations for existing and new sources of pollution | 403 |
| Pretreatment standards, steam electric power generating | 423 |
| Pulp, paper, and paperboard | 430 |
| Rubber manufacturing | 428 |
| Seafood processing, canned and preserved | 408 |
| Soap and detergent manufacturing | 417 |
| Sugar processing | 409 |
| Tars and asphalt paving and roofing materials, existing and new sources, performance standards and pretreatment standards | 443 |
| Textile mills | 410 |
| Timber products processing | 429 |

TABLE 18.2    Common Wastewater Treatment
Concepts

---

Concept 1: Settling and oil removal
Concept 2: Chemical feeding
Concept 3: Mixing
Concept 4: Aeration
Concept 5: Neutralization
Concept 6: Flocculation
Concept 7: Clarification
Concept 8: Filtration
Concept 9: Dewatering and solids handling

---

## Treatment Concepts

Treatment concepts should fit the particular wastewater stream and the desired effluent objective. Treatment facilities can vary from a small neutralizing pit to a multistep process requiring acres of land. Typical treatment methods are listed in Table 18.2. Brief descriptions follow.

### Discharging to public sewers

Discharging to public sewers that connect to publicly owned treatment works (POTW) is one means to reduce the amount of treatment necessary. Limitations for these discharges are specified under *CFR* 40, Part 403, "General Pretreatment Regulations for Existing and New Sources of Pollution." The pretreatment guidelines specified limit pollutants that are objectionable in discharges from the POTW. Generally, only biodegradable and inert suspended solid pollutants are allowed, and these are limited in concentration so as not to "slug" the POTW. The POTW may place a surcharge on the excess amounts of pollutants it receives.

Treatment also may be done in stages. *Primary* treatment involves simple separation. *Secondary* treatment includes chemical and physical changes preceding additional separation. *Tertiary* treatment may be necessary if the secondary treatment effluent still does not meet the permit limits.

### Settling and oil removal

Quiescent settling allows both settleable and floating substances to separate from the wastewater. Laboratory settling tests in vertical tubes can determine settling rates for design. Flow-through settling pits or basins must be long enough to allow separation of the coarse particles and oily floatables. Both steel and oil industries use well-developed settling facilities. Steel mill scale pits are used for large flows containing metal oxide scale and oil. The American Petroleum Institute (API) has designed settlers that are excellent for oil separation in small to moderate amounts.

Sufficient depth should be provided for solids storage and 1 to 2 m (3 to 6 ft) for clear settling. Width should be sized for the solids removal equipment. Entry design is critical to provide uniform flow patterns across the basin. Exit design must prevent solids and oil reentrainment using under and over baffles. Selection of solids and oil removal equipment will depend on the rate of collection and frequency of removal. Cleaning out the settled solids is done during no-flow periods to avoid disrupting the settling process.

### Chemical feeding

The first step following primary treatment may be the addition of ingredients to effect a chemical or physical change in the pollutants in the wastewater. Unless the amounts of the additives are small and the feeding is intermittent, the method of handling and feeding these ingredients should minimize materials handing. Continuous flow requires automatic feeding. Selection of equipment must take into account the cost, shipment, receiving, and temporary storage of the additives, as well as the feed-control method.

### Neutralization

Adjustment of the pH (the acidity or alkalinity) of the waste stream may be needed to obtain optimal conditions for the formation and/or settling of solids. For example, iron hydroxide settles best at a pH of 8.3 but will dissolve completely below a pH of 6. Metal equipment will corrode at a pH below 6, and masonry will dissolve at a pH above 11. Discharges to POTW and to public waterways must be maintained at a pH between 6 and 9. Neutralizing agents are inexpensive and act rapidly. Caustic soda (NaOH) is rapid, whereas lime (impure $CaCO_3$) is inexpensive but slow in dissolving and may introduce undesirable substances such as magnesium, which can be more difficult to settle. It is apparent that the data gathered on the pollutant(s) in the wastewater must be correct and treatment by chemical additives must be understood thoroughly.

### Mixing

The rate of feeding chemical additives must be accurate to achieve the desired result in wastewater treatment. In addition, to complete the treatment process, thorough mixing must follow. Mixing is accomplished by mechanical agitation or a static method. Agitating the liquid may be done by surface impellers that float on the liquid. Rotating mixers are used most commonly in large systems, and they can be used to produce various blends. The selection of agitator types, locations in the tanks, and mixer motor horsepower is important.

Static mixing can be accomplished by a series of stationary blades mounted in a pipe. The blades can split, reverse, and blend the flow in several stages to achieve mixing. This method is effective and economical with small streams.

### Aeration

*Aeration* is the oxidation of the wastewater using air. The air causes chemical or biological reactions among some of the pollutants and degrades them. For example, ferrous ions are readily oxidized to ferric ions in neutral solutions by dissolved oxygen.

Aeration is achieved by a special type of mixing in which air is passed into the water by such methods as spraying the liquid in the air, bubbling air through the liquid, or agitating the liquid to promote surface absorption of air. Spraying the liquid in the air is done by water pumps and spray nozzles located above the surface of the liquid. Bubbling air through the liquid is done by locating dispersion nozzles at the bottom of the tanks or basins and supplying the air with a plant compressed air supply main or a small air blower. Since the solubility of air in water is low, fine bubbles are desirable for dissolving the air into solution.

### Flocculation

*Flocculation,* sometimes called *agglomeration* or *coagulation,* is a process of contact and adhesion of small particles to form larger particles to promote reasonably rapid settling. This is done by adding flocculating agents. Mixers again are used to blend the agent gently, with tip speeds not exceeding 0.6 to 0.9 m/s (2 to 3 ft/s) to prevent the breakup of the floc. The agents may be cationic, nonionic, or anionic, and they can be tested on site by water-treatment vendors. Alum, aluminum sulfate, and ferric sulfate are some common flocculants.

### Clarification

*Clarification* is the process of removing suspended solids by quiescent settling to produce a clear effluent. It requires a slow-moving sludge rake and an end-overflow clear-liquid weir. Flocculation may precede clarification or occur in the central zone of the clarifier.

A thickener is similar to a clarifier but its desired product is the underflow sludge.

A clarifier is rated by its ability to remove solids. It is related to settling rate expressed in distance per time, meters per minute or feet per minute, but it is usually expressed as flow rate per surface area of the settling zone. Thus, if flow is in cubic meters per minute and the surface area is expressed in square meters, dividing the flow by the area results in square meters canceling out and leaving meters per minute (feet per second).

The sludge is usually raked down a sloping bottom to a central discharge point. The pushing movement tends to densify the sludge. Oily scum that rises out of the solution can be skimmed to a scum box and drained off for disposal. Overflow weirs, such as V-notch weirs, uniformly distribute the flow across a considerable length, reducing reentrainment of solids.

Inclined-plate settlers have been developed recently to provide clarification in a small space. The settler features plates spaced several centimeters (inches) apart and inclined 45 to 60 degrees from the horizontal. As the flow rises between the plates, the solids drop out onto the plate below. The solids then slide down the plate into a pyramidal bottom. The projected areas of each plate overlap, providing more area in a small space. These inclined-plate settlers are particularly suitable for small to moderate flows. Biological solids do not separate well in these settlers.

### Filtration

Filtering the solids out of a wastewater stream is also another method used to remove suspended solids. The filter medium can be either a replaceable porous membrane or granular material such as sand. Medium selection involves effluent clarity, solid storage capacity on the medium without plugging, and nominal run time between backwashes. Granular media are sized so that interstitial spaces between the media will trap the particulates. Typical media are sand and anthracite (hard coal) that are specially graded to specific sizes. Close grading is desirable to avoid reclassification, which would leave medium fines on top of the filter that would quickly plug during the succeeding filter run. While filtration produces an excellent effluent, the backwash slurries must be stored, probably mixed, and the solids dewatered in some manner for disposal.

### Dewatering and solids handling

The ultimate in solids handling is to concentrate or densify the solids as much as possible to minimize the transportation and final

**TABLE 18.3    List of Dewatering Equipment**

Sludge beds
Rotary vacuum filters
Belt presses
Filter presses
Centrifuges
Strainers
Hydroclones
Flotation

---

disposal costs. Inert nonhazardous solids may be sent to a sanitary landfill, but hazardous solids fall under the Resource Conservation and Recovery Act (RCRA) (see Chap. 19). Dewatering equipment is listed in Table 18.3.

A *sludge bed* has a base of sand and gravel underlain with drainage tiles. A layer of slurry is allowed to accumulate for a number of days. As the water in the slurry drains down through the sand, the solids are left to dry in the air. This method is typical of older sanitary sewage treatment systems. The solids are then scraped off and shipped to a sanitary landfill if they are not hazardous. Sludge beds require space and drying weather days. Operations are batch type and have intervals of weeks between operations.

A *rotary vacuum filter* consists of a hollow drum rotating horizontally in a shallow tank. The drum is covered with cloth. As vacuum is applied to the drum interior and a slurry is fed into the tank, a cake of dewatered solids collects on the surface of the cloth and is subsequently scraped off. Sludge conditioning may be necessary for optimal capacity. Rotary vacuum filtration is a continuous operation, and filtration rates can be large.

A *belt press* has a continuous fabric belt that passes between rollers through various stages of slurry application, sludge compression, solids discharge, and belt washing. This method is good for difficult to dewater solids, such as metal hydroxides. Operations are continuous.

A *filter press* has a number of leaves covered with fabric. Slurry is pumped through ports and spaces between alternate leaves. Solids build up on the fabric as the water passes through. A high pump pressure can be applied to produce a dry cake. The press must be partially disassembled to drop the cakes out. Although a dry cake can be produced, this is a batch operation that requires more manpower than other methods. In addition, sturdy construction is required to withstand the high pressures, and this results in higher capital costs.

A *centrifuge* separates slurries or liquids of different densities by centrifugal action. High rotation speeds are required. Operations are continuous, but flow capacities are small. The equipment for these high speeds must be sturdy and is expensive. Applications to wastewater are few.

A *strainer* separates solids on a perforated medium. The perforations obviously must be smaller than the solids. The solids are removed by continuous or intermittent manual cleaning.

A *hydroclone* is a funnel-shaped device into which the flow is directed tangentially. The solids spin out of suspension through the apex, and the effluent leaves from the votex. Higher velocities through the hydroclone improve removal. Coarse particles can be removed continuously with this equipment.

*Flotation* is a process in which sparging fine air bubbles through an oily emulsion lifts the oily substance to the surface. Conditioning agents may be added to improve the removal. Operation is continuous.

## Storm Water Discharges

Regulations pertaining to storm water discharges were published in the *Federal Register* (55 *Fed. Reg.* 47990) in 1990 and were amended in 1991 (56 *Fed. Reg.* 12098). *Storm water* is defined as runoff, snowmelt runoff, surface runoff, and drainage [see 40 *CFR* 122.26(b)(13)]. Permits are required for storm water discharges associated with industrial activity. NPDES permits are required for storm water discharges from areas such as access roads and rail lines that are used to transport hazardous materials, even when they discharge into municipal storm sewers that already have discharge permits. The Clean Water Act requires that storm water discharges not presently included in its regulations be included in future amendments.

# Hazardous Waste Regulations

## Stephen R. Sabatini

This chapter provides an outline for use by plant engineers when they are confronted with a project that involves hazardous waste regulations. For information on the origin of these regulations, see Chap. 2. The Environmental Protection Agency (EPA) and many state environmental regulatory agencies have promulgated regulations to comply with the federal Resource Conservation and Recovery Act (RCRA). These regulations specify how facilities that generate, store, transport, treat, or dispose of hazardous wastes must operate to ensure that the public and the environment are not harmed or endangered. This chapter also discusses disposal requirements for nonhazardous solid wastes.

## The Resource Conservation and Recovery Act (RCRA)

The Resource Conservation and Recovery Act (RCRA) includes

1. A complete ban on land disposal of hazardous waste unless no migration from the waste facility will occur for as long as the waste remains hazardous or the waste is treated to EPA-established levels.

2. Legally mandated deadlines.

3. More stringent standards for the handling of hazardous waste.

4. A schedule for EPA listing of additional categories of chemicals (see Chap. 2).

With most environmental concerns, facilities must comply with both state and federal regulations. However, with hazardous waste regulations, either the state or the federal agency has jurisdiction, not both. In many cases, the state agency has been granted the authority to regulate hazardous waste by the EPA. Such states must have regulations that are at least as stringent as those of the EPA. In these states the EPA's regulations do not apply; however, the EPA reserves the right to review permits and associated applications and make comments. Facilities must comply only with the state's regulations. Ohio,

TABLE 19.1   Summary or Regulations Governing Hazardous Waste Treatment, Storage, and Disposal Facilities

| Ohio regulation | Federal regulation* | Ohio regulation title or description |
|---|---|---|
| 3745-54 | 40 *CFR* 260 | Standards for the Management of Hazardous Wastes |
| 3745-55 | 40 *CFR* 264, Subpart G | Management of Hazardous Wastes; Closure and Post-Closure |
| 3745-56 | 40 *CFR* 264, Subparts G, J, K, and L | Standards for Surface Impoundments, Waste Piles and Tanks; Closure and Post-Closure |
| 3745-57 | 40 *CFR* 264, Subparts G and J | Standards for Incinerators; Closure |
| 3745-58 | 40 *CFR* 264, Subpart X | Miscellaneous Methods of Waste Treatment |
| 3745-59 | 40 *CFR* 268 | Identifies hazardous wastes that are restricted from land disposal |
| 3745-65 | 40 *CFR* 265, and 40 *CFR* 267 | Interim Standards for Hazardous Waste Facilities Operating Prior to October 9, 1980 |
| 3745-66 | 40 *CFR* 264, Subparts G, I, and J | Closure and Post-Closure Requirements; Containers, Tanks |
| 3745-67 | 40 *CFR* 264, Subparts K, L, and M | Surface Impoundments, Waste Piles and Land Treatment Facilities |
| 3745-68 | 40 *CFR* 264, Subparts N, O, and X | Landfills, Incinerators,Thermal Treatment, Open Burning and Detonation of Waste Explosives |
| 3745-69 | 40 *CFR* 264, Subparts W and X | Describes the standards for TSDs other than tanks, surface impoundments, and land treatment |

*In addition to the specific subparts listed here, other subparts may apply to certain facilities. All the regulations should be considered in determining which apply to a facility.

for example, has been given authority to regulate hazardous waste within its boundaries. Interstate transportation of hazardous wastes is still regulated by the EPA and the Department of Transportation (DOT), however. For a summary of EPA regulations, see Table 19.1.

## The Ohio Regulations

This chapter uses the Ohio regulations as a model to illustrate how to deal with hazardous waste regulations. However, the same steps can be used in dealing with the regulations of the EPA or any other state. It should be noted that not all the hazardous waste regulations are mentioned in this chapter. However, this chapter will indicate the sections of the regulations that should be investigated for industrial facilities that involve the disposal of hazardous waste.

States that have been granted authority to regulate their own hazardous waste have typically patterned their regulations after the EPA regulations and have made modifications to meet their specific situation. Some states have even simply adopted the federal regulations either by copying them verbatim or by reference.

### Types of facilities

Several types of facilities fall under the Ohio hazardous regulations:

- Those that create the waste (generators)
- Those that haul the waste (transporters)
- Those that manage the waste (treatment, storage, and disposal facilities, TSDs)

Any facility that deals with hazardous waste falls into one or more of these categories and must comply with the regulations that apply to those types of facilities. Some of the regulations apply to all types of facilities (see below).

### Determining whether a material is hazardous waste

The first step in determining if any of the regulations apply to a facility is to determine if any hazardous waste is present at your facility, even in very small quantities. This is somewhat complicated. The regulations are very detailed as to what is a waste and if the waste is hazardous. Materials that are recycled, reclaimed, or used as a fuel may not be subject to the regulations. However, a waste can be hazardous simply if it has any one of four characteristics: toxicity, corrosivity, ignitability, or reactivity. Table 19.2 lists the Ohio rules that should be used to determine if a material is a hazardous waste.

### Minimum quantities exempt

Waste generators may be exempt from some or all of the regulations if they produce only small quantities of waste. For example, a facility that generates between 100 and 1000 kg (approximately 220 to 2200 lb) per month of waste is exempt from many of the recordkeeping and reporting requirements. Table 19.3 is a checklist that can assist facilities that generate waste in determining if they are in compliance with the regulations.

### Types of hazardous waste

The regulations specify two types of hazardous wastes, listed and characteristic. A *listed waste* is one that is specifically mentioned, by chemical name or by process description, in the regulations as being hazardous. Listed wastes are contained in Ohio EPA Rules 3745-51-30

**TABLE 19.2    Rules That Define Which Wastes Are Hazardous**

| Rule | Title | Description |
|------|-------|-------------|
| 3745-51-02 | Definition of Waste | Defines which substances at a facility are wastes. It also discusses materials that are recycled, reclaimed, or used as fuels. |
| 3745-51-03 | Definition of Hazardous Waste | Defines which wastes at a facility are hazardous. Refers to the rules listed below. |
| 3745-51-04 | Exclusions | Describes specific wastes that are excluded from Ohio EPA rules. |
| 3745-51-06 | Requirements for Recyclable Materials | Describes materials that are considered recycled and are therefore not subject to the hazardous waste regulations. |
| 3745-51-20 | Characteristics of Hazardous Waste, General | Describes the general properties of a waste that is a characteristic hazardous waste. |
| 3745-51-21 | Characteristic of Ignitability | Describes the properties of ignitable characteristic hazardous wastes. |
| 3745-51-22 | Characteristic of Corrosivity | Describes the properties of corrosive characteristic hazardous wastes. |
| 3745-51-23 | Characteristic of Reactivity | Describes the properties of reactive characteristic hazardous wastes. |
| 3745-51-24 | Characteristic of EP Toxicity | Describes the properties of toxic characteristic hazardous wastes as determined by a chemical extraction procedure. |
| 3745-51-30 | List of Hazardous Wastes, General | Lists hazardous wastes by chemical name. |
| 3745-51-31 | Hazardous Waste from Nonspecific Sources | Lists raw materials and chemical intermediates that, when they are spent, are hazardous wastes. Also lists some wastes by process that are hazardous. |
| 3745-51-32 | Hazardous Waste from Specific Sources | Lists hazardous wastes by production process name. |
| 3745-51-33 | Discarded Commercial Chemical Products, Off-Specification Species, Container Residues and Spill Residues Thereof | Lists hazardous wastes by chemical name. |

through 3745-51-33. *Characteristic wastes* are those which meet certain chemical or physical criteria when submitted to specific tests. These tests are described in the EPA publication entitled, *Test Methods for Evaluating Solid Waste* (document no. SW-846). Characteristic wastes are considered hazardous if they are ignitable, corrosive, reactive, or contain toxic levels of heavy metals or organic constituents when subjected to a chemical leaching test. Characteristic wastes are discussed in Rules 3745-51-20 through 3745-51-24.

TABLE 19.3    Checklist for Hazardous Waste Generators

1. What wastes are generated?
2. Are the wastes generated listed as hazardous?
3. Are the wastes generated toxic, ignitable, corrosive, or reactive?
4. Has the plant implemented a program to minimize the amount of hazardous wastes generated?
5. Does the plant provide adequate security?
6. Does the plant generate less than 100 kg per month of hazardous wastes?
7. Are wastes incinerated, landfilled, or otherwise treated or disposed on site? (If yes, plant is subject to transportation, storage, and disposal requirements.)
8. Does the plant use the Uniform Waste Manifest for each off-site shipment?
9. Is the shipper that hauls the hazardous waste off site licensed as a hazardous waste transporter?
10. Is the off-site disposal facility licensed to accept the hazardous wastes?
11. Does the plant store wastes more than 90 days? (If yes, the plant is considered a hazardous waste storage facility.)
12. If wastes are not to be stored more than 90 days, what steps are taken to ensure that wastes are not kept longer?
13. Is each container marked with an approved hazardous waste label?
14. Are the containers inspected for leakage and/or corrosion at least weekly?
15. Are the containers holding ignitable or reactive wastes stored at least 50 ft from the property line?
16. Are the reactive wastes handled and stored so as to prevent chemical reactions?
17. Are the corrosive wastes stored in containers made of materials that are compatible with the waste?
18. Are incompatible wastes adequately separated?
19. Is secondary containment provided?
20. Does the plant have a contingency plan?
21. Is the secondary containment volume equal to the largest tank or 10 percent of the drum-storage volume plus a 24-hour or 25-year rainfall?
22. Are the ignitable wastes handled and stored in a manner that will prevent fires or explosions?
23. Is a written operating record of the following kept for three years?
    a. Wastes analysis results
    b. Location and quantity of each hazardous waste
    c. Waste manifest
    d. Incident reports of when the contingency plan had to be implemented
    e. Inspection results

If none of the wastes, as defined in Ohio EPA Rule 3745-51-02, at a facility meet any of the criteria of a hazardous waste in the rules listed in Table 19.2, then none of the hazardous waste regulations apply. If, however, one or more of the wastes meet at least one of the criteria, then the facility is subject to the hazardous waste regulations. The corresponding federal regulations can be found in 40 *CFR* 261, particularly Subparts C and D.

## Variances

Facilities that have what is normally considered a hazardous waste may, under special conditions, be granted a variance from the regula-

TABLE 19.4  Exceptions to the Rules

| Rule | Title | Description |
|------|-------|-------------|
| 3745-50-311 | Variance from Classification as a Solid Waste | Describe conditions under which a material that is normally considered a waste may be reclassified as a recycled or reclaimed material because small amounts are accumulated speculatively with the intent to recycle them. |
| 3745-50-312 | Standards and Criteria for Variances from Classification as a Waste | |
| 3745-50-313 | Variance to be Classified a Boiler | Describe conditions under which a facility that burns hazardous waste to generate steam may be considered a boiler. |
| 3745-50-314 | Procedures for Variances from Classifications as a Waste or to be Classified a Boiler | |
| 3745-50-315 | Additional Regulation of Certain Hazardous Waste Recycling Activities on a Case-by-Case Basis | Describe conditions under which, on a case-by-case basis, materials that are normally considered hazardous waste may be considered recycled. |
| 3745-50-316 | Procedures for Case-by-Case Regulation of Hazardous Recycling Activities | |

tions. The facility must apply for the variance in writing, just as it must apply for a permit if it is subject to the regulations.

Table 19.4 lists the rules that govern circumstances under which a facility may be granted a variance. The corresponding federal regulations are contained in 40 *CFR* 261.

### Permits

Any facility, no matter the type, that is subject to the hazardous waste regulations must apply for and obtain a permit to operate. The application consists of two parts, A and B. Part A is primarily a notification to the agency of the facility's intent to handle hazardous waste. Part B contains by far the largest portion of the application. For treatment, storage, or disposal facilities, Part B is often contained in several volumes, whereas Part A is a form consisting of only a few pages. The process by which a facility applies for and is granted a permit is often quite labor intensive for both the facility and the regulatory agency. The amount of effort spent completing the application and the application fee will vary depending on the facility type.

### Hazardous waste facilities

Three types of hazardous waste facilities are specified, and all of them are subject to different sections of the regulations. The facility types are generator, transporter, and treatment, storage, and disposal (TSD) facilities. Any facility that deals with hazardous waste falls into at least one of these categories and may actually be more than one type. Each facility must comply with all the regulations that apply to all the categories under which it is classified.

**Generators**  *Generators* are facilities that regularly create waste materials that are hazardous based on the criteria discussed earlier. Basically, generators are ultimately responsible for the safe handling of the waste until its final disposition.

The regulations specify how the waste is to be packaged, how the packages are to be labeled and marked, and the procedures that must be followed to ensure that the waste is safely shipped to the disposal site. The generator must make sure that the waste generated is disposed of properly at a facility licensed to accept the waste. If it is sent offsite, the generator also must ensure that the waste is carried by a company licensed to transport it to its destination.

To haphazardly dispose of the waste is economically impractical, because, for example, if the waste is buried in a mismanaged landfill and it must be excavated and redisposed, the generator may be required to pay the cost, just as the EPA is making the waste generators pay to clean up many of the Superfund sites under CERCLA.

Generators must comply with Ohio EPA Rule 3745-52, "Standards for Generators of Hazardous Waste." Table 19.5 lists the sections of Rule 3745-52 and provides a brief explanation of each section. The corresponding federal regulations for hazardous waste generators are contained in 40 *CFR* 262. Facilities that generate hazardous waste must decide carefully how to manage that waste. The regulations are simpler for a generator than they are for a storage facility. If a facility stores its waste onsite for more than 90 days, it also must comply with the TSD (treatment, storage, and disposal) facility regulations, which are much more complex, and the permit application is much more extensive.

**Transporters**  The regulations for hazardous waste transporters are simpler than those for other types of hazardous waste facilities. Basically, transporters must ensure that the waste is shipped safely, register with the Ohio EPA, use placards to indicate the material(s) being transported, and comply with the manifest requirements. Transporters that keep hazardous wastes at a transfer facility more than 10 days are also subject to the storage facility regulations (A transfer facility is a location at which a transporter temporarily holds a waste after it is picked up at the generator and before it is hauled to the disposal facility.) Table 19.6 lists the Ohio EPA regulations that apply to hazardous waste transporters. As with many states, in addition to the

**TABLE 19.5   Standards for Hazardous Waste Generators**

| Rule | Title | Description |
|------|-------|-------------|
| 3745-52-10 | Applicability | Describes the facilities that are and are not subject to this rule. |
| 3745-52-11 | Evaluation of Wastes | States that any waste generated in or imported into Ohio must be evaluated to determine if it is hazardous. |
| 3745-52-12 | Generator Identification Numbers | States that generators must register with Ohio EPA and obtain an identification number. |
| 3745-52-20<br>3745-52-21 | Manifest, General Requirements<br>Manifest, Required Information | Describes the paperwork that must be completed by the generator for any offsite shipments of hazardous waste. |
| 3745-52-22<br>3745-52-23 | Manifest, Number of Copies<br>Manifest, Use | Describes how the manifest is to be used to track the waste "from cradle to grave." |
| 3745-52-30 | Packaging | Incorporates U.S. DOT regulations (49 *CFR*, Parts 173, 178, and 179) by reference. They describe the minimum packaging requirements for wastes. |
| 3745-52-31<br>3745-52-32 | Labeling<br>Marking | Incorporates U.S. DOT regulations (49 *CFR*, Part 172) by reference. It describes how the packages containing the waste must be labeled to indicate what is in the containers and marked with the generator's name, address, and manifest number. |
| 3745-52-33 | Placarding | Incorporates U.S. DOT regulations (49 *CFR*, Part 172 Subpart F) by reference. It describes how the vehicle carrying the waste must be marked to indicate the type of waste it is carrying. |
| 3745-52-34 | Accumulation Time of Hazardous Waste | Generators may not accumulate hazardous waste onsite for more than 90 days without obtaining a permit as a storage facility. Storage facilities must then comply with the regulations that apply to TSDs. |
| 3745-52-40 | Recordkeeping | Generators must keep the returned manifests and any other pertinent information for 3 years. |
| 3745-52-41 | Annual Report | Generators must report annually to Ohio EPA the total quantity of each waste they generated. |
| 3745-52-42 | Exception Report | Generators must report to Ohio EPA anytime they ship waste to a disposal facility and do *not* receive a copy of the manifest within 35 days of the shipment. |
| 3745-52-43 | Additional Reports | Ohio EPA may request other reports at any time about the types and quantities of wastes generated. |
| 3745-52-44 | Special Requirements for Generators of Between 100 and 1000 Kilograms per Month | Indicates portions of the requirements that generators of small quantities need not follow. |
| 3745-52-50<br>through<br>3745-52-60 | Various sections | Describes the requirements for facilities that import or export waste from or to a foreign country. |
| 3745-52-70 | Farmers | Exempts farmers with waste pesticides from the regulations if they follow certain procedures. |

**TABLE 19.6    Standards for Hazardous Waste Transporters**

| Rule | Title | Description |
|------|-------|-------------|
| 3745-53-11 | Registration of Hazardous Waste Transporters | Describes the registration requirements for companies that haul hazardous waste. |
| 3745-53-12 | Transfer Facility Requirements | Lists regulations from which transfer facilities that store waste less than 10 days are exempt. |
| 3745-53-20 | Acceptance and Handling of Hazardous Waste and the Manifest System | Describes the procedures transporters must follow in accepting a waste shipment. |
| 3745-53-21 | Compliance with the Manifest | Describes how the paperwork is to be used to track the waste "from cradle to grave." |
| 3745-53-22 | Recordkeeping | Requires that transporters keep their copies of the manifests for a certain period of time. |
| 3745-53-30 | Immediate Action | Describes the steps that transporters must take immediately in the event of an accident involving the vehicle carrying the waste. |
| 3745-53-31 | Discharge Cleanup | Requires that transporters clean up any waste that they spill. |

state regulations, Ohio regulations incorporate by reference the federal Department of Transportation (DOT) regulations. The corresponding federal regulations for hazardous waste transporters are contained in 40 *CFR* 263. The applicable DOT regulations are contained in 49 *CFR,* Parts 172, 173, 178, and 179.

**Treatment, storage, and disposal (TSD) facilities.**    Facilities that treat, store, or dispose of hazardous wastes are subject to the most complex regulations of all hazardous waste facility types. Treatment facilities are those which process a waste to render it nonhazardous. For example, biodegradation is sometimes used to change the chemical composition of a waste. A storage facility is one that keeps a hazardous waste onsite for more than 90 days. Some transfer facilities operated by hazardous waste transporters also may be considered storage facilities. Disposal facilities are those which permanently get rid of the waste, typically by burial or incineration.

The regulations establish minimum construction, administrative, and operational requirements for TSD facilities. For example, the regulations specify the minimum thickness of the clay walls of a landfill; they require that facilities prepare detailed emergency response plans; and they state the minimum destruction efficiency of incinerators. The regulations that apply to a TSD facility will depend on the treatment, storage, and/or disposal processes employed.

Facilities that have incinerators must plan and conduct a trial burn to demonstrate that the incinerator will achieve the designed destruction efficiency. The trial burn is very expensive and sometimes causes facilities to abandon their plans to install an incinerator. In addition, the public is usually opposed to hazardous waste disposal facilities being located in their area. Public relations costs can be excessive, causing the owner to reevaluate the facility.

The regulations require TSD facilities to consider and account for all phases of their operations, including the design, operation, closure, and even postclosure of their sites. Each facility must be designed to minimize the possibility of exposure of people or the environment to the hazardous waste while it is being treated or stored, as well as after its disposal. Each facility must be operated safely and have a contingency plan describing what will be done if an emergency arises. TSD facilities must plan the closure of their sites to ensure that no hazardous waste remains onsite once the plant is closed or that the hazardous waste cannot cause harm to people or the environment after closure. Finally, if hazardous waste will remain onsite after closure, as in the case of a landfill, the owner will have to monitor the site to document that no waste is migrating offsite for at least 30 years. If waste is discovered to be migrating offsite, the owner will have to determine the cause, correct the problem, and remove any contamination.

The Ohio regulations covering TSD facilities and the corresponding federal regulations are summarized in Table 19.1. In addition to the federal regulations listed in Table 19.1, others may apply to a facility. All the regulations should be considered when deciding which apply to a facility.

## Other Regulations

In addition to the regulations promulgated as a result of the Resource Conservation and Recovery Act (RCRA), other regulations may apply. The Toxic Substances Control Act (TSCA) regulates some materials not covered under RCRA. Most notably, PCBs are regulated under TSCA, not RCRA. Regulations covering the land disposal of PCBs and other toxic wastes, including those also covered under the RCRA regulations, are included in 40 *CFR* 268.

The Comprehensive Environmental Response, Compensation and Liability Act (CERCLA, or Superfund) regulates the cleanup of abandoned sites that are contaminated. The sites also must be inactive; otherwise, they are still regulated under RCRA. CERCLA gives the EPA the authority to force the parties responsible for the contamination to pay for the cleanup. A hazardous waste generator is often considered a responsible party, even though it shipped its waste offsite. If a disposal site is contaminated, the EPA can go after the disposal site operator and the waste generators that sent waste to the site.

The Superfund Authorization and Reauthorization Act (SARA) also regulates the discharge of 190 hazardous chemicals to the atmosphere or water. Any facility that manages any of the chemicals, including hazardous waste facilities, also must comply with the SARA regulations. Many of the 190 chemicals are regulated under RCRA as hazardous wastes when they are considered wastes.

## Industrial Nonhazardous Solid Waste

The Solid Waste Disposal Act was passed in 1976 and was amended by the Hazardous and Solid Waste Amendments of 1984 (P.L. 98-616), the Safe Drinking Water Act Amendments of 1986 (P.L. 99-339), and the Superfund Authorization and Reauthorization Act of 1986 (P.L. 99-499). All these laws govern nonhazardous industrial solid waste.

# Environmental Audits and Underground Storage Tanks

The first part of this chapter deals with environmental audits. The second part outlines the regulations for new and existing underground storage tanks (USTs).

## Emergency Information

The EPA reports that 50 percent of the U.S. population takes drinking water from groundwater sources. Consequently, the EPA established the following procedure: Hazardous chemical spills or overfills that meet or exceed "reportable quantities" must be reported immediately to the National Response Center at (800)-424-8802 or (202)-267-2675. Information on "reportable quantities" of leaks and spills is available from a RCRA/CERCLA hotline at (800)-424-9346 or (202)-382-3000.

## Environmental Audits

Superfund liability can be inherited from the purchase of a previously contaminated site and/or building. Hazardous waste contamination is seldom apparent and requires the review of experienced environmental engineers. Costs of cleaning up polluted groundwater, soil, or structures can be formidable. Older properties can be likely sources of environmental problems.

Environmental audits for hazardous material contamination must be performed, by qualified personnel, for new sites and for existing buildings to avoid the extensive costs of cleanup. An *environmental audit,* as defined by the EPA, is a "systematic, documented, periodic and objective review by regulated entities of facility operations and practices related to meeting environmental requirements." Such audits involve the regulations specified by CERCLA, RCRA, SARA, TSCA, and OSHA and must include the items listed in Table 20.1.

TABLE 20.1   Items Included in an Environmental Audit

1. Unpermitted emissions into the air and improper registration and equipment maintenance
2. Unpermitted discharges into water or discharges that exceed the national pollution discharge elimination system limits or sewer ordinances
3. Unpermitted storage of hazardous waste, incompatible wastes, uncovered reactive waste tanks, plugged floor drains, and incomplete contingency, personnel training, and closure plans
4. Old contamination of soil, groundwater, or surface water
5. Old contamination of building(s) with any hazardous materials
6. Inadequate ventilation, potential work hazards, and inadequate right-to-know programs
7. Asbestos

NOTE: Also see Property Transfer Inspections in Chapter 21 for inspection for asbestos.

### Regulations and historical review

There is presently a multi-industry committee working under the auspices of the American Society for Testing and Materials (ASTM) to develop professional standards for those who do environmental assessments. Both the grounds and buildings of a facility are audited for environmental contamination. The Resolution Trust Corporation (RTC) has established some guidance in the *RTC Environmental Guidelines and Procedures*. The past owners and their activities are reviewed. A thorough review is also made of what is already available in the public records of various government agencies. This is a critical starting point for these audits. Additionally, any aerial photographs that are available are carefully examined (see Table 20.2).

### Available databases

Since 1988, at least a half dozen national database firms have been started, and these organizations apply computer recordkeeping and sorting techniques to the vast number of documents that have been filed with state and federal environmental agencies over the past decade. This has resulted in the availability of a host of electronic databases that can be searched far more quickly and comprehensively than would be possible by hand.

TABLE 20.2   Three Steps of an Environmental Site Assessment

1. A review of federal, state, and local records for any permitted activities and releases of hazardous materials
2. A review of the chain of title for the past 50 years to determine ownership and use
3. A review of available aerial photographs

## Sites

Lagoons, underground storage tanks, railroad and truck unloading or loading stations, and all locations suspected of hazardous waste storage and handling should be tested. Both soil and groundwater samples must be laboratory tested and reported. Soil borings also must be taken of any area that is suspected of having a history of dumping or fill dirt to check for any toxic substances.

For example, contaminants on one property purchased for a highrise building have been found in the soil to 55 ft (16.76 m) below the surface. The contamination was caused by a previous owner's underground gasoline storage tanks. Tested soil samples had contaminants ranging from 37,000 ppb to 1 million ppb. Anything more than 5 ppb required cleanup or filing of a risk assessment.

## Buildings

Buildings must be checked for asbestos. Tile floors, ceilings materials, pipe insulation, and structural fireproofing must be inspected, and the air must be sample tested, if necessary, to ensure that an excessive amount of asbestos fibers are not present (see Chap. 21). Inspecting a building for asbestos prior to transferring ownership is not required by federal regulations, nor is it required by state or local regulations. However, in many cases, lending institutions will not loan money for the purchase of a building unless an environmental audit of the property is conducted.

## Environmental audits for current operations

Environmental audits of operating plants is now considered a risk management tool. Environmental risks have become increasingly difficult to manage because of complex regulations, expensive litigation, and close public scrutiny. Environmental audits can

1. Provide an early warning system to identify potential and hidden liabilities and compliance deficiencies
2. Confirm a facility's current compliance status
3. Control the cost of insurance and economic compliance

## Underground Storage Tanks (USTs)

### Financial responsibility

In 1984, Congress responded to the problem of leaking underground storage tanks (USTs) by adding Subtitle I to the Resource Conservation and Recovery Act (RCRA). Subtitle I requires the EPA to develop regulations to protect human health and the environment from leaking USTs and specifically mandates requirements for financial responsibility. *Financial responsibility* means that an owner or operator of a UST must ensure, either through insurance or bonding, that money is available to help pay the costs of third-party liability and corrective action caused by a leak from a tank. Such costs can include cleaning up the leak, correcting environmental damage, supplying drinking water, and compensating people for personal injury or property damage.

### Petroleum USTs

In October of 1988, the EPA published underground storage tank (UST) regulations by adding Subtitle I to RCRA, which applies to tanks containing petroleum products. These regulations affect most tanks and provide minimum standards on which states must base their laws. Complete regulations appear in the *Federal Register* of October 26, 1988. The regulations apply only to USTs storing either petroleum or certain hazardous chemicals. The requirements for both petroleum and chemical USTs are similar.

New petroleum USTs must have the following:

1. Proper installation

2. Spill and overfill protection

3. Corrosion protection

4. Leak detection

### Chemical USTs

The UST regulations apply to the same hazardous chemicals identified by CERCLA in Section 101(14), except those listed as hazardous wastes. Hazardous wastes are already regulated under Subtitle C of RCRA and are not included in UST regulations (see 40 *CFR*, Parts 260 to 270, for this). Chemical USTs have to meet the same requirements as petroleum USTs, but in addition, they *must* have (1) secondary containment and (2) interstitial monitoring. *Secondary containment* consists of one of the three methods described in Table 20.3. *Interstitial monitoring* is leak-detection devices that detect the presence of a leak in the space between the two tank walls or between the tank wall and the concrete vault or liner.

A summary of the federal regulations is contained in two publications issued by the EPA Office of Underground Storage Tanks: *Musts for USTs,* which describes technical standards for tanks and piping,

**TABLE 20.3   Three Secondary Containment Methods**

1. Double-walled tanks
2. Single-walled tank in a concrete vault
3. Line excavation with a chemically resistant liner

**TABLE 20.4   Purposes of *Musts for USTs***

*Item 1:* Prevent leaks and spills
*Item 2:* Find leaks and spills
*Item 3:* Correct problems created by leaks and spills
*Item 4:* To be sure that owners and operators of USTs can pay for correcting the problems created by leaks and spills
*Item 5:* To make sure that every state has a regulatory program for USTs that is at least as strict as the federal regulations

**TABLE 20.5   Tanks Not Included in UST Regulations**

Type 1: Farm and residential tanks holding 1100 gallons or less of motor fuel oil used for noncommercial purposes
Type 2: Tanks storing heating oil used on the premises where it is stored
Type 3: Tanks on or above the floor of underground areas, such as basements or tunnels
Type 4: Septic tanks and systems for collecting storm water and waste water
Type 5: Flow-through process tanks
Type 6: Tanks holding 110 gallons or less
Type 7: Emergency spill and overfill tanks

and *Dollars and Sense,* which discusses financial responsibility. The purposes of *Musts for USTs* are listed in Table 20.4. See the Supplemental Sources at the end of this book. However, UST regulations do not include the tanks listed in Table 20.5.

## State environmental laws

EPA regulations establish minimum guidelines that states must enforce. Additional conditions can be required by state laws. Compliance with state environmental regulations governing the installation, operation, and monitoring of USTs containing petroleum products is required of all industrial companies.

State UST regulations usually contain the items listed in Table 20.6. It was mentioned in Chapter 12 that one state's UST regulations are found under the state fire code because the state fire marshal is delegated the responsibility for the UST program.

An *underground storage tank* is, by definition, any tank, including underground piping connected to the tank, that has at least 10 percent

**TABLE 20.6    Items Contained in State UST Regulations**

1. Design of tanks and piping systems
2. Installation of underground storage systems
3. Secondary containment
4. Leak detection
5. Overfill protection and transfer spill prevention
6. Storage tightness testing
7. Storage tank rehabilitation
8. Closure of underground storage facilities

of its volume underground. The regulations apply only to USTs storing either petroleum or certain hazardous chemicals. (See previous paragraph on chemical USTs.) Information on the CERCLA hazardous chemicals is available from EPA through the RCRA/CERCLA Hotline at 1-800-424-9346.

**New USTs.**    USTs installed after December of 1988 must meet the requirements of the regulations. For USTs installed before that date, the following requirements must be met:

1. Corrosion protection

2. Spill and overfill prevention

3. Leak detection

General factors to consider when designing an underground storage tank installation are

1. Soil condition

2. Foundation or tank support and anchoring

3. Corrosion resistance of the tank to both the soil and the product inside

Tanks suitable for underground petroleum storage in order preference in terms of underground water protection are

1. Double-walled steel or fiberglass-reinforced plastic tanks

2. Steel tanks that are clad with fiberglass-reinforced plastic

3. Single-walled fiberglass-reinforced plastic tanks

4. Single-walled cathodically protected steel tanks

The local authority must be consulted to be certain you are complying with local rules. Soil conditions and underground drinking water locations vary with each locality. Double-walled tanks with leak detection sensing in the inner space provide the safest installation. Local authorities will require these in all environmentally critical locations.

Chemical USTs installed after 1988 must meet two requirements: (1) the UST must prevent releases due to corrosion or structural failure, and (2) the stored contents must be compatible with the tank's interior wall. Variances are considered for both secondary and interstitial monitoring, but they are difficult to obtain.

**TABLE 20.7  Industry Codes and Standards***

| Installation | Corrosion Protection |
|---|---|
| API Publication 1615, 1987, "Installation of Underground Petroleum Storage Systems, Recommended Practice," 4th ed. | API Publication 1632, 1987, "Cathodic Protection of Underground Petroleum Storage Tanks and Piping Systems, Recommended Practice," 2d ed. |
| PEI RP-100-90, 1990, "Recommended Practices for Installation of Underground Liquid Storage Systems" | NACE RP-0169-83, 1983, "Recommended Practice: Control of Corrosion on Underground or Submerged Metallic Piping Systems" |
| **Tank Filling Practices** | |
| API Publication 1621, 1977, "Recommended Practice for Bulk Liquid Stock Control at Retail Outlets," 3d ed. (A revised edition is now available.) | NACE RP-0285-85, 1985, "Recommended Practice: Control of External Corrosion on Metallic Buried, Partially Buried, or Submerged Liquid Storage Systems" |
| NFPA 385, 1985, Standard for Tank Vehicles for Flammable and Combustible Liquids | **General (Repair, Spill and Overfill, Installation, Compatibility)** |
| **Closure** | API Publication 1626, 1985, "Storing and Handling Ethanol and Gasoline-Ethanol Blends at Distribution Terminals and Service Stations" |
| API Bulletin 1604, 1987, "Removal and Disposal of Used Underground Petroleum Storage Tanks, Recommended Practice," 2d ed. | API Publication 1627, 1986, "Storage and Handling of Gasoline-Methanol/Cosolvent Blends at Distribution Terminals and Service Stations" |
| **Lining** | API Publication 1635, 1987, "Management of Underground Petroleum Storage Systems at Marketing and Distribution Facilities, Recommended Practice," 3d ed. |
| API Publication 1631, 1987, "Interior Lining of Underground Storage Tanks, Recommended Practice," 2d ed. | |
| NLPA Standard 631, 1990, "Spill Prevention: Minimum 10 Year Life Extension of Existing Steel Underground Storage Tanks by Lining without the Addition of Cathodic Protection" | NFPA 30, 1987, Flammable and Combustible Liquids Code |
| | NFPA 30A, 1987, Automotive and Marine Service Station Code |

*This list includes the most relevant codes and standards for underground storage tank systems.

**TABLE 20.8  Selected National Consensus Codes and Recommended Practices for UST Management**

| Document number | Major technical topics of the final EPA UST rule | | | | | | | |
| --- | --- | --- | --- | --- | --- | --- | --- | --- |
| | Design and construction | Corrosion protection | Installation | UST system repair and retrofit | Operating requirement | Release detection | Release reporting and corrective action | Closure |
| ANSI B31.4 | X | American National Standards Institute (ANSI) | X | | X | X | X | X |
| | | | | | | | | |
| | American Petroleum Institute (API) | | | | | | | |
| *API 50 | X | | | | | | | |
| *API 125 | X | | | | | | | |
| API 650 | X | | | | | | | |
| API 1604 | | | | | | | | X |
| *API 1615 | | X | X | | X | | | |
| API 1628 | | | | | | X | X | |
| API 1631 | | X | | X | X | X | | |
| API 1632 | X | X | | X | X | | | |
| API 2202 | | | | | | | | X |
| | American Society for Testing and Materials (ASTM) | | | | | | | |
| ASTM (Steel Piping, Tubing, and Fittings) | X | | | | | | | |
| *ASTM A 53-87b | X | | | | | | | |
| *ASTM A182/A182M-87 | X | | | X | | | | |
| *ASTM D 4021-86 | X | | | | | | | |
| | Association of Composite Tanks (ACT) | | | | | | | |
| *ACT 100 | X | X | X | | X | | | |
| | Factory Mutual (FM) | | | | | | | |
| FM 1920 | X | | X | | | | | |
| | National Association of Corrosion Engineers (NACE) | | | | | | | |
| NACE RP-0169-83 | X | X | | | | | | |
| NACE RP-0172-72 | X | X | | | | | | |
| NACE RP-0184-84 | | X | | | | | | |

| | National Fire Protection Association (NFPA) | National Leak Prevention Association (NLPA) | Owens Corning (OC) | Petroleum Equipment Institute (PEI) | Underwriters Laboratories (UL) | Western Fire Chiefs Association |
|---|---|---|---|---|---|---|
| NACE RP-0275-75 | x | | | x | | |
| NACE RP-0285-85 | x | | | x | | |
| NACE RP-0572-85 | x | | x | | | |
| *NFPA 30 | x | | x | x | x | x |
| *NFPA 321 | x | | | x | | |
| *NFPA 327 | | | | x | | |
| *NFPA 328 | x | | x | x | x | x |
| *NFPA 329 | x | | x | x | x | x |
| *NFPA 385 | x | | | | | |
| †NLPA 631 | x | | x | x | | x |
| OC 3-PE-9632-A | x | | x | | | |
| *PEI/RP100 | x | | x | x | x | x |
| Steel Tank Institute (STI) | | | | | | |
| STI (Installation of STI-P3) | x | | x | | | |
| STI (interior Corrosion Control) | x | | x | | | |
| STI (Exterior Corrosion Protection) | x | | x | | | |
| STI (Dual Wall USTs) | x | | x | | | |
| UL 58 | x | | | | | |
| UL 567 | x | | | | | |
| UL 1316 | x | | x | | | |
| *UFC 1985 | x | | x | x | x | x |

*Revised in 1987.
†Drafted in 1987.
x = There is a code or recommended practice.

SOURCE: From "Rules and Regulations," *Federal Register*, 53(185), Sept. 23, 1988.

Several hundred chemicals also were designated as hazardous in Section 101(14) of the Comprehensive Environmental Response, Compensation and Liability Act of 1980, better known as CERCLA or Superfund. The UST regulations apply to the same hazardous chemicals identified by CERCLA, except for those listed as hazardous waste. Such hazardous wastes are regulated under Subtitle C of RCRA (see 40 *CFR,* Parts 260 to 270, for the hazardous waste regulations).

Nationally recognized industry installation standards must be followed when installing new USTs. See Tables 20.7 and 20.8. Complete final rules can be found in the September 23, 1988, and Wednesday, October 26, 1988, issues of the *Federal Register.*

**Existing USTs.**    Existing USTs are those installed before December of 1988. Existing tanks must have leak detection installed, as shown in Table 20.9. In addition, the deadline for corrosion protection and for devices to prevent spills and overfills was December of 1988. However, you can be liable for any leaking tank before that time. In addition, chemical USTs also must immediately employ tank-filling procedures that prevent spills and overfills.

TABLE 20.9    Leak Detection Requirement Dates for Existing Chemical USTs

| Must have leak detection by | Installation date |
|---|---|
| 1989 | Before 1965 |
| 1990 | Between 1965 and 1969 |
| 1991 | Between 1970 and 1974 |
| 1992 | Between 1975 and 1979 |
| 1993 | Between 1980 and December of 1988 |

**Closing of existing USTs.**    If a tank is not protected from corrosion and remains out of service for more than 12 months, it must follow the requirements for permanent closure, which include

1. Notifying the local authority 30 days in advance.

2. Determining if leaks have damaged the environment.

3. Either removing the UST or following EPA's procedure for permanent closure (see Table 20.7).

In addition, see Table 20.8 for recommended practices for UST management.

## NFPA 30 and reclaiming

NFPA 30, Flammable and Combustible Liquids Code, is enforced by most state and local communities. NFPA 30, Paragraph 2-3.4, "Abandonment or Reuse of Underground Tanks," requires that the reuse of existing tanks comply with the latest provisions of the code and receive approval of the local authority. Appendix C of NFPA 30 specifies the procedures for the abandonment or removal of underground tanks. NFPA 30 also specifies requirements for tanks located in basements.

# Asbestos Regulations

## Stephen R. Sabatini

This chapter outlines federal regulations regarding asbestos. Three federal agencies regulate asbestos: the EPA, OSHA, and the Department of Transportation (DOT). EPA regulations are contained primarily in 40 *CFR* 763. OSHA regulations are contained in 29 *CFR* 1910 and 1926. And DOT regulations are contained in 49 *CFR* 173 through 176. Table 21.1 lists many of the federal regulations that govern asbestos management.

In addition, many state and local agencies have regulations that apply to asbestos and its management. Both the states and the federal government have the authority to regulate asbestos. Some states' regulations are more strict than others. Therefore, regulations from all the governing bodies in your area must be considered in determining compliance. In some cases, even municipalities may regulate asbestos.

Asbestos and its removal constituted one of the most important environmental issues in the 1980s, and while much of the asbestos has been removed, it is still a major concern to industry (see Variances in Chap. 1). Asbestos regulations cover several areas: use of asbestos in manufacturing, worker exposure, inspections and testing, certifications, removal methods, disposal, and transportation. In addition, while property transfers are not regulated, many lending institutions will not loan money for the purchase of a property unless that property has been inspected for asbestos.

## Background

The primary concern for industry in dealing with asbestos is as a building material. Because it was an inexpensive material, asbestos became popular in a host of industrial uses, as shown in Table 21.1. Asbestos also has been used frequently in adhesives, asbestos-cement pipes, and vehicle brake shoes.

Asbestos was first used in building construction around the time of World War II. In the late 1960s, regulatory agencies began proposing regulations limiting the use of asbestos. By the early 1970s, asbestos

**TABLE 21.1  Common Locations of Asbestos in Industrial Facilities**

Thermal insulation on pipes
Fireproofing on structural metals
Sound deadening in areas where noise was a concern
Architectural materials such as transit panels, ceiling tiles, floor
  tiles, and moldings

could no longer be used in pipe insulation or fireproofing. Tighter regulations have continued to be developed. One of the last uses of asbestos, as a vehicle brake lining component, will be eliminated in the late 1990s.

Asbestos is regulated as dangerous because it presents a potential health hazard when it is inhaled. It is generally a fibrous material that becomes caught in the lungs and can cause cancer, asbestosis, and other respiratory diseases. Another concern is that the disease may not manifest itself until 20 years or more after the individual is exposed. This makes dealing with asbestos an extremely difficult problem, and the liabilities are long term. Therefore, many who deal with asbestos have taken the conservative approach very seriously, which means, essentially, the removal of all asbestos and asbestos products.

Since the problems from asbestos arise when it is inhaled, friable materials are of greatest concern. Friable materials are those which are easily crushed in the hand and become powdery or fluffy. The fibers in friable asbestos products are much more likely to become airborne than those which are trapped in a cementlike or adhesive substrate. In keeping with the very conservative attitudes toward managing asbestos, many facilities have decided to remove all the asbestos, not just that which is friable.

## Regulations on the Use of Asbestos in Manufacturing

Few industries still manufacture products that contain asbestos. Some automobile brake shoe manufacturers still use asbestos, but many have already started phasing out its use. Asbestos may no longer be used in original-equipment brake shoes after the 1993 model year or in replacement shoes after the 1996 model year.

A few other industries may still use asbestos, including the manufacture of asbestos-cement pipe and roofing materials. The regulations covering products that contain asbestos include 40 *CFR* 763.160 through 179. These regulations cover

- Automotive parts
- Prohibition of manufacturing, importing, processing, and distribution of certain asbestos-containing products
- Asbestos-cement pipes and sheets
- Asbestos floor tiles
- Asbestos millboard
- Asbestos paper
- Asbestos roofing materials
- Asbestos textiles

Table 21.2 presents a summary of asbestos regulations.

TABLE 21.2    Summary of Asbestos Regulations

| Regulation | Topic |
| --- | --- |
| 29 *CFR* 1910.1001(b) | Airborne concentrations |
| 29 *CFR* 1910.1001(c) | Compliance |
| 29 *CFR* 1910.1001(d) | Personal protective equipment |
| 29 *CFR* 1910.1001(e), (f) | Monitoring and measurement |
| 29 *CFR* 1910.1001(g) | Caution signs and labels |
| 29 *CFR* 1910.1001(i), (j) | Recordkeeping and medical examinations |
| 29 *CFR* 1910.1001(h)(2) | Disposal |
| 29 *CFR* 1926.50–59 | Exposure limits |
| 29 *CFR* 1926.103 | Respiratory protection |
| 40 *CFR* 61.140–156 | National emission standard for asbestos |
| 40 *CFR* 763, Subpart E, Appendix A* | Interim transmission electron microscopy analytical methods, mandatory and nonmandatory, and mandatory section to determine completion of response actions |
| 40 *CFR* 763, Subpart E, Appendix B* | Work practices and engineering controls for small-scale, short-duration operations, maintenance, and repair activities involving ACM |
| 40 *CFR* 763, Subpart E, Appendix C* | EPA model contractor accreditation plan |
| 40 *CFR* 763, Subpart E, Appendix D* | Transport and disposal of asbestos waste |
| 40 *CFR* 763, Subpart E, Appendices E and H* | Medical requirements |
| 40 *CFR* 763.120–126 | Asbestos abatement projects |
| 40 *CFR* 160–179 | Prohibition of the manufacture, importation, processing, and distribution in commerce of certain asbestos-containing products; labeling requirements |
| 49 *CFR* 172–175 | Transportation |

*These regulations deal specifically with asbestos-containing materials in schools.

## Exposure regulations

The amount of asbestos that workers and the general public may be exposed to is regulated by the Occupational Safety and Health Administration (OSHA) in 29 *CFR* 1910.1001(b). This regulation covers the exposure of abatement workers while they remove the asbestos as well as the exposure of the employees and the general public in a building that has asbestos.

As long as the exposure level to employees in an area is below the action level (see 29 *CFR* 1910.1001), nothing must be done. Otherwise, the facility must either remove the asbestos or institute a program of engineering controls to reduce the exposure. Engineering controls include repairing damaged areas, encapsulating asbestos that may be released to the air, and periodically inspecting the asbestos to ensure that it remains in good condition. Engineering controls of asbestos are also discussed in the 40 *CFR* 763, Subpart E Appendices, and 29 *CFR* 1926.50 through 1926.59.

## Inspections and testing

As mentioned earlier, in order to properly administer engineering controls, the asbestos must be inspected periodically. Also, inspections are conducted frequently to determine the location(s), if any, of all the asbestos at a facility. These inspections include taking samples of suspect materials. It should be noted that few people can accurately determine if a material contains asbestos simply by looking at it without the aid of a microscope. Many materials that look like they contain asbestos do not, and conversely, many materials that look like they may not contain asbestos do contain it. Because of this, the EPA has developed standard sampling and analytical methods for determining the presence of asbestos in materials. These standards are contained in 40 *CFR* 763.120 through 763.126.

In addition to the procedures that must be followed, the inspectors, the laboratory, and its workers often must be certified. These certifications are discussed in the next section.

## Certifications

In addition, many states require that inspectors be certified. Certification typically requires that inspectors attend a 40-hour training course and pass a written test. The training must be refreshed annually. Certification requirements for other people involved in asbestos varies depending on their degree of contact and their responsibility for its proper handling. For example, the laboratory workers who analyze samples must pass a test demonstrating that they can accurately determine the asbestos concentrations in samples. Certification for analyzing air samples is independent from that for analyzing bulk samples because the analytical methods are very different.

Most states require similar certifications for those who analyze samples. Some states also require certifications for the owners' representatives who oversee the abatement or write asbestos abatement specifications. All employees of the abatement company must be certified, including the workers, the field supervisors, and the project supervisor. Texas even considered regulations that would have required those who reviewed the specifications to be certified.

In order to determine the certification requirements in a state, contact the agency that regulates asbestos. The appropriate agency varies from state to state. For example, in Ohio it is the Ohio EPA; in Texas it is the Water Commission.

Because of the liabilities involved, it is often prudent to require the people involved to be certified even if the regulations do not require it. If a civil lawsuit is filed 20 years later, the possibility of an unfavorable ruling is minimized if the most stringent current regulations have been followed, even those which do not apply to a particular situation. For example, some government facilities are not subject to the OSHA requirements. However, if they do not meet the OSHA standards while abating asbestos and someone sues them because they became exposed during that facility's abatement project, the court ruling is more likely to be in favor of the complainant and the award will probably be much higher.

### Asbestos removal methods

The most detailed of the asbestos regulations concern its removal or abatement, because during the removal the potential for releasing asbestos to the air is the greatest. If the removal is conducted improperly, people in the area during and after the removal may become exposed to high levels of asbestos.

The regulations cover all phases of removal from the construction of an enclosure to procedures to ensure that all the asbestos is removed and the air is not contaminated. Decontamination of personnel and equipment is also regulated. The OSHA regulations covering asbestos abatement are contained in 29 *CFR* 1910.1001. The EPA regulations are contained in 40 *CFR* 763.120 through 763.126.

The OSHA regulations cover not only the removal procedures but worker protection as well. Exposure limits are contained in 29 *CFR* 1910.1001(b). Personnel protective equipment requirements based on the level of asbestos concentration in the work area are contained in 29 *CFR* 1910.1001(d), and requirements for medical monitoring of the workers are contained in 29 *CFR* 1910.1001(i).

### Transportation and disposal

Some of the requirements for transporting asbestos are similar to those for hazardous waste. For example, manifests must be completed, and trucks must be lined to prevent contamination. The U.S. Department of Transportation (DOT) regulates the shipment of asbestos in 49 *CFR* 174 and 175.

In order to dispose of asbestos waste properly, it must first be packaged properly. The asbestos must be "double bagged." In other words, it must be sealed inside a plastic bag shortly after being removed from the structure and while still inside the containment. When the bag is being removed from the containment, the outside of it is cleaned and that bag is placed in a second bag. Then the second bag is sealed. After the bags are removed from the containment, they are placed in fiber drums for shipment to the disposal facility. The packaging of the waste for shipment is regulated in 40 *CFR* 763 and 29 *CFR* 1910.1001.

The requirements are not as stringent for asbestos disposal facilities as those for hazardous waste facilities because asbestos will not migrate through soil like some hazardous wastes. The primary requirements are that asbestos must be disposed at a facility licensed to accept it and that the bags containing asbestos must be covered with soil within 24 hours of being placed in the landfill. The disposal regulations are contained in 29 *CFR* 1910.1001(h)(2) and the Appendices to 40 *CFR* 763, Subpart E. Also, many states and local regulatory agencies regulate the types of facilities that may accept asbestos. To ensure compliance with all the regulations, check with all the agencies that regulate waste disposal in your area.

### Property transfer inspections

To have a building inspected for asbestos prior to transferring ownership is not required by federal regulation, and it is probably not required by state or local regulations. However, in many cases, lending institutions will not loan money for the purchase of a building unless an environmental audit of the property is conducted.

The environmental audit is designed to protect all parties involved in the sale. It involves inspecting the property for indications of any environmental problems, including the presence of asbestos. Even though it is not required by regulation, certified inspectors should be used to conduct environmental audits. This will minimize the chance of future liabilities from using unqualified inspectors. As mentioned earlier, most people involved in the management of asbestos elect to follow the very conservative approach, and they often exceed the regulatory requirements. See Chapter 20 for information on environmental audits.

# Supplemental Sources

A. National enforced standards
   1. *Catalog of American National Standards, 1990–1991.* (Lists standards of over 90 standards-writing organizations by title and number in almost 200 pages and is the best source of enforced references. Contact American National Standards Institute, 1430 Broadway, New York, N.Y. 10018.)
B. Process safety
   1. Chemical Safety Data Sheets, available from the Manufacturing Chemists' Association, 2501 M St. N.W., Washington, D.C. 20037.
   2. NFPA. *Fire Protection Guide to Hazardous Materials,* 10th ed. Quincy, Mass.: National Fire Protection Association, 1991. (Contains the complete texts of NFPA 49, 325M, 491M, and 704.)
   3. AIChE. *Guidelines for Hazard Evaluation Procedures,* 2d ed., New York, AIChE, 1991. (Covers process/system checklists, safety reviews, relative ranking, hazard and operability studies, failure modes, effects and criticality analysis, fault-tree analysis, guidelines for selecting hazard evaluation procedures, and human error analysis with easy-to-follow examples.)
   4. AIChE and National Safety Council. *Hazard Control in the Chemical and Allied Industries.* New York: AIChE, 1979. (Presents extensive guidelines for safe storage and handling of high toxic hazard materials; prepared by Arthur D. Little, Inc.).
   5. Industrial Risk Insurers. *Plant Layout and Spacing for Oil and Chemical Plants* (IM.2.5.2). IRI, 1991. (See Appendices A and B of this book.)
   6. NFPA. *Industrial Fire Hazards Handbook,* 3d ed. Quincy, Mass.: National Fire Protection Association, 1991.
   7. NFPA. *Liquefied Petroleum Gases Handbook,* 3d ed. Quincy, Mass.: National Fire Protection Association, 1992.

8. American Society of Mechanical Engineers (ASME). *Boiler and Pressure Vessel Code*. New York: ASME, 1992.

9. American Petroleum Institute (API) publishes standards for mechanical equipment, plant layout, and process instrument. A publications catalog is available. Contact American Petroleum Institute, 1220 L Street, NW, Washington, D.C. 20005.

10. NFPA. *National Electrical Code*. Quincy, Mass.: National Fire Protection Association, 1990. (Includes requirements for hazardous (classified) locations with extensive specifications for the manufacture of electrical devices and installations in hazardous areas; see Chap. 15 for more information.)

11. Instrument Society of America (ISA) publishes standards for the manufacture, calibration, and application of process instruments. Contact the Instrument Society of America, P.O. Box 12277, 67 Alexander Dr., Research Triangle Park, N.C. 27709.

12. National Fire Protection Association (NFPA) publishes a number of handbooks explaining standards, many of which are enforced by building codes, that apply to the processing and storage of hazardous materials. Contact the National Fire Protection Association, Batterymarch Park, P.O. Box 9101, Quincy, Mass. 02269-9101.

13. U.S. Environmental Protection Agency Clean Air Act Amendments, Title III, List of Initial Extremely Hazardous Substances. Washington, D.C.: U.S. Government Printing Office, 1991.

14. Stoess, H. A., Jr. *Pneumatic Conveying*. New York: Wiley, 1970.

15. NFPA. *Electrical Installations in Hazardous Locations*. Quincy, Mass.: National Fire Protection Association, 1991.

16. *Fire Protection Guide on Hazardous Materials*. Quincy, Mass.: National Fire Protection Association, 1990.

17. Factory Mutual Systems. *Loss Prevention Data: Spacing of Facilities in Outdoor Chemical Plants*. Factory Mutual System, 1151 Boston-Providence Turnpike, Norwood, Mass. 02062.

18. NFPA. *Hazardous Materials Response Handbook*. Quincy, Mass.: National Fire Protection Association, 1991.

C. NFPA Standards

| 1991 NFC Contents: Alphabetical Listing | | |
|---|---|---|
| 51A | Acetylene Cylinder Charging Plants—1989 | Vol 2 |
| 1904 | Aerial Ladder and Elevating Platform Fire Apparatus—1991 | Vol 8 |
| 30B | Aerosol Products, Manufacture and Storage—1990 | Vol 1 |
| 61D | Agricultural Commodities, Milling of—1989 | Vol 2 |
| 90A | Air Conditioning and Ventilating Systems—1989 | Vol 4 |
| 296 | Air Operations for Forest, Brush and Grass Fires—1986 | Vol 10 |

## 1991 NFC Contents: Alphabetical Listing (*Continued*)

D. Insurers' standards
  1. Industrial Risk Insurers. *Standards*. (See Appendices A and B in this book.)
  2. Factory Mutual Systems List of Data Sheets.
E. Building code references
  1. NFPA. *Life Safety Code Handbook*. Quincy, Mass.: National Fire Protection Association, 1991.
  2. BOCA. *National Building Code Commentary*, Vols. 1, 2, and 3. Country Club Hills, Ill.: BOCA, 1990.
  3. BOCA. *National Building Code Plan Review Checklists*. Country Club Hills, Ill.: BOCA.
  4. *Fire Resistance Design Manual*. Washington, D.C.: Gypsum Association. (Shows many diagrams of fireproofing with fire ratings.)
  5. The National Conference of States on Building Codes and Standards Inc. (NCSBCS) [505 Huntman Park Dr., Herndon, Va., 22070] publishes a directory of state building codes.
F. Fire codes
  1. Solomon, R. E. *Automatic Sprinkler Systems Handbook*, 5th ed. Quincy, Mass.: National Fire Protection Association, 1991.
  2. NFPA. *Flammable and Combustible Liquids Code Hand-*

*book,* 4th ed. Quincy, Mass.: National Fire Protection Association, 1990.

3. NFPA. *Fire Protection Handbook,* 7th ed. Quincy, Mass.: National Fire Protection Association, 1991.
4. Fleming, R. P. *Sprinkler Plan Review Guide.* Patterson, N.Y.: National Fire Sprinkler Association, 1983.
5. A fire protection system checklist is included in the BOCA *National Building Code Plan Review Checklist,* E.3 above.
6. SFPE. *Handbook of Fire Protection Engineering.* Boston, Mass.: Society of Fire Protection Engineers, 1988.
7. Bryan, J. L. *Automatic Sprinkler and Standpipe Systems,* 2d ed. Quincy, Mass.: National Fire Protection Association, 1991.
8. Hilado, C. J. *Flammability Handbook for Plastics,* 4th ed., 1982.
9. Mowrer, D. S. (Consulting Specifying Engineer) *Selecting Pipe for Buried Fire Protection Water Supplies.* April 1990.
10. NFPA. *Fire Protection Systems—Inspection, Testing, and Maintenance Manual.* Quincy, Mass.: National Fire Protection Association, 1986.
11. *Industrial Fire Protection.* Fire Protection Publications, Oklahoma State University, validated by the International Fire Service Training Association. (Describes all types of systems in Chapter 8 and inspection and testing of all systems in Chapter 9.)
12. NFPA. *Fire Alarm Signaling Systems Handbook.* Quincy, Mass.: National Fire Protection Association, 1987.
G. Mechanical codes references: Ventilation
1. ACGIH. *Industrial Ventilation: A Manual of Recommended Practice,* 20th ed., Cincinnati, Oh.: American Conference of Governmental Industrial Hygienists, 1989.
2. U.S. Environmental Protection Agency. *Air Pollution Engineering Manual* (Publication No. AP-40). Washington, D.C.: U.S. Government Printing Office, 1970.
3. Stoess, H. A., Jr. *Pneumatic Conveying.* New York: Wiley, 1970.
4. Kolte, J. H. *Design of Smoke Control Systems for Buildings.* Washington, D.C.: Center for Fire Research, National Engineering Laboratory, National Bureau of Standards, 1983.
5. AABC Associated Air Balance Council Standards, 2146 Sunset Boulevard, Los Angeles, CA 90026.
6. Sheet Metal and Air Conditioning Contractors' National Association Standards. Contact SMACNA, P.O. Box 70, Merrifield, Va., 22116.
7. National Association of Fan Manufacturers Standards. Con-

tact AMCA (formerly NAFM), 30 W. University Dr., Arlington Heights, Ill. 60004.

8. ANSI. Practices for Ventilation and Operation of Open Surface Tanks (Standard 29.1). New York: American National Standards Institute.

9. ANSI. Fundamentals Governing the Design and Operation of Local Exhaust Systems (Standard 29.2). New York: American National Standards Institute.

10. Factory Mutual Systems. *Loss Prevention Data: Industrial Exhaust Systems.*

11. ASHRAE, *Indoor Air Quality,* Standard #62. Atlanta, Ga.: American Society of Heating, Refrigerating, and Air Conditioning Engineers, 1989. This manual identifies indoor air quality problems and gives methods and procedures for solving them.

12. ANSI. Standard on Laboratory Ventilation (Standard 29.5). New York: American National Standards Institute.

G. Mechanical codes references: Heating and air conditioning

1. ASHRAE. *Fundamentals Handbook.* Atlanta, Ga.: American Society of Heating, Refrigerating, and Air Conditioning Engineers, 1989.

2. ASHRAE. *Systems Handbook.* Atlanta, Ga.: American Society of Heating, Refrigerating, and Air Conditioning Engineers, 1987.

3. ASHRAE. *Equipment Handbook.* Atlanta, Ga.: American Society of Heating, Refrigerating, and Air Conditioning Engineers, 1988.

4. ASHRAE. *Applications Handbook.* Atlanta, Ga.: American Society of Heating, Refrigerating, and Air Conditioning Engineers, 1991.

5. Reitz, K. *CFCs for Water Chillers.* Carrier Corp. Heating, Piping, and Air Conditioning Association, 1990.

6. ASHRAE. *Alternative Refrigerants.* Atlanta Ga.: American Society of Heating, Refrigerating, and Air Conditioning Engineers, 1991. This manual contains nine papers on alternatives to CFCs and HCFCs.

7. Lorenz, M. R., and Goswami, D. *CFCs: The Designers Dilemma.* Heating, Piping, and Air Conditioning Association, 1990.

8. Thumann, A. *Handbook of Energy Audits,* 3d ed.

9. Payne, W. *Efficient Boiler Operators Sourcebook,* 3d ed.

10. Thumann, A. *Plant Engineers and Managers Guide to Energy Conservation,* 5th ed.

11. American Society of Mechanical Engineers (ASME). *Boiler and Pressure Vessel Code.* ASME, 1989.

12. ASHRAE. Safety Code for Mechanical Refrigeration (Standard 15-1989). Atlanta, Ga.: American Society of Heating, Refrigerating, and Air Conditioning Engineers, 1989.
13. Air Moving and Conditioning Association Standards, AMCA, 30 W. University Dr., Arlington Heights, Ill. 60004.
14. Standards of the Tubular Exchange Manufacturers Association. Contact TEMA, 25 N. Broadway, Tarrytown, N.Y. 10591.
15. BOCA. *National Mechanical Code Plan Review Checklist.* Country Club Hills, Ill.: BOCA.
16. BOCA. *National Energy Conservation Code Checklist.* Country Club Hills, Ill.: BOCA.

G. Mechanical codes references: Plumbing
1. American Society of Plumbing Engineers (ASPE). *DataBook,* Vols. 1 and 2.
2. Manas, W. *National Plumbing Code Handbook.* New York: McGraw-Hill, 1957.
3. BOCA. *National Building Code Commentary,* Vol. 3, Article 28: Plumbing. Quincy, Mass.: BOCA.
4. BOCA. *National Plumbing Code Plan Review Checklist.* Quincy, Mass.: BOCA.
5. *Uniform Plumbing Code Interpretations Manual.*
6. NFPA. *National Fuel Gas Handbook.* Quincy, Mass.: National Fire Protection Association, 1988.
7. CGA. *Handbook of Compressed Gases,* 3d ed. Arlington, Va.: Compressed Gas Association, 1981.

H. Electrical codes references
1. NFPA. *The National Electrical Code Handbook.* Quincy, Mass.: National Fire Protection Association, 1990.
2. NFPA. *Electrical Installations in Hazardous Locations.* Quincy, Mass.: National Fire Protection Association, 1988.
3. American Petroleum Institute (API). *Recommended Practice for Classification of Locations for Electric Installations at Drilling Rigs and Production Facilities on Land and on Marine Fixed and Mobile Platforms,* 3d ed. (RP500B). American Petroleum Institute, Washington, D.C., annually.
4. American Petroleum Institute. *Recommended Practice for Classification of Areas for Electric Installations at Petroleum and Gas Pipeline Transportation Facilities.* (RP500C). American Petroleum Institute, Washington, D.C., annually.
5. NFPA. *Fire Alarm Signaling Systems Handbook.* Quincy, Mass.: National Fire Protection Association, 1987.
6. IAEI. *Source Book on Grounding,* 4th ed., periodically.

I. OSHA regulation references
1. Cralley, L. V., and Cralley, L. J. *In-Plant Practices for Job-Related Health Hazards Control,* Vol. 2: *Engineering Aspects.*

Cincinnati, Oh.: American Conference of Governmental Industrial Hygienists, 1981.

J. Environmental regulation references

1. ACGIH. *Industrial Ventilation: A Manual of Recommended Practice,* 20th ed. Cincinnati, Oh.: American Conference of Governmental Industrial Hygienists, 1989.

2. U.S. Environmental Protection Agency. *Air Pollution Engineering Manual* (Publication No. AP-40). Washington, D.C.: U.S. Government Printing Office, 1973.

3. Lund, H. F. (Ed.). *Industrial Pollution Control Handbook.* New York: McGraw-Hill, 1971.

4. Metcalf & Eddy, Inc. *Wastewater Engineering: Treatment, Disposal, Reuse.* New York: McGraw-Hill, 1979.

5. Liptak, B. G. (Ed.). *Environmental Engineers' Handbook,* Vol. 1: *Water Pollution.* New York: Chilton Book Company, 1974.

6. U.S. Environmental Protection Agency. *Design Manual for Onsite Wastewater Treatment and Disposal Systems.* Washington, D.C.: U.S. Government Printing Office, 1980.

7. U.S. Environmental Protection Agency. *Musts for USTs* (530/UST-88/008). Washington, D.C.: U.S. Government Printing Office, 1990.

8. U.S. Environmental Protection Agency. *Dollars and Sense* (530/UST-88/005). Washington, D.C.: U.S. Government Printing Office, 1988.

9. U.S. Environmental Protection Agency. *Guidance for Controlling Friable Asbestos Containing Materials in Buildings* (560/5-83-002). Washington, D.C.: U.S. Government Printing Office, 1991. (See paragraphs 5.1.3, "Encapsulation with Sealants," 5.2, "Abatement Methods for Pipe and Boiler Insulation," and Appendix E for additional EPA publications on this subject.)

# Plant Layout and Spacing for Oil and Chemical Plants

## Introduction

Loss experience clearly shows that fires or explosions in congested areas have resulted in very extensive loses. Wherever explosion or fire hazards exist, proper plant layout and adequate spacing between hazards are essential to loss prevention and control. Layout relates to the relative location of equipment or units within a given site. Spacing pertains to minimum distances between units or equipment.

IRI layout and spacing recommendations are for property loss prevention purposes only and are intended for oil and chemical facilities. IRI guidelines only address spacing and layout within a plant and are only applicable to open structures. An open air design favors vapor dissipation, provides adequate ventilation, reduces the size of the classified electrical area and increases firefighting accessibility.

This IRInformation manual section replaces the previous guidelines titled "General Recommendations for Spacing in Refineries, Petrochemical Plants, Gasoline Plants, Terminals, Oil Pump Stations and Offshore Properties" published by Industrial Risk Insurers and adapted from Oil Insurance Association No. 631. Additional information can be found in several publications.[1]

A good layout and sufficient spacing between hazards, equipment and units will have the following benefits:

- Lower explosion damage. Over pressures created by an explosion decrease rapidly as the distance from the center of the explosion increases. The mathematical relationship between overpressures and their distances from the explosion center is given in IM.8.0.1.1.[2]
- Lower fire exposure. Radiation from a fire quickly decreases as the separation distance increases.
- Higher dilution of gas clouds or plumes. Gas concentration decreases as the distance from the emission source increases.
- Easier access of equipment for maintenance, inspection and firefighting purposes.
- Easier spill and spill fire control in open areas, reducing the overall exposure.
- Lower concentration of values, resulting in a lower property damage loss should a given incident occur. IRI typically establishes a probable maximum loss (PML) based upon a vapor cloud explosion where such a hazard exists. A good spread of values and a good spacing between explosion hazard areas will lower the PML.

Extensive spacing might increase the investment required to build a given plant due to the following:

- More land may be required.
- More piping, cabling, roads and larger drainage systems may be required.
- Additional or larger pumps or compressors might be required as friction loss increases with the piping length and, therefore, operating costs increase.

Proper layout and separation distances should be designed into a plant during the very early planning stages of the project. This will require preliminary identification of hazards inherent to the operations or to the natural hazards. A good layout may not automatically increase the construction cost because proper separation between hazards can decrease the exposure protection required. For example, a control room unexposed by a process unit would have no need to be explosion resistant. Optimum layout will achieve a balance among loss prevention, construction, maintenance and operation requirements.

Computer-aided design (CAD) generates three dimensional layouts which have proven very effective for visualizing the proposed spatial arrangement of a unit or plant. High equipment concentration, plant congestion, etc., are spotted easily by these computer generated techniques. The use of CAD allows operators, maintenance and loss prevention personnel to easily comment and make appropriate recommendations. Reduced scale plastic models, while more difficult to build, offer similar benefits.

### IRI Position

The layout and spacing guidelines are based on fire and explosion loss experience.

The following factors should be considered when determining the layout and the separation required:

- High hazard operations
- Grouped operations
- Critical operations
- Concentration of values
- Fire and explosion exposures
- Vapor cloud explosions
- Maintenance and emergency accessibility
- Drainage and grade sloping
- Natural hazards and climate
- Future expansions

A review of various hazards and loss potentials will help establish the degree of separation required between units and equipment. Tables A.1, A.2, and A.3 provided in this guide are minimum spacing guidelines and are mainly based on fire and vessel explosion hazards.

Where large amounts of flammable vapors could be released and a vapor cloud explosion could occur, a more detailed hazard analysis and evaluation would be required per IM.8.0.1.1. The vapor cloud explosion overpressure circles should be calculated. The minimum spacing required between units would be based upon the following criteria:

- Critical equipment from adjacent units should not be located within the 3 psi (0.21 bar) overpressure circle.
- Equipment or structures from adjacent units within the 1 psi (0.07 bar) overpressure circle should be designed to withstand the given vapor cloud overpressure.

If the minimum spacing requirements based on a vapor cloud explosion incident appear to be less than the minimum spacing required by the spacing tables, the spacing from tables should be used.

Vapor cloud study results could indicate that an even higher separation between some units is needed because of higher than normal explosion damage potential and business interruption.

Other hazard analysis methods can provide good loss potential evaluations and are described in various Center for Chemical Process Safety publications[3] or in the DOW Fire & Explosion Index.[4]

## Overall plant layout

The site selection is quite critical as it can seriously affect exposure from uncontrollable factors such as floods, earthquakes, tidal waves, subsidence and hurricanes. Information pertaining to site selection and natural hazards evaluation will be found in other IRInformation sections.

Once a site has been selected, layout and spacing can reduce the effect of some of the following controllable and uncontrollable factors that contribute to losses:

- Site slope, climate, exposure to natural hazards, wind direction and force are among the uncontrollable factors. However, locating ignition sources upwind of potential vapor leaks or building the tank farm downhill of essential units will reduce the likelihood of an explosion or fire ignition. Figure A.1 illustrates a good layout based on the prevailing wind.

- Flammable liquid holdups, spill control and the type of process are among the controllable factors. Proper drainage and separation will control spills and fire spread.

Adjusting the plant layout to the physical requirements of the site, the process flow, the operational hazards and the loss prevention considerations is difficult.

The hazard assessment of each plant operation should help establish the relative position or orientation of blocks or units within the plant. The possible loss events and their consequences should be reviewed for each proposal. The selected layout should minimize the overall property damage and elated business interruption should an incident occur.

The overall site should be subdivided into general areas dedicated to process units, utilities, services, and offices. Each area or unit block generally has a rectangular shape. A maximum unit size of 300 ft (92 m) by 600 ft (183 m) is generally recommended for firefighting purposes.

Access roadways should be provided between blocks to allow each sec-

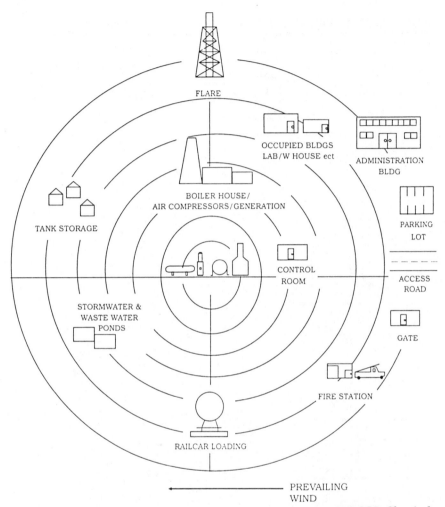

FLARE

OCCUPIED BLDGS
LAB/W HOUSE ect

ADMINISTRATION
BLDG

BOILER HOUSE/
AIR COMPRESSORS/GENERATION

PARKING
LOT

TANK STORAGE

CONTROL
ROOM

ACCESS
ROAD

STORMWATER &
WASTE WATER
PONDS

GATE

FIRE STATION

RAILCAR LOADING

PREVAILING
WIND

**Figure A.1** Good layout example. (*Reprinted by permission of NOVACOR Chemical Ltd.*)

tion of the plant to be accessible from at least two directions. Dead end roads should be avoided. Road widths and clearances should be sized to handle large moving equipment and emergency vehicles. Trucks and cranes may also require large overhead and lateral clearances to avoid hitting piping racks, pipe ways, tanks or hydrants. Roads should be unexposed by drainage ditches and pipe ways. Slightly elevated roads may be required in areas subject to local flooding. Hydrants and monitors are often located along these roads to allow easy hook-up of firefighting trucks. There should be at least two entrances to the plant for emergency vehicles to prevent the possibility of vehicles being blocked during an incident, e.g., open bridge, railway.

**TABLE A.1    Inter-Unit Spacing Requirements for Oil and Chemical Plants**

The diagonal headers (rows/columns, in order) are:

1. SERVICE BUILDINGS
2. MOTOR CONTROL CENTERS AND ELECTRICAL SUBSTATIONS
3. UTILITIES AREAS
4. COOLING TOWERS
5. CONTROL ROOMS
6. COMPRESSOR BUILDINGS
7. LARGE PUMP HOUSES
8. PROCESS UNITS MODERATE HAZARD
9. PROCESS UNITS INTERMEDIATE HAZARD
10. PROCESS UNITS HIGH HAZARD
11. ATMOSPHERIC STORAGE TANKS
12. PRESSURE STORAGE TANKS
13. REFRIGERATED STORAGE TANKS DOME ROOF
14. FLARES
15. UNLOADING AND LOADING RACKS
16. FIRE WATER PUMPS
17. FIRE STATIONS

| | 1 | 2 | 3 | 4 | 5 | 6 | 7 | 8 | 9 | 10 | 11 | 12 | 13 | 14 | 15 | 16 | 17 |
|---|---|---|---|---|---|---|---|---|---|---|---|---|---|---|---|---|---|
| 1 | / | | | | | | | | | | | | | | | | |
| 2 | / | / | | | | | | | | | | | | | | | |
| 3 | 50 | 50 | / | | | | | | | | | | | | | | |
| 4 | 50 | 50 | 100 | 50 | | | | | | | | | | | | | |
| 5 | / | / | 100 | 100 | / | | | | | | | | | | | | |
| 6 | 100 | 100 | 100 | 100 | 100 | 30 | | | | | | | | | | | |
| 7 | 100 | 100 | 100 | 100 | 100 | 30 | 30 | | | | | | | | | | |
| 8 | 100 | 100 | 100 | 100 | 100 | 30 | 30 | 50 | | | | | | | | | |
| 9 | 200 | 100 | 100 | 100 | 200 | 50 | 50 | 100 | 100 | | | | | | | | |
| 10 | 400 | 200 | 200 | 200 | 300 | 100 | 100 | 200 | 200 | 200 | | | | | | | |
| 11 | 250 | 250 | 250 | 250 | 250 | 250 | 250 | 250 | 300 | 350 | * | | | | | | |
| 12 | 350 | 350 | 350 | 350 | 350 | 350 | 350 | 350 | 350 | 350 | * | * | | | | | |
| 13 | 350 | 350 | 350 | 350 | 350 | 350 | 350 | 350 | 350 | 350 | * | * | * | | | | |
| 14 | 300 | 300 | 300 | 300 | 300 | 300 | 300 | 300 | 300 | 300 | 300 | 400 | 400 | / | | | |
| 15 | 200 | 200 | 200 | 200 | 200 | 200 | 200 | 200 | 200 | 300 | 250 | 350 | 350 | 300 | 50 | | |
| 16 | 50 | 50 | 50 | 50 | 50 | 200 | 200 | 200 | 300 | 300 | 350 | 350 | 350 | 300 | 200 | / | |
| 17 | 50 | 50 | 50 | 50 | 50 | 200 | 200 | 200 | 300 | 300 | 350 | 350 | 350 | 300 | 200 | / | / |

1 ft = 0.305 m

/ = no spacing requirements

* = spacing given in Table A3

Table A.1 provides minimum inter-unit spacing guidelines but should not be considered as a substitute guideline where a hazard analysis shows that larger separation distances are required. Unfavorable conditions, such as inadequate sloping, poor drainage, and critical operations, can increase the exposure between units, thus requiring higher separation distances. All distances between units are measured from battery limits. "Battery limits" as defined by IRI are imaginary lines surrounding a unit. This line is typically box shaped and encloses equipment required for the operation of the unit. It generally does not include cooling towers, maintenance buildings or other structures not considered as being part of this unit. This line crosses utility, service, raw material, and finished product piping.

The space between battery limits of adjoining unit should be kept clear and open. The clear area between units should not be regarded as a future area for process expansion.

### Process units

The processing units are generally the most hazardous operations in a plant. For operational purposes, the process units are generally grouped together and arranged in accordance with the general process flow.

Process hazards should be evaluated and, depending on the results of such review, be classed high, intermediate, moderate and minimum hazard groups as shown in IM.2.5.2.A. The relative hazard of each process should determine the spacing required between the various blocks. Hazardous units should be separated from other hazardous hazard units to avoid fire spread. Adequate separation, "separating" or "buffering" high hazard units by moderate or even lower hazard units is a way to reduce such exposure, e.g., a catalytic cracker should be separated from the alkylation unit.

Equipment or structures common to multiple process units, such as large compressors and turbines, central control rooms and fired heaters, should be properly located to prevent a single event from impairing the overall operation and causing extensive business interruption.

The equipment within a unit can be laid out in two general ways or a combination thereof:

- Grouped layout, where similar equipment is grouped together to ease operation, maintenance and control.

- Flow line, where equipment is arranged in a sequence similar to the process flow diagram.

Maintenance and operations accessibility will be a governing spacing and layout factor. Equipment needing frequent overhaul, maintenance or cleaning should be preferably located at unit boundaries. Large vessels or equipment should be located close to unit boundaries to allow easy access of cranes.

In some cases, fire protection spacing requirements will exceed maintenance accessibility requirements. The relative location of equipment depends on its probable release of flammable materials, its flammable liquid holdup and its potential to be a source of ignition. A domino effect loss is possible within process units.

Table A.2 provides minimum spacing guidelines for spacing within process units. The recommended separations are the clear, horizontal

**TABLE A.2    Intraunit Spacing Requirements for Oil and Chemical Plants**

| COMPRESSORS | INTERMEDIATE HAZARD PUMPS | HIGH HAZARD PUMPS | HIGH HAZARD REACTORS | INTERMEDIATE HAZARD REACTORS | MODERATE HAZARD REACTORS | COLUMNS | ACCUMULATORS, DRUMS | FIRED HEATERS | AIR COOLED HEAT EXCHANGER | HEAT EXCHANGERS | PIPE RACKS | EMERGENCY CONTROLS | UNIT BLOCK VALVES | ANALYZER ROOMS |
|---|---|---|---|---|---|---|---|---|---|---|---|---|---|---|
| 30 | | | | | | | | | | | | | | |
| 30 | 5 | | | | | | | | | | | | | |
| 50 | 5 | 5 | | | | | | | | | | | | |
| 50 | 10 | 15 | 25 | | | | | | | | | | | |
| 50 | 10 | 15 | 25 | 15 | | | | | | | | | | |
| 50 | 10 | 15 | 25 | 15 | 15 | | | | | | | | | |
| 50 | 10 | 15 | 50 | 25 | 25 | 15 | | | | | | | | |
| 100 | 100 | 100 | 100 | 100 | 100 | 100 | 100 | | | | | | | |
| 50 | 50 | 50 | 50 | 50 | 50 | 50 | 100 | 25 | | | | | | |
| 30 | 15 | 15 | 25 | 15 | 15 | 15 | 100 | 50 | / | | | | | |
| 30 | 10 | 15 | 25 | 15 | 10 | 10 | 100 | 50 | 15 | 5 | | | | |
| 30 | 10 | 15 | 25 | 15 | 10 | 10 | 100 | 50 | / | 10 | / | | | |
| 50 | 50 | 50 | 100 | 50 | 50 | 50 | 100 | 50 | 50 | 50 | 50 | / | | |
| 50 | 50 | 50 | 100 | 50 | 50 | 50 | 100 | 50 | 50 | 50 | 50 | / | / | |
| 50 | 50 | 50 | 50 | 50 | 50 | 50 | 100 | 50 | 50 | 50 | 50 | / | / | / |

1 ft = 0.305 m
/ = no spacing requirements

distances between adjacent edges of equipment. The following classifications are for equipment and processes:

- Process reactors are classed as moderate, intermediate or high hazard. The relative hazard classification is detailed in IM.2.5.2.A.
- High hazard pumps:
  - Handle flammable and combustible liquids, operate at temperatures above 500°F (260°C) or above the product autoignition temperature.
  - Handle flammable and combustible liquids and operate at pressures above 500 psi (34.5 bar).

- Handle liquefied flammable gases.

- Intermediate hazard pumps: All other pumps handling flammable or combustible liquids. Canned and magnetic pumps have a lower fire hazard, and therefore, there are no specific spacing requirements.

Proper intra-unit layout should include the following principles:

- Pumps and compressors handling flammable products should not be grouped in one single area nor should they be located under pipe racks, air cooled heat exchangers and vessels. Pump and driver axis should be oriented perpendicular to pipe racks or other equipment to minimize fire exposure in case of a pump seal failure. High pressure charge pumps should be separated from any other major process equipment and other pumps by at least 25 ft (7.5 m).

- Compressors should be at least 100 ft (30 m) downwind from fired heaters and at least 25 ft (7.5 m) from any other exposing equipment. To avoid unnecessary exposure, lube oil tanks and pumps should not be located directly under the compressor.

- Heaters and furnaces should be detached from the unit or at least located at one corner of the unit. Such continuous ignition sources should be upwind of the process units.

- Some very high hazard equipment susceptible to explosions, such as reactors, can be separated from other areas by blast resistant walls instead of increased spacing.

- Flammable products storage should be minimized within the process unit boundaries. Tanks, accumulators or similar vessels with flammable liquid holdups should be installed at grade, if possible.

The preferred layout of a process unit is a pipe rack located in the center of the unit with large vessels and reactors located outwards of the central pipe rack. Pumps should be placed at the outer limits of the process area. The practice of stacking equipment in process structures should be limited to equipment with no fire potential.

### Utilities

Central services, such as cooling towers, boilers, power stations and electrical substations, should be located away from hazardous areas. They should not be affected by a fire or explosion within the plant nor be a source of ignition for any potential flammable liquid or gas release. Adequate separation between different utility services is recommended because utility losses could then lead to unsafe conditions in other plant units, possibly creating fires or explosions. Safe spacing between boilers or generators will increase the reliability of the utilities.

Electrical substations and motor control centers are generally scattered throughout the plant. They can be a potential ignition source if not properly pressurized or separated. Locating substations away from hazardous areas will increase the reliability of the power supplies should a loss occur. Electrical distribution cables should be buried to limit their exposure to explosions, fires, storms, and vehicles, and to ease firefighting accessibility.

### Control rooms

Traditionally, control rooms were located at the edge or within the process unit, but technological developments have allowed a more remote location. The control room is an essential element in the process control; its location and construction should allow operators to safely shut down units under emergency conditions. The control room should be unexposed by fires or explosions, otherwise the control building should be designed to withstand potential explosion overpressure. Where control rooms are exposed, the emergency loss control coordination center should be relocated to a safe area.

Unmanned satellite computer rooms, terminal rooms, rack rooms etc., should be considered equivalent to motor control centers for the purpose of this guideline.

### Services

Warehouses, laboratories, shops, fire brigade stations and offices could be unduly exposed if located too close to process areas. Welding equipment, cars and trucks as well as large numbers of people are "uncontrollable ignition sources."

Loading racks, piers and wharfs should be well spaced from other areas due to large numbers of trucks, railcars, barges or ship carrying large amounts of flammable or combustible liquids. To limit vehicle traffic within the plant, loading and off-loading operations should be located at the plant perimeter close to the entry gate. Reducing plant traffic will ease emergency vehicle movement and limit accident hazards.

The location of flares depends on their height and flare load. Specific spacing requirements can be found in API 521.[5]

### Tank farms

Large fires have spread quickly within tank farms because of poor spacing, diking, drainage or layout.

Generally, the following layout recommendations should be considered:

- Different types of tanks and contents should not be grouped or diked together.

- Storage tanks should be located at a lower elevation than other occupancies to prevent liquids or gases from flowing toward equipment or buildings and exposing them. Tanks should be located downwind of other areas.

- Atmospheric storage tanks and pressure vessels should be arranged in rows not more than one or two deep and should be adjacent to a road or accessway for adequate firefighting accessibility.

- Piping involved in ground fires usually fails within 10 or 15 minutes of initial exposure. Therefore, piping, valves, and flanges should be held to an absolute minimum when located within dikes. Pumps, valve manifolds, and transfer piping should be installed outside dikes or impounding areas.

- Tanks should be properly diked or drainage to a remote impounding provided.

- Where large tanks are present, minimum distances should be greatly increased and 500–1000 ft (153–305 m) spacing could be recommended. Table A.1 provides minimum spacing between tank farms and other units.

Tanks should be spaced so that the thermal radiation intensity from an exposing fire is low enough to prevent the contents of the adjacent tanks from igniting. Tolerances of tanks to thermal radiation can be increased by:

- Painting vessels with a reflective color (generally white or silver).

- Providing a fixed water spray or tank shell cooling system. Refer to IM.12.2.1.2[6] for additional guidance.

- Insulating or fireproofing the tank shell. Guidance can be found in IM.2.5.1.[7]

Table A.3 provides general recommendations for spacing above-ground storage tanks in the oil and chemical industry. The spacing is given as a tank shell to tank shell separation distance and is a function of the largest tank diameter. Adverse conditions such as poor fire water supply, difficult firefighting, poor accessibility, poor diking, poor drainage, etc., will require additional spacing.

NFPA 30 defines flammable liquids as Class I materials, and combustible liquids as Class II & III materials. The classification

**TABLE A.3    Storage Tank Spacing Requirements for Oil and Chemical Plants**

| FLOATING & CONE ROOF TANKS < 3000 BARRELS | FLOATING & CONE ROOF TANKS > 3000 < 10,000 BARRELS | FLOATING ROOF TANKS > 10,000 < 300,000 BARRELS | JUMBO FLOATING ROOF TANKS > 300,000 BARRELS | CONE ROOF TANKS CLASS II, III PRODUCT > 10,000 < 300,000 BARRELS | CONE ROOF TANKS INERTED CLASS I PRODUCT** > 10,000 < 150,000 BARRELS | PRESSURE STORAGE VESSELS SPHERES AND SPHEROIDS | PRESSURE STORAGE VESSELS DRUMS AND BULLETS | REFRIGERATED DOME ROOF STORAGE TANKS |
|---|---|---|---|---|---|---|---|---|
| 0.5 D* | | | | | | | | |
| 0.5 D | 0.5 D | | | | | | | |
| 1 X D | 1 X D | 1 X D | | | | | | |
| 1 X D | 1 X D | 1 X D | 1 X D | | | | | |
| 0.5 D | 0.5 D | 1 X D | 1 X D | 0.5 D | | | | |
| 1 X D | 1 X D | 1 X D | 1 X D | 1 X D | 1 X D | | | |
| 1.5 D 100' MIN | 1.5 D 100' MIN | 1.5 D 100' MIN | 2 X D | 1.5 D 100' MIN | 1.5 D 100' MIN | 1 X D 50' MIN | | |
| 1.5 D 100' MIN | 1.5 D 100' MIN | 1.5 D 100' MIN | 2 X D | 1.5 D 100' MIN | 1.5 D 100' MIN | 1 X D 100' MIN | 1 X D | |
| 2 X D 200' MIN | 2 X D 200' MIN | 2 X D 200' MIN | 2 X D | 2 X D 200' MIN | 2 X D 200' MIN | 1 X D 100' MIN | 1 X D 100' MIN | 1 X D 100' MIN |

D = Largest Tank Diameter
1 Barrel = 42 Gallons = 159 L
$^0C = (^0F - 32) \times 0.555$
1 ft = 0.305 m

*For Class II,III products, 5 ft spacing is acceptable.
**Or Class II or III operating at temperatures T> 200$^0$ F

depends on the flash point of the product. Crude oil should be treated as a flammable liquid. In some very hot climates, Class II liquids could behave as flammable liquids because the storage temperature could exceed the flashpoint temperature. Unstable liquids or gases, and monomer storage require special precautions and are not addressed in Table A.3.

### Atmospheric storage tanks

Open top floating roof tanks limit product evaporation and have little or no vapor space above the liquid because the pontoon floats on the stored liquid. Internal floating roof tanks should be considered as floating roof tanks when pontoon roofs are provided. When plastic, aluminum, or a steel pan are used in the construction of the internal floater, the tank should be classified as a cone roof tank for spacing purposes.

- Floating roof tanks: Crude oil and flammable liquids (Class I) should be stored in floating roof or internal floating roof tanks.
- Floating roof tanks in excess of 300,000 barrels (47,700 m³) should be arranged in a single row. If multiple rows are necessary, tanks should be spaced farther than one diameter apart.
- Cone roof tanks: Combustible liquids (Class II & III) may be stored in cone roof tanks with the following limitations or exceptions:
  - Cone roof tanks in excess of 300,000 barrels (47,700 m³) present an unacceptable amount of potentially explosive vapor space, even if storing heavy oils. In such cases, floating roof tanks are recommended.
  - Liquids with boilover characteristics should not be stored in cone roof tanks larger than 150 ft (45.8 m) in diameter, unless an inerting system is provided.
  - Storage of flammable liquids (Class I) in cone roof tanks should be avoided. Cone roof tanks less than 150,000 barrels (23,850 m³) could be used for flammable liquids storage, if an inert gas blanket is provided. Increased spacing will be required.
  - Cone roof tanks storing Class IIIB liquids with a flash point above 200°F (93°C), operating at ambient temperatures, should be spaced as "floating and cone roof tanks smaller than 3000 barrels (480 m³)."
  - Cone roof tanks in excess of 10,000 barrels (1590 m³) containing combustible liquids stored at a temperature higher than 200°F (93°C) will require a greater separation.

### Pressure and refrigerated storage tanks

- *Spheres and spheroids:* The spacing between groups of vessels should be at least 100 ft (30 m) or the largest tank diameter. A tank group should be limited to a maximum of 6 vessels. The minimum spacing between vessels is given in Table A.3.
- *Drums and bullets:* Horizontal pressurized storage vessels should be limited to not more than 6 vessels or 300,000 gals (1136 m³) combined capacity in any one group. The spacing between groups should be at least 100 ft (30 m) or the largest tank diameter. Vessels should be aligned so that their ends are not pointed toward process areas or other storage areas. These vessels tend to rocket if they fail during a

fire. Multiple row configuration is not recommended. Pressurized storage vessels should not be located above each other.

- *Refrigerated dome roof tanks:*   The spacing between groups of vessels should be at least 100 ft (30 m) or the largest tank diameter. A tank group should be limited to a maximum of 6 vessels. Greater spacing could be required if exposed combustible insulation is used on the tanks.

## References

1. Hazard Survey of the Chemical and Allied Industries, *Technical Survey No. 3,* 1968, American Insurance Association, New York, NY.
   An *Engineer's Guide to Process-Plant Layout,* F. F. House, July 28, 1969, Chemical Engineering, McGraw-Hill, New York, NY.
   *Process Plant Layout,* by J. C. Mecklenburgh, John Wiley & Sons, New York, NY.
   *Loss Prevention in the Process Industries,* F. P. Lees, Volumes 1 & 2, Butterworths, Boston, MA.
   *Loss Prevention Fundamentals for the Process Industry,* O. M. Slye Jr., Loss Prevention Symposium, March 1988, American Institute of Chemical Engineers, New York, NY.
   NFPA 30-1990, *Flammable and Combustible Liquids Code,* National Fire Protection Association, Quincy, MA.
   NFPA 59A-1990, *Liquefied Natural Gas,* National Fire Protection Association, Quincy, MA.
2. IRInformation IM.8.0.1.1, *Oil and Chemical Properties Loss Potential Estimation Guide,* Industrial Risk Insurers.
3. Center for Chemical Process Safety, American Institute of Chemical Engineers, New York, NY.
4. *Fire & Explosion Index, Hazard Classification Guide,* Dow Chemical Company, Sixth edition, available from the American Institute of Chemical Engineers, New York, NY.
5. API RP 521-1982: *Guide for Pressure-Relieving and Depressurizing Systems,* American Petroleum Institute, Washington, DC.
6. IRInformation IM.12.2.1.2, *Water Spray and Deluge Protection for Oil and Chemical Plants,* Industrial Risk Insurers.
7. IRInformation IM.2.5.1, *Fireproofing for Oil and Chemical Properties,* Industrial Risk Insurers.

# Hazard Classification of Process Operations for Spacing Requirements

## Introduction

Processes differ from each other because of their inherent hazards. Processes and operations can be empirically classified into one of the three classes according to their explosion and fire hazards.

There are three hazard groups:

- Moderate
- Intermediate
- High

These classifications do not substitute for a proper hazard identification or analysis method. They are intended only to be used in determining spacing requirements. Many additional factors and judgements can still affect the class to which the process is assigned. Therefore, it may be desirable to classify a process in a higher class if the materials, size of unit or hazards associated with the process are higher than normal. Typical process examples are given for each classification.

An evaluation method for estimating damage from a vapor cloud or vessel explosion can be found in IM.8.0.1.1.

## Fire and Explosion Hazard Classification

### Moderate

Processes or operations having a limited explosion hazard and a moderate fire hazard are included. This category generally includes endothermic reactions and other operations, such as distillation, absorption, mixing and blending of flammable liquids. Exothermic reactions with no flammable liquids or gases are also included in this hazard group. Typical process examples include:

- Acetic anhydride (carbonylation of methyl acetate)
- Acetone (dehydrogenation of alcohol)
- Adiponitrile
- Ammonia
- Crude distillation
- Dimethyl formamide
- Chloromethanes
- Ethanol (from methanol)
- Ethylene glycol
- Formaldehyde (methanol oxidation)
- Methyl amines
- Methyl ethyl ketone (dehydrogenation of alcohol)
- Solvent extractin
- Styrene
- Urea
- Visbreaking

### Intermediate

Processes or operations having an appreciable explosion hazard and a moderate fire hazard are included. This category generally includes slightly exothermic reactions. Typical process examples include:

- Acetic anhydride (from acetic acid)
- Alkylation (Refinery)

- Benzene (from toluene-xylene)
- Benzene-Toluene-Xylene (BTX)
- Cumene
- Cyclohexane
- Ethyl benzene
- Methanol (Reforming)
- Polyethylene HD (small units)
- Polypropylene
- Polystyrene
- Polyvinylchloride
- Reforming (Refinery)
- Terephtalic acid

## High

Processes or operations having a high explosion hazard and moderate to heavy fire hazard are included. This category includes highly exothermic or potential runaway reactions and high hazard products handling. Typical process examples include:

- Acetic acid
- Acetaldehyde (oxidation)
- Acetone (cumene oxidation)
- Acrolein
- Acrylic acid
- Acrylonitrile
- Butadiene (oxidation)
- Caprolactam
- Cumene hydroperoxide
- Dimethyl terephtalate
- Ethylene
- Ethylene oxide
- Hydrocracking (Refinery)
- Maleic anhydride (butane oxidation)
- Methyl metacrylate

- Phenol (cumene oxidation)
- Phtalic anhydride
- Polyethylene LD (high pressure)
- Polyethylene HD (large units)
- Propylene oxide
- Vinyl acetate
- Vinyl chloride (VCM-EDC)

# Basic Preventive and Protective Features

Many of these features should be provided regardless of the magnitude of the Fire and Explosion Index. When they are not, the existing hazard exposure will be greater than the F&E Index indicates.

A number of these features would be provided regardless of the type of operation.

This list is not all-inclusive as other features may be used, depending upon the specific installation.

A. Adequate water supply for fire protection. This is determined by multiplying the length of time that the worst possible fire can be expected to last by its water demand. The supply deemed adequate will vary with different authorities and may range from enough for a two-hour fire to enough for one lasting eight hours.

B. Structural design of vessels, piping, structural steel, etc.

C. Overpressure relief devices.

D. Corrosion resistance and/or allowances.

E. Segregation of reactive materials in process lines and equipment.

F. Electrical equipment grounding.

G. Safe location of auxiliary electrical gear (transformers, breakers, etc.).

H. Normal protection against utility loss (alternate electrical feeder, spare instrument air compressor, etc.).

---

From *Fire and Explosion Index Hazard Classification Guide*, 5th ed., New York: AIChE, 1981. Reprinted by permission.

I. Compliance with various applicable codes (ASME, NEC, ASTM, ANSI, Building Government, etc.).

J. Fail-safe instrumentation.

K. Access to area for emergency vehicles and exits for personal evacuation.

L. Drainage to handle probable spills safely plus fire-fighting water from hose nozzles and sprinkler heads and/or chemicals.

M. Insulation of hot surfaces that heat to within 80% of the autoignition temperature of any flammable in the area.

N. Adherence to the National Electric Code. The Code should be followed except where variances have been requested/approved.

O. Limitation of glass devices and expansion joints in flammable or hazardous service. Such devices are not permitted unless absolutely essential. Where used, they must be registered and approved by the production manager and installed in accordance with Dow standards and specifications.

P. Building and equipment layout. Separation of high-hazard area must be recognized especially as it relates to both property damage and interruption of business. Separation of tanks must be at least in accordance with U.S. NFPA No: 30.

Q. Protection of pipe racks and instrument cable trays as well as their supports from exposure to fire.

R. Provision of accessible battery limit block valves.

S. Cooling tower loss prevention and protection.

T. Protection of fired equipment against accidental explosion and resultant fire.

U. Electrical classification. Division 2 electrical equipment will be required for outside flammable liquid handling where congestion is minimal and natural ventilation is unobstructed. Division 1 equipment is required only for special chemicals and/or special building or process handling conditions, or where ventilation is inadequate.

V. Process Control Rooms shall be isolated by one hour fire walls from process control laboratories and/or electrical switch-gear and transformers.

# Engineer's Check List

The following check list is intended as a guide for use when assessing the fire hazards and reviewing the fire protection requirements of a chemical plant. It may also be used to particular advantage in planning new facilities. No such check list can ever be entirely complete or meet the needs of every situation. Care should be taken in using such a list to make sure that other pertinent items not included here are not overlooked.

A. *Location*
1. Accessibility
2. Traffic—vehicular and pedestrian
3. Parking areas—entrances, exits, drainage, lighting, enclosures
4. Clearances—buildings for railroad traffic and vehicles (overhead width turnarounds)
5. Drainage, impounding areas
6. Road locations, markings
7. Entrances, exits—pedestrian, vehicular, railroad
8. Location furnaces, units for DOWTHERM heat transfer agent, flare stacks

B. *Building's*
1. Wind pressure, snow loads, floor loads, earthquake design
2. Roof material, anchorage
3. Roof vents and drains, smoke dispersal
4. Stairwells, ramps, lighting
5. Elevators and dumbwaiters
6. Fire walls, openings, fire doors
7. Explosion relief
8. Exits—fire escapes, identification, safety tread
9. Record storage

From *Fire and Explosion Index Hazard Classification Guide,* 5th ed. New York: AIChE, 1981. Reprinted by permission.

10. Ventilation—fans, blowers, air conditioning, scrubbing of toxic vapors, location of exhausts inlets, smoke and heat ventilation dampers, fire curtains
11. Lightning protection, structural and equipment grounding for electrical dischargers
12. Building heaters (hazardous or nonhazardous area), vents
13. Locker rooms including need for separate lockers for work and street clothes, required number of each and air changes (ASA)
14. Building drainage—inside and out
15. Structural steel and equipment fireproofing
16. Access ladders to roofs from outside level, escape ladders, fire escapes
17. Bearing capacity of subsoil

C. *Sprinklers, Hydrants, and Mains*
1. Water supply including secondary supplies, pumps, reservoirs and tanks
2. Mains—adequate looping, cathodic protection, coated and wrapped when needed, sectional valves
3. Hydrants—location
4. Automatic sprinklers—occupancy classification, wet systems, dry systems, deluge systems
5. Standpipes and tanks
6. Type, size, location, and number of fire extinguishers needed
7. Fixed automatic extinguishing systems, $CO_2$, $N_2$, foam, dry powder
8. Special fire protection systems—rise in temperature alarms, sprinkler system flow alarms, photoelectric smoke and flame alarms, snuffing steam

D. *Electrical*
1. Hazard classification
2. Accessibility of critical circuit breakers
3. Polarized outlets and grounded systems
4. Switches and breakers for critical equipment and machinery
5. Lighting—hazardous or nonhazardous areas, light intensity, approved equipment, emergency lights
6. Telephones—hazardous or nonhazardous areas
7. Type of electrical distribution system—voltage, grounded or ungrounded, overhead, underground
8. Conduit, raceways, enclosures, corrosion considerations
9. Motor and circuit protection
10. Transformer location and types
11. Fail safe control devices protection against automatic restarting
12. Preferred busses for critical loads

13. Key interlocks for safety and proper sequencing, duplicate feeders
14. Accessibility of critical breakers and switch gear
15. Exposure of process lines and instrument trays to fire damage

E. *Sewers*
1. Chemical sewers—trapped, accessible cleanouts, vents, locations, disposal, explosion hazards, trap tanks, forced ventilation automatic flammable vapor detectors and alarms
2. Sanitary sewers—treatment, disposal, traps, plugs, cleanouts, vents
3. Storm sewers
4. Waste treatment, possible hazards from stream contamination including fire hazard from spills into streams and lakes
5. Drain trenches—open, buried, accessible cleanouts, presence of required baffles, exposure to process equipment
6. Disposal of wastes, air water-pollution safeguards

F. *Storage*
1. General
   a. Accessibility—entrances and exits, sizes
   b. Sprinklered
   c. Aisle space
   d. Floor loading
   e. Racks
   f. Height of piles
   g. Roof venting
2. Flammable Liquids—Gases, Dusts and Powders, Fumes and Mists
   a. Closed systems
   b. Safe atmospheres throughout system
   c. Areas to be sprinklered or provided with water spray
   d. Emergency vents, flame arrestors, relief valves, safe venting location including flares
   e. Floor drains to chemical sewers properly trapped
   f. Ventilation—pressurized controls, etc., and/or equipment
   g. Tanks, bins, silos—underground, above ground, distances, fireproof supports, dikes and drainage, inert atmospheres
   h. Special extinguishing systems, explosion suppression— foam, dry chemicals, carbon dioxide
   i. Dependable refrigeration systems for critical chemicals
3. Raw Materials
   a. Hazard classification of material including shock sensitivity
   b. Facilities for receiving and storing
   c. Identification and purity tests
   d. Provisions to prevent materials being placed in wrong tanks, etc.

   4. Finished Products
      a. Identification and labeling to protect the customer
      b. Conformance with ICC and other shipping regulations
      c. Segregation of hazardous materials
      d. Protection from contamination, especially in the filling of
         tank cars and tank trucks
      e. Placarding of shipping vehicles
      f. Routing of hazardous shipments
      g. Data sheets for safety information for customers
      h. Safe storage facilities, piling height
      i. Safe shipping containers
G. *Inert Gas Blanketing of All Hazardous Products*
   1. Consider raw material, intermediates, and products
   2. Consider storage, material handling and processes
H. *Materials Handling*
   1. Truck loading and unloading facilities
   2. Railroad loading and unloading facilities
   3. Industrial trucks and tractors—gasoline, diesel, liquefied pe-
      troleum gas
   4. Loading and unloading docks for rail, tank trucks and truck
      trailer—grounding system for flammable liquids
   5. Cranes—mobile, capacity marking, overload protection, limit
      switches
   6. Warehouse area—floor loading and arrangement, sprinklers,
      height of piles, ventilation
   7. Conveyors and their location in production areas
   8. Flammable liquid storage—paints, oils, solvents
   9. Reactive or explosive storage—quantities, distance separation,
      limited access
  10. Disposal of wastes—incinerators, air and water pollution safe-
      guards
 I. *Machinery*
   1. Accessibility, Maintenance, and Operations
      a. Provision to prevent over-heating, including friction heat
      b. Possible damage to fire protection equipment from machine
         failures
      c. Protection of pipe lines from vehicles, including lift trucks
   2. Emergency Stop Switches
   3. Vibration Monitoring
J. *Process*
   1. Chemicals—fire and health hazards (skin and respiratory), in-
      strumentation, operating rules, maintenance, compatibility of
      chemicals, stability, etc.
   2. Critical pressures and temperatures

3. Relief devices and flame arresters
4. Coded vessels and suitable piping material
5. Methods for handling runaway reactions
6. Fixed fire protection systems—$CO_2$, foam, deluge
7. Vessels properly vented, safe location
8. Permanent vacuum cleaning systems
9. Explosion barricades and isolation
10. Inert gas blanketing systems—listing of equipment to be blanketed
11. Emergency shutdown valves and switches, location from critical area, action time for relays
12. Fireproofing of metal supports
13. Safety devices for heat exchange equipment—vents, valves, and drains
14. Expansion joints or expansion loops for process steam lines
15. Steam tracing—provision for relief of thermal expansion in heated lines
16. Insulation for personnel protection—hot process, steam lines and tracing
17. Static grounding for vessels and piping
18. Cleaning and maintenance of vessels and tanks—adequate manholes, platforms, ladders, cleanout openings and safe entry permit procedures
19. Provisions for corrosion control
20. Pipe line identification
21. Radiation hazards including personal protection for fire fighters—processes and measuring instruments containing radioisotopes, X-rays, etc.
22. Redundant instruments with alarms

K. *Safety Equipment General*
1. Dispensary and equipment
2. Ambulance
3. Fire truck
4. Fire alarm system
5. Fire whistle and siren—departments, inside and outside
6. Sanitary and process waste treatment
7. Snow removal and ice control equipment
8. Safety showers and eye wash fountains
9. Safety ladders and cages
10. Emergency equipment locations—gas masks, protective clothing, fire blankets, inside hose streams, stretchers, etc.
11. Laboratory safety shields
12. Hose houses—type, location, hose and allied equipment
13. Instruments—continuous analyzers for flammable vapors and gases, toxic vapors, etc.

14. Communications—emergency telephones, radio, public address systems, paging systems, safe location and continuous manning of communication center
15. Guards on Rotating Equipment
16. Combustion safeguards on furnaces
17. Fuel gas shut off valves

# Index

## ABOUT THE AUTHOR

JOSEPH N. SABATINI is president of J&S Engineering
Consultants, Cincinnati, Ohio, specializing in industrial
hazards and code consulting. He was formerly resident code
consultant with the MK Ferguson Company, Cleveland,
designers and builders of industrial facilities. He has more
than 20 years' experience in the field, is a frequent leader
of professional Code Seminars, and has authored numerous
trade articles.